The Rhetoric of Cool

# The Rhetoric of Cool

## Composition Studies and New Media

Jeff Rice
With a Foreword by Gregory L. Ulmer

Southern Illinois University Press / *Carbondale*

10  09  08      4  3  2

Library of Congress Cataloging-in-Publication Data
Rice, Jeff (Jeff R.)
The rhetoric of cool : composition studies and new media
  / Jeff Rice.
p. cm.
Includes bibliographical references and index.
ISBN-13: 978-0-8093-2752-2 (pbk. : alk. paper)
ISBN-10: 0-8093-2752-X (pbk. : alk. paper)
1. English language—Rhetoric—Computer-assisted
instruction. 2. English language—Rhetoric—Study and
teaching. 3. Cool (The English word) 4. Communication—
Philosophy. 5. Language and culture. 6. Interactive
multimedia. I. Title.
PE1404.R5127 2006
808′.0420285—dc22                    2006032031

Printed on recycled paper. ♻

The paper used in this publication meets the minimum
requirements of American National Standard for Information Sciences—Permanence of Paper for Printed Library
Materials, ANSI Z39.48-1992. ∞

*To Jenny*

Comes the darn
An My L'il
Sun-Flowa
Will rise in the yeast again,
"Dollin"

# Contents

# Foreword: Elementary Cool

*Gregory L. Ulmer*

To understand where *The Rhetoric of Cool* is coming from, it may be helpful to know where Jeff Rice came from, if only to provide reassurance that his convictions developed "honestly," so to speak. Some of the assumptions guiding the argument of *Cool* may be made explicit by describing an intellectual climate that Rice experienced during his graduate studies at the University of Florida. There are multiple dynamics in progress at any graduate program, but the one Rice picked up on was associated with the Networked Writing Environment (NWE), which opened in 1994. The NWE began as a gift of UNIX servers and work stations from IBM, enough to supply five classrooms. The university refurbished a building and provided several staff lines, and, most surprisingly, the administration decided that the facility would be used for writing instruction. Rice took graduate seminars in the NWE, working with the Website as the medium of study, and taught his own general education writing courses there as well.

Part of the excitement of those early years, coinciding with the emergence of the Internet as a public institution, and the growth of the World Wide Web as a popular medium of everyday life, was that nobody knew exactly what this technology could do (the capabilities were and are in continuous transformation), and there was no established wisdom about how it could be put to work in the service of humanities teaching, research, and service. The approach taken by Florida's English Department, and specifically by the writing program (first under the direction of Carolyn Smith, and then Sid Dobrin), was that "computers and writing" are relevant to everyone in the discipline, not just those working with composition or with media studies. The practicum was taught in the NWE so that teaching with technology could be part of every Teaching Assistant's training, related both to pedagogy and to research in the TA's area of specialization. Meanwhile, under President Lombardi, the university pushed toward an ever more wired campus, including requirements that all students own computers, with specific capabilities set by each college, and a long-term investment to upgrade classrooms and provide all faculty with computers. Although budget and vision have not always been in synch from year to year, the trend was established that computing is a part of every aspect of our educational enterprise.

The English Department was well positioned to take advantage of the opportunity afforded by the NWE. Film Studies was already established when I arrived on campus in 1972, and the curriculum continued to expand through the 1980s, when we introduced some production courses into the program and began hiring faculty to teach them. The principle justifying this expansion into "making" derived from the history of rhetoric. The analogy was that image-based media needed to be studied in the same way that we studied texts: by writing as well as by reading. Students should be producers as well as consumers of writing or of media. In a context in which English majors conduct inquiry in video and 16mm film, the addition of Web site design did not seem unusual. Each shift of the Department away from the traditional model of the discipline was not without controversy, however, from the mid-1970s when the required bibliography course was replaced by a course in critical theory, continuing today with the recent addition of game studies.

Among the faculty Rice met during his years at Florida, he would have encountered colleagues representing the full range of attitudes toward new media—a range that breaks down roughly along the lines of a battle of the ancients and the moderns. The conservative view was that the NWE should be used strictly to supplement conventional education in literacy: teaching the essay, the research paper, argumentative and expository writing, technical writing. The liberal view was that new media are the technological manifestation of a shift in the language apparatus of our civilization that has been underway at least since the invention of photography and involving a cultural adaptation to the industrial and information revolutions. To rehearse the argument that Rice heard in my seminars, we work in a research university one of whose purposes is to help society and the community meet the challenges of our world. Disciplines are organized around paradigmatic problems, to focus attention and resources on the most pressing issues relevant to the field of knowledge. The theorists of literary study have identified "the spectacle"—the culture of commodified entertainment images increasingly responsible for our imagined community—as one of the chief problems/opportunities facing our culture.

The "spectacle" within the frame of grammatology (the disciplinary background for my seminars) is understood as a manifestation of the apparatus of "electracy," which is to digital media what literacy is to alphabetic writing. Alphabetic writing is not just a technology, obviously, but also an institution formation founded by the Classical Greeks to promote the invention and dissemination of the practices of writing. The University of Florida is a direct heir of the first school as we understand the term—Plato's Academy. We are all familiar with this history: *Phaedrus* as the first discourse on method, the invention of dialectic, continuing in Aristotle's Lyceum, with the invention of topical logic, the conceptual category (metaphysics), poetics, rhetoric. These inventions are still recognizable in any handbook or textbook used in general education writing courses today, including McCrimmon (the book taught in my freshman writing course at the University of Montana in 1962). The motto for the grammatological approach to new media, central to the rationale for teaching new media in English departments, comes from the Japanese poet Basho, who observed that one should not follow in the footsteps of the masters but seek what they sought.

The research (and teaching) challenge for the language and literature disciplines today is not to follow in the footsteps of Plato and Aristotle but to seek what they sought. Electracy is not against literacy but is the means to assist our society in adding a new dimension to our language capabilities. This project does not replace the other things that we do or responsibilities that we have for literacy but proposes that our discipline also has primary responsibility for inventing the practices of reasoning and communicating in ways native to new media. A review of the works on new media will show that this dimension of the apparatus is (with some exceptions) neglected if not ignored completely. The literature in the field covers in detail matters of technology, art experiments, philosophical contexts, scientific research, narrative forms, and the like. They rarely acknowledge the fundamental historical fact that the logic, rhetoric, poetics of electracy have to be invented every bit as much as does the equipment. Moreover, the sources supporting that invention have little to do with science and technology, and everything to do with the humanities. One may learn all the tricks of Photoshop, Dreamweaver, Illustrator, CSS/DHTML and still be anelectrate. *The Rhetoric of Cool* is an invitation to Composition Studies to take up this paradigmatic project: the invention of electracy.

When studies do call for the invention of a new logic or rhetoric corresponding to the new capacities of digital media, they usually do so at the end of the book, stopping just before they explain how this invention might be undertaken. The other methodology that Rice picked up at Florida and that he uses to good effect is heuretics is the logic of invention. Heuretics (the term is related to "eureka" and "heuristics") uses theory for the generation of new kinds of works, as distinct from hermeneutics, which applies theory to the interpretation of existing texts. The operating procedure of heuretics was derived from an analysis of the tradition of discourses on method, from Plato to the present. This analysis showed a pattern recurring through most works with the ambition of introducing a new mode of thinking and writing. The poetic generator producing these innovations may be described with an acronym: CATTt, standing for Contrast, Analogy, Theory, Target, and tale. We may see how the generator works by applying it to the rhetoric of cool.

The problem to which heuretics responds is articulated between the Contrast and the Target. The Target in this case is the saturation of our society with new technologies of recording. Aristotle's logic became possible and necessary in response to the power of alphabetic writing to record (store and retrieve) the flow of human speech. Aristotle's name is on the invention, but he is the culmination of a long process covering several generations, from the first recordings of the epic bards, passing through the pre-Socratics, Hesiod, the Academy. Electracy similarly has been in progress since the nineteenth century, producing not only a continuing series of new recording technologies but also new institutionalizations, primarily Entertainment (within which the spectacle has emerged as our paradigmatic problem), and now the Internet. The Internet is an institution, meaning that it has officially established political and administrative organizations that set its policies and rules, and direct its development. This institution is unstable and in process and needs a practice adequate to its technical and social conditions. Nor is there a technological determinism that allows one to read off a Web logic from the technical features of hypermedia. Rather, an inventory of these features is one dimension of the CATTt. Rice chooses (as I did in *Internet Invention*) to assume the readers' familiarity with these features, and to evaluate the legitimacy of a rhetoric of cool with such features in mind.

The other register of the problem addressed heuretically is Contrast, provided in this case by textbooks of literacy, of which McCrimmon is the prototype foregrounded here. This function of Aristotelian textbooks as Contrast should not be misunderstood, especially in the context of Composition Studies. Plato contrasted his dialectic in the largest sense with epic, and more narrowly with sophistry. At the same time, he borrowed features of his Contrast, the Eleusinian mysteries for example, either as metaphors (the winnowing basket) or directly (some aspects of myth). The first rule of innovation, in any case, is to "make it new." If the existing practices of literacy were adequate to new media, there would be no need for a new rhetoric. There is nothing bad or wrong with literacy (needless to say), but only that literacy is relative to its alphabetic apparatus. This apparatus will not disappear, any more than did orality, including its institution formation (School) and identity structures (individual self, collective nation-states). The discussion of composition studies in 1963, with the list of all the things coexisting in that historical moment, serves just to say that at that time we considered our responsibility to be "literacy" only. We were then following in the footsteps of the masters. The task today, however, is to seek what they sought (to invent electracy).

The problem is now set: We need a practice of writing adequate to the Internet/Web, and it will not look very much like what is recommended in most composition textbooks. Some poetics only get this far and are satisfied to fill the slots of the Target by proposing the opposite of whatever stands as Contrast. In fact this shortcut does produce some useful results but misses the big picture. The real sources of the solution—a rhetoric of cool in this case—comes from inventories of Analogy and Theory. In the case of Theory, Plato drew directly upon Socrates, but more broadly upon the Pythagorean legacy available to him, and that made number and hence mathematics (geometry) the theoretical guide for his invention. For Rice this slot is filled by the various grammatologists he cites. There is no need to look at the bibliography to see the influences of Walter Ong, Eric Havelock, Jack Goody, not to mention Marshall McLuhan, to name only the most obvious. Indeed one of the organizing strategies of the argument is to use the year 1963, based on Havelock's recommendation, as the moment when the limits or edges of "literacy" appeared as such, this being a symptom that apparatus shift was already underway. To read these authors and others telling the history and theory of writing is to appreciate both the extraordinary inventiveness of our tradition and the expectation that the point of being in Composition Studies is not (only) to curate this legacy but to contribute to it. Enough has happened between 1963 and today to make it seem obvious to Rice and his generation that of course it is possible and necessary to innovate in the fields of rhetoric and composition, just as it is in any other disciplinary field.

Paired with this guidance from Theory is an inventory of Analogy. Analogy in this case is filled with an array of the creative practices that Rice summarizes in the term *cool,* defined, as he notes, chorally (that is, using every meaning of the term). What the heuretic CATTt allows us to appreciate is that these manifestations of "cool" do not by themselves provide the rhetoric of new media, any more than does an inventory of the features of hypermedia. Rather, Rice extracts from this array a set of devices—appropriation, juxtaposition, commutation, and the like—that do not exist together in any one of his sources, but that these sources as a whole demonstrate to be relevant to the convergence of demands generated by the other elements of the CATTt. At one level the approach reminds us of one of the peculiarities of our discipline, which is that we study about our inventors but rarely consider learning anything from them with respect to our own practices. Recent studies, for example, have indicated a growing consensus that William Burroughs may be the most important American author of the twentieth century (if not the most popular). Why are we not teaching the cut-up in our composition classes? Why is the macaronic pun perfected in *Finnegans Wake,* to take another obvious example, not introduced as an inference procedure along with the more conventional modes, especially now that Jacques Derrida proved its applicability to the most complex philosophical questions? These devices are available for further use.

The final element of the CATTt is the tale—the form borrowed from one of the other registers and used to organize and make receivable the results of the hybrid developed from a convergence and integration of the four inventories (CATT). *Cool* is a "handbook" that, as any good tale must, does (performs) at least in part what it says. *Cool* is cool in this way, persuasively insisting upon the modesty of its proposals. Part of the persuasiveness comes from the fact that the handbook covers applications of the devices based on the author's classroom experience. The product has been tested. It is not saying that we should forget everything we learned from literacy, but only that the devices extracted from the Analogy, applied to the potentialities of the Target, guided by the proposals of the Theory, make up for the limitations of the Contrast. We still want our students to achieve the goals of literacy (turn information into knowledge; perform the critical thinking required of citizens in a free democracy; experience the full humanity that comes from self-knowledge). We recognize, however, that these goals must be transported into electracy. *The Rhetoric of Cool* is an exemplary performance of this move.

# Acknowledgments

I acknowledge the influence of many friends and colleagues on this project who, no doubt, understand me as living out the definition of unhip as it is outlined in Cab Calloway's *Cab Calloway's Cat-ologue: A Hepster's Dictionary*. Calloway, the great bandleader of the 1930s, describes anyone who is unhip as "not wise to the jive, an icky, a jeff, a square," incidentally naming me (identifying my first name) as unhip, or what we might call uncool, a geek, a nerd. I accept that role—the nerd and the computer person are now equal terms in our culture—as I'm sure my colleagues and friends have accepted that role I play as well.

Notably, in his role as mentor and inspiration for all things "out there" and unconventional, Gregory Ulmer has provided invaluable insight and supported a rhetoric of cool where others may have been dismissive. Ulmer's influence on my work cannot be overstated, and I am grateful for the opportunity I had to study with him at the University of Florida, where I learned about rhetoric, media studies, critical theory, writing, pedagogy, and invention. From the first seminar I took with Ulmer, I entered into the world of technology, rhetoric, and writing. And there has been no looking back. I have learned a great deal from his mentorship and scholarship. Most importantly, I learned that there is no distinction between theory and pedagogy. Theory *is* pedagogy.

Similarly, Sid Dobrin, Jim Paxson, and William Tilson also supported my work while I was at UF and understood my interest in cool as rhetoric as a serious, and not a trivial, topic. Readers and critics (who double as friends) of various essays and presentations relevant to this project also have helped shape it. I thank Victor Vitanza, Geoffrey Sirc, Bradley Dilger, Denise Cummings, Jenny Edbauer, the Weblog community blogrolled on my Weblog and other Weblogs, and the chora-1 group (i.e., The Florida School) at the University of Florida for their comments in this regard. I also thank the editors of journals who published various versions of my project and have allowed me to reprint these revised versions: *Ctheory* ("What Is Cool? Notes on Intellectualism, Popular Culture, and Writing," May 10, 2002), *Composition Studies* ("The 1963 Composition Revolution Will Not Be Televised, Computed, or Demonstrated by Any Other Means of Technology," Spring 2005, 55–73), *Computers and Composition* ("Writing about Cool: Teaching Hypertext as Juxtaposition," Sept. 2003, 221–36, copyright 2003, with permission from Elsevier), *College Composition and Communication* ("The 1963 Hip Hop Machine: Hip Hop Pedagogy as Composition," Feb. 2003, 453–71, copyright 2003 by the National Council of Teachers of English, reprinted with permission), *WPA: Writing Program Administration* ("Cooltown: The Place of Intellectual Work," 2007), *Composition Forum* ("1963: Collage as Writing Practice," Winter 2001, 19–39), *Kairos* ("The Handbook of Cool" 7.2, Summer 2002), *Enculturation* ("The Street Finds Its Own Use for Things: Hypertext, DJing, and the New Composition Program" 4.2, 2002), and *M/C—A Journal of Media and Culture* ("They Put Me in the Mix: Williams S. Burroughs, DJs, and the New Cultural Studies," No. 2, April 2001). To Victor I owe extended gratitude for his assistance in publishing the textbook I wrote for Longman Publishers, *Writing about Cool: Hypertext and Cultural Studies in the Computer Classroom,* a pedagogical approach for teaching cool writing in the classroom. And I owe him extra thanks for the insightful comments he provided on an earlier version of this book. Victor has served as a second mentor to my scholarship over the years, and I am grateful for his insights and friendship. To the University of Detroit Mercy, I still marvel over its decision to hire as director of writing someone devoted to teaching a rhetoric of cool. To Wayne State University, I marvel again that another school has brought me and my ideas about cool into its faculty. I thank Richard Grusin, Ellen Barton, and Richard Marback for their continuing friendship and support at Wayne. And I thank Karl Kageff, Marie Maes, and Southern Illinois University Press for the support in seeing this project through. Finally, I acknowledge the continued support my family has given to a project they no doubt recognize as just another one of my eccentricities. In their voice, I adopt the truism of Bob Dylan's "Gonna Change My Way of Thinking," which asks which is worse: doing your own thing, or just being cool.

And to Koom Koom, I quote: "Let me out, human!"

And to Jenny, who I owe so much, I dedicate this writing and all of my love.

# The Rhetoric of Cool

# Introduction

The truth is that this art of composition, like any other, is one that must be
practiced with deliberate coolness.
                                —Wendell Barrett, *English Composition:*
                          *Eight Lectures Given at the Lowell Institute*

"It's cool, Sister Heavenly," he said in the voice of a convert giving a testimo-
nial. "I got the real cool faith."
                                    —Chester Himes, *The Heat's On*

One could argue that I am merely joining the queue of those in our field per-
petually dissatisfied with everything.
                                  —Cynthia Haynes, "Writing Offshore:
                       The Disappearing Coastline of Composition Theory"

Early in 2001, I read a newspaper advertisement for Broward County Community College entitled "Cool School/Hot Credits." Broward County
Community College, eager to tap into the surrounding, fashionable environment of Las Olas Boulevard and South Florida in general, attempts to lure
prospective students to its campus by promoting the school as cool, as hip
and different, as an institution rebelling against traditional instruction, and,
consequently, as worthy of students' time and money. Featuring a surfboard
on the beach covered with descriptive text, the advertisement contrasts fun
(surfing) with promised educational benefits ("Outstanding professors teach
smaller classes"). Having grown up in South Florida, I can understand this
advertisement's rhetorical value for local students, many of whom, like me,
have at some point identified the beach's value as trumping anything education might offer. In what might be triumphed as an incident of visual rhetoric,
Broward County Community College's promotional material is suggestive
and alluring through its placement of iconic imagery; it fuses South Florida
excitement with the promise of extraordinary education. But what, I thought
as I read over the ad, can we find in the college's curriculum or educational

philosophy that indicates this school as a center for alternative teaching and learning? What is it about Broward Community College that makes it cool? What does a student who attends a "cool school" expect from that institution? Surfing? Fun? Or something different entirely?

The connection between cool and school is the subject of this book, particularly in regard to writing instruction and technology. Since my initial encounter with this one advertisement, I have spent considerable time wondering about a persistent, ambiguous educational investment in cool. Not long after reading the Broward County Community College ad, for instance, I noticed that Education World,[1] an online Web site sponsored by Hewlett Packard, offers Cool School awards for public schools that successfully integrate technology into teaching. The benefits of being named a Cool School are outlined on the organization's Web site:

> Cool School award winners at CS will receive exclusive Cool School T-shirts and mouse pads, two commemorative plaques, Cool School award certificates, plus a Cool School award winner button for their Web site. All Cool School award winners are also eligible to win the title of "Cool School of the Year."

Like the college's advertisement, the Cool School award equates consumerism (surfing for the community college, trinkets for the public school) with cool. But unlike the ad's focus, Cool Schools are situated within cyberculture. Cool Schools, like October 17, 2005, winner Midland High School of Midland, Michigan,[2] put student work, school information, and other related items online. These schools are cool because, supposedly, they are plugged into the Web. They are cool because, like Cyber Oregon Online's COOL School program,[3] they embrace some aspect of online learning as an alternative to or rebellion against the status quo (what we might imagine as bricks and mortars places of learning or non-online teaching). They are cool, one might assume, for how they merge the traditional attitudes of cool (rebellion) with the increasing attractiveness of technological influence. These schools are not so much cool, then, as they are rhetorical; these sites of learning refigure a commonplace position and situate it as pedagogical.

Like these educational examples, I am interested in how cool functions as a rhetorical act. My interests, however, are not entirely with being online and are not at all with winning awards but are more concerned with how cool shapes an emerging technological apparatus we are living, working, studying, and teaching within. Unlike the college's advertisement, I am interested in other meanings associated with this term (those other than "fun" or "sun"), meanings different from cool's definition of popularity, status, or fashion. I am interested in meanings that are more reflected in the advertisement's choice of iconic representation, juxtaposition, and nonlinear reasoning (i.e., "a cool school equates a better education") and the public schools' associations with technology and learning. These other meanings, I claim, can be found not only in an ad like the one I introduce or the Web sites I direct attention to; these meanings already exist within a specific moment that runs parallel to a composition studies' history that begins in 1963. And each meaning, as I will explain in this book, deals with cultural studies, technology, and visual writing, three areas vital to electronic writing. When we bring these meanings together, I will show, we invent a new electronic rhetoric. Why composition studies has not integrated these meanings into its curriculum and why composition studies has not felt cool to be an important rhetoric are questions that motivate the development of what I call the rhetoric of cool.

These kinds of questions are difficult to ask and to answer because of the specific ways composition studies views writing and popular culture terminology, like cool. Within the popular view, cool is typically understood as what Edward Schiappa calls in *Defining Reality* "a fact of usage," the lexical meaning we accept as definitive (6). To introduce what Schiappa also names a "definitional rupture," a rhetorical gap unaccounted for in the definitive meaning (7), is to explore more fully a term's boarder effective value. In rhetorical studies, we are familiar with this line of thinking in terms of language (deconstruction) and critique (cultural studies). Both practices ask us to locate definitional ruptures. Indeed, my work with cool stems from these traditions but notably follows the work of Jacques Derrida, whose breakdown of terms like pharmakon, friendship, specter, or even one's name demonstrates the convolution of everyday discourse and the need to work with that convolution for purposes of invention. To rephrase Derrida's deconstruction of the pharmakon in "Plato's Pharmacy," language "is caught in a chain of significations . . . communications are established, through the play of language, among diverse functions of the word and, within it, among diverse strata or regions of culture" (95). Cool, I contend, is one such chain.

Within that chain, my experience teaching cool as writing leans toward the latter position Schiappa proposes (ruptured meaning), even though the former view (definitive meaning) often arises when I discuss my work. When I first began teaching a series of courses about cool at the University of Florida (where I received my graduate training), typically comments like "So you're the one who teaches cool?" accompanied my introduction around the school's campus. Those asking the question referred to the Writing About Cool classes I taught to freshmen and sophomores as part of the university's general writing requirement. The mystique of a course dealing with the term cool attracts students looking to supplement their studies with interesting subject matter and perplexes other instructors who ponder over such a course's overall significance. Coupled with its status as a *writing course*, confusion immediately sets in, and doubt follows: What does writing have to do with cool? What does the syllabus mean when it says that students learn about cool and how to write cool? Aren't the two areas of cool and writing completely unrelated? Doesn't your course neglect the composition requirements the university demands of its writing courses? Do you tell your students that *you're* cool?

I found similar reactions upon graduation. During MLA interviews in my first year on the academic job market, responses to my work often abandoned whatever discussion we were having regarding pedagogy and technology in order to return to the idea of cool as personality: "So, are your students cool?" "Are you a cool instructor?" "How does one stay cool in the classroom?" "What's the coolest computer application you know?" "What's the coolest Web site you've seen?" "By the way, be cool!" These remarks suggest my interest in cool fixates not on rhetoric but rather on status symbols, the way I or others walk, whether or not I or students speak slang, what's our take on the latest fashion or trend, and what we might wear to class. These remarks, when they do engage with technology, reduce technology to a flashy Web site or a new application gaining in popularity among Web users. These remarks, therefore, reinforce a definitive meaning of cool, for they focus only on the *easily recognizable* meaning in circulation. Similarly, early reader reviews of many of the essays I have published, and which precede this book, often asked why I wasn't writing specifically about Chet Baker (a member of the cool jazz school in the late 1950s), African-American slang, or Madonna. Each of these areas depicts, in some way or another, a topos of cool. Joel Dinnerstein places this topos firmly in the American musical tradition of jazz.

> Contemporary American usage of the word "cool" has its roots in the jazz culture of the early 1940s, and the legendary tenor saxophonist Lester Young probably used it first to refer to a state of mind. When Young said, "I'm cool" or "that's cool," he meant "I'm calm," "I'm OK with that," or just "I'm keeping it together in here." (Dinnerstein 239)

That topos has extended into any number of popular publications on cool, such as, for example, Lewis McAdams's *Birth of the Cool: Beat, Bebop, and the American Avant-Garde,* which reduces cool to the biographies of supposedly "cool" people. I don't disparage the inclination to think of cool as slang, hip figures, cool jazz, celebrity, or any other popular perception of the term. The larger issue, though, and the one never approached when such questions come up, is what does cool refer to when we use it ubiquitously? How can it mean everything and nothing at once? What do we mean when we note cool language, dress, or people? How is this notation part of a way of writing? Are these namings meaningful significations, or do they suggest a disciplinary quandary regarding how we come to accept language as an uncomplicated process? How is cool an electronic form of writing, as Marshall McLuhan and others have since argued, and how are these popular manifestations writing as well? How empty of a rhetorical gesture is the expression "I know what is cool when I see it"?

It is that final point that this book works against. When Alan Liu writes in his recent *The Laws of Cool* that "cool is information designed to resist information," he makes an error regarding the rhetorical power of cool (179). Liu, like many others who discover interest in this popular word, struggles to find a connection between cool and the networked society he spends much time critiquing as "cold." Through a discussion of cool, Liu proposes a quest for the "future literary," the mix of knowledge work and artistic practice that will rejuvenate the Humanities. His work is prompted by a series of questions that, he argues, revolve around the concept of cool: "What is knowledge work? How does information sustain it? And how might the culture of such information—self-named 'cool'—challenge knowledge work to open a space, as yet culturally sterile (coopted, jejune, anarchistic, terrorist), for a more humane hack of contemporary knowledge?" (9). Cool, in this definition, is something to be avoided for how it hinders the production of information. Despite the text's "Laws of" title (an implicit reference to McLuhan's Laws of Media), the laws Liu outlines and traces represent various technology and cultural issues important to academic life, but far removed from the challenges cool poses for discourse. These are not laws of cool but laws for how to resist or avoid cool. Cool, Liu writes, hampers technological innovation and rhetorical production. "The friendship of the Web, and everything it represents in the long history of work leading up to current knowledge work, is also strangely cold. It is from this coldness—remoteness, distantiation, impersonality—that *cool* emerges as the cultural dominant of our time" (76). Cool, as Liu understands it, has nothing constructive to do with rhetoric or with writing; it's a throwaway term best left to popular culture, teenagers, consumerism, and anything else Liu finds antithetical to what he calls "knowledge work." If you engage with cool, this argument follows, then you engage with the superficial. If you engage with cool, Liu argues, then the cultural dominant you succumb to will make you cold, remote, and impersonal. Knowledge, the enthymematic gesture suggests, will suffer, too, the same fate.

That composition studies has replicated Liu's argument to some extent and that it views cool as just a throwaway or superficial term is probably best exemplified in the title of Christine Farris's essay "Too Cool for School? Composition as Cultural Studies and Reflective Practices." Since neither the word *cool* nor those items typically associated with it appear in the essay's content,

Farris does not clarify why she chooses its inclusion in the title. The phrase *too cool for school* does sustain a strong relationship with popular culture as topos for wanting nothing to do with education (I'm too good to be involved) or for dropout practices (school's not the place for me). The phrase materializes in, among other places, contemporary rock music, such as the Ben Folds Five song "That's Robert Sledge," which repeats "Too cool for school" throughout its chorus. The phrase, as well, is prominent in the Eagles' 1974 hit "James Dean," which demonstrates the actor's tragic character and eventual downfall through an emphasis on Dean's foray through high school clichés (dances, jobs in a local garage) as representative of Dean being too cool for school (as the song's chorus claims) while he broke all the rules.

While Farris's description of Indiana University's training of graduate students begins from the position of cool, the kinds of cultural moments these songs project, and the meanings they circulate, never appear in her discussion. After reading Farris's work, who are we to believe is "too cool for school"? The teachers or the students? Is the discipline of cultural studies, which Farris exposes to her graduate students so that they will be better informed teachers, too cool for school because of its, at times, contentious relationship with the university and writing instruction? Or is composition studies itself too cool for school?

> In most English departments, composition is marginalized; the teaching of writing is separated from the teaching of reading. Consequently, the practicum or proseminar, like the freshman composition course, by virtue of who takes it and who teaches it, may be viewed as a-disciplinary and un-theorized by those first coming to teaching. TAs may assume that the teaching of writing to freshmen will not be as fraught with complexity as the "sacred" texts, theories, and rituals they are encountering in the rest of the profession. (Farris 101)

If anything, being too cool for school implies a complexity, a complication of expectations (how writing should be taught) by introducing unfamiliar elements into writing instruction (like, for instance, cultural studies or even the word *cool*). Like the Broward County Community College advertisement, Farris's essay title introduces a term that supposedly is unfamiliar to academic culture. The usage of that term, unfortunately, does not create a tension or "independent" reading because such usage still depends on the notion of status (being too cool). A *status* quo remains in place.

In this book, I am attempting to write against that status quo by arguing the cool writer as not cool for her identity (or how she has adopted the popular cool identity) but rather how she is cool for the ways she uses specific rhetorical practices to make meaning in electronic environments. These practices do not depend on a specific Web platform or technology tool; they are generalizable to new media overall. And while I admit that generalizing new media might appear hyperbolic, my overall point is not to emphasize a given application or approach but rather to consider rhetorical gestures relevant to new media practices, much as rhetorical and writing instruction have done with rhetoric for quite some time. Similarly, my writing style as well won't sound cool; it won't be interrupted by hip sayings, cursing, or any other culturally "in" way of speaking.[4] By writing about cool (and writing about how to write cool), I don't profess to be cool. Such status is irrelevant because, as I will show, there does not exist one single signifier we can acknowledge as cool. What cool offers writing instruction is not so much its content (popularity or slang) but instead its rhetoric. In this sense, my work is more aligned with recent publications like Steven Johnson's *Everything Bad Is Good for You: How Today's Popular Culture Is Actually Making Us Smarter*. Johnson's argument (in McLuhanist fashion) is that the *content* of media, like video games and television, does not affect us so much as the *form* and *rhetoric* of media do. Media that encourage multithreaded thinking, interactivity, complexity, and other features, Johnson argues, have caused changes in how we structure and generate information. Instead of focusing on the violence or nudity such media display, we should think about how these media generate new rhetorical moves. Johnson notes,

> The sharpening of the [average person's] mind can't be measured at the extremes of intellectual achievement. Instead, we should detect that improvement somewhere else, in the everyday realm of managing more complex forms of technology, mastering increasingly nuanced narrative structures—even playing more complicated video games. (156)

Following that thinking, I am doing the same for cool; I am asking for a new kind of rhetorical understanding that begins with cool's structures. I am asking for an understanding much akin to Johnson's appreciation of the complexities media and popular culture pose for new learning practices.

> For decades, we've worked under the assumption that mass culture follows a steadily declining path toward lowest-common-denominator standards, presumably because the "masses" want dumb, simple pleasures and big media companies want to give the masses what they want. But in fact, the exact opposite is happening: the culture is getting more intellectually demanding, not less. (9)

The culture is getting more demanding, and so are the pedagogical practices needed to engage with new media in general. Cool's rhetorical complexity demands its breakdown through theoretical and pedagogical application.

Cool, I have come to discover, consists of a variety of rhetorical gestures and moves. With cool, I find that chora, appropriation, juxtaposition, commutation, nonlinearity, and imagery are the rhetorical moves that comprise a specific new media writing I am inventing. In this book, I break each rhetorical feature down chapter by chapter, offering historical, theoretical, and pedagogical justifications along the way.

The rhetoric I am constructing emerges from the complex ways cool as signifier is put into discursive practice. I will try to do for cool what Diane Davis does for laughter in *Breaking Up (At) Totality*: "Here, however, we will attempt to make a space for a composition pedagogy of an/Other kind, one that puts itself into the service of writing rather than the other way around" (Davis 6). I am arguing for *another* kind of composition pedagogy, a pedagogy whose focus stems from a word popularly believed to have no connection to writing. That other kind of pedagogy I argue for is not a definitive pedagogy. Nor is the historical reading of composition studies I perform throughout this book definitive. Instead, I am arguing for an *alternative* to the status quo we have maintained—a status quo that extends outward from a term like *cool* and comes to include a disciplinary view of writing and new media. That view, I will show, emerges out of a specific temporal moment in composition studies' history. This moment, 1963, has given birth to an ideological and practical way of teaching with technology, one that has ignored the rich rhetorical possibilities cool poses for new media work and has instead settled on very nonmedia, or only slightly media, methods and teachings. In order to critique and respond to that moment, what I offer is "a" theory of writing and new media, not "the" theory of writing and new media.

Finding "a" theory of new media to work with has proven difficult for composition studies, particularly regarding what any rhetoric of new media might entail or offer teaching and research. Even though, for instance, the field has seen the publication of numerous textbooks devoted to technology or visuality over the last few years—texts like *Picturing Texts, Seeing & Writing, Convergences*, and *Writing in a Visual Age*—none completely engage with a rhetoric of new media. Each book continues the project of print culture to some extent, carrying over the very specific assumptions and ideological positions associated with print (writing topic sentences, paragraph-based structuring, interpretation over production, logical reasoning and ordering, referential-based argumentation, the question of purpose, audience recognition) and kept alive through the 1963 composition studies trope of rebirth. And even though a subdiscipline of composition studies, computers and writing, has done excellent work since the late 1970s/early 1980s drawing attention to innovative methods for teaching with technology (particularly regarding MOOs, word processing, and hypertext), the field, as a whole, still lacks a substantive rhetoric of new media. The rhetoric of cool is meant as a first step toward inventing a new media rhetoric by recognizing that the terms that shape writing differ significantly within new media than they have within print. Part of that recognition is that we have to invent new practices for new media. But what makes this project different from others that attempt to fashion new media rhetorics or approaches to writing is that I invent the rhetoric of cool out of the very same time period that led to a completely different outlook regarding pedagogy and new media. Because of this outlook that I critique, the discipline has never seen 1963 as relevant to new media. My task is to foreground the relevant moments we have not yet paid attention to.

To do that, I am a bit performative as well as explanatory and argumentative. In a rhetorical tradition of performance actualized by Jacques Derrida, Roland Barthes, Marshall McLuhan, and Gregory Ulmer, among others, I often demonstrate what I am explaining. As these writers have shown, instrumental application often reveals less about the potential of new media than theoretical performance does. Such performativity is still not the norm in most writing about technology, a norm that often explains or theorizes at the expense of also showing. Contrary to what I perform and how I perform my theoretical assumptions in this book, the majority of computers and writing scholarship still resists performativity, opting instead to focuses mostly on either the "this is what I do with this tool/this is how this tool affects our students" scholarship (often through anecdotal or empirical foundations) or hermeneutical readings of media texts ("this is what the media artifact means") or continued laments regarding the technology gap ("we must first address access"). I am not disparaging these kinds of scholarship, but instead I am looking to generate an alternative approach that is both critical and performative. Therefore, this is not a book that surveys the field of computers and writing or new media in general; it is instead a book fashioning a theory out of a very specific critique and performativity.

My alternative approach stems from a historical discrepancy (1963) I find extremely relevant toward inventing a new media practice. In general, in discrepancy, I contend, is where the possibility of an alternative is most prominent and most promising. For out of difference, we invent. For out of "missed moments," we find completely new possibilities. Those possibilities are, however, sometimes difficult to identify or to work with in terms of disciplinary work because of our dependence on familiar texts and ideas. In this particular project, I look beyond the canonical texts that we believe have shaped our discipline in order to draw upon areas not normally considered relevant to composition studies, but which I find pose long-term possibilities toward inventing new media-based writing practices. My decision to do so is not eccentric; rather I recognize that rhetoric and rhetorical invention emerge out of a number of influences: art, film, literature, music, record covers, cultural studies, imagery, technology, and, of course, writing. Our challenge is to foreground that acknowledgment, not resist it because of its unfamiliarity or because it doesn't fit what we assume writing should entail.

# 1

## The Story of Composition Studies and Cool

We sat in English class and we dissected the stories that I'd escaped into, laid open their abdomens and tagged their organs, covered their genitals with polite, sterile drapes, recorded dutiful notes en masse that told us what the story was about, but never what the story *was*. Stories are propaganda, virii that slide past your critical immune system and insert themselves directly into your emotions. Kill them and cut them open and they're as naked as a nightclub in daylight.

—Cory Doctorow, *Eastern Standard Tribe*

Rhetoric: The use of words by agents to form attitudes or induce actions in other human agents. Accordingly, what we want is not terms that avoid ambiguity, but terms that clearly reveal the strategic spots at which ambiguities necessarily arise.

—Kenneth Burke, *A Grammar of Motives*

What we need and desire is not just terms that reveal the strategic spots at which ambiguities arise, *but terms that create, detonate, and exploit those ambiguities.*

—Victor Vitanza, "Critical Sub/Versions of the History of Philosophical Rhetoric"

I want to tell a story about composition studies and cool. My story isn't about how composition *is* or *isn't* cool. My story is about how cool and composition studies maintain overlapping narratives that commence in 1963. My story is about how this overlap offers composition studies a pedagogy for teaching electronic writing. The story I want to narrate is not typically told in composition circles, nor is it the one most popularly attributed to composition studies' supposed rebirth in 1963. In *The Making of Knowledge in Composition: Portrait of an Emerging Field*, Stephen North tells that story by noting that 1963 marks the moment when composition studies earns its capital C. Nineteen sixty-three, North claims, finds composition studies' dependence on lore, the academic practice of reporting classroom activities and anecdotal experience, yielding to more theoretical concerns as writing instructors struggle to perceive their work as academic. "We can therefore date the birth of modern Composition, capital C, to 1963. And what marks its emergence as a nascent academic field more than anything else is this need to replace practice as the field's dominant mode of inquiry" (North 15). To back his claim, North notes how 1963 events like the annual meeting of the Conference on College Composition and Communication (CCCC)—themed "The Content of the English Course"—as well as the influential publications of Richard Braddock, Richard Lloyd-Jones, and Lowell Schoer's *Research in Written Composition* and Albert Kitzhaber's *Themes, Theories, and Therapy* pushed composition studies away from oral reporting of student work habits and instead encouraged instructors to be theoretical about writing itself. That push gave birth to new theoretical principles and interest in empirical study of writing habits and practices.

Like North, Eric Havelock found 1963 an important date for writing theory. As Havelock worked to map the transformation from oral to alphabetic cultures, he found that in the time period leading up to and including 1963 the near simultaneous publication of several works interested in the history of writing (*La Pensé Sauvage* by Lévi-Strauss, "The Consequences of Literacy" by Jack Goody and Ian Watt, *Animal Species and Evolution* by Ernst Mayr, *The Gutenberg Galaxy* by Marshall McLuhan, and *Preface to Plato* by Havelock) highlighted a renewed interest in how writing defines culture. Havelock discovered that the temporal juxtaposition of different writers with conflicting research agendas produced a pattern, and that pattern, in turn, produced an insight. "The year 1963 provides a convenient watershed date," Havelock writes, "or perhaps better a date when a dam in the modern consciousness appears to burst, releasing a flood of startled recognitions of a host of related facts" (*The Muse Learns to Write* 24).

Havelock's insight into 1963 compliments North's observations regarding composition studies. Yet, when we consider a temporal date as a "watershed" for the way it "startles" common assumptions and disciplinary recognition, we might benefit by expanding the juxtaposition to include other moments as well. Havelock, a prominent figure in writing theory, is himself not a component of North's remarks regarding composition in 1963. Havelock's absence alone might spark suspicion concerning whether or not North's paradigm is inclusive of all or the most significant writing moments in 1963. In fact, a closer look at the time period leading up to and including 1963 reveals three other areas relevant to composition studies unmentioned in North's study:

technology, cultural studies, and visual writing. Even more so, three writers from these areas of study use the same term, *cool*, in order to define their observations regarding communication practices. Interested in how electronic communication reshapes thought and experience, Marshall McLuhan employed "cool" to describe the high-participatory nature of certain media forms (TV, the telephone, comic books) as opposed to the low-participatory characteristic of other forms he called "hot" (film, radio, print). At the same time, in *Blues People*, Amiri Baraka used "cool" to describe the African-American reaction to a white, oppressive authority as calm, noninvolved, detached. Meanwhile, Robert Farris Thompson, working in West Africa and later recording his observations in *Flash of the Spirit*, discovered that African-American terms like *cool* have their origins in indigenous, African societies such as the Yoruba, who use it as a form of visual writing in order to express in art and aesthetics a lifestyle characteristic of appeasement, conciliation, and calmness. Together, these writers discover cool as something beyond its immediate and established connotations of popularity or personality. Together, these writers explore the same word in the areas that, I believe, have become the most important to composition studies today. Yet why have these moments found themselves excluded from composition studies' historical narrative? What are the consequences of not recognizing cool's relationship to writing? Such questions comprise the basis of the story I want to tell in this book, for these are the questions that lead me to invent an electronic writing practice I have come to call the rhetoric of cool. To begin my own story regarding cool and composition studies, however, I first must explore further the grand narrative of composition studies.

## The Grand Narrative

This book begins with a polemic: What is the story of composition studies? The narrative, or story, often told in composition studies is that the field experienced a rebirth in 1963. This narrative follows what Jean-François Lyotard names as the modernist impulse for "grand narratives," sweeping definitions used in order to legitimate meaning. Lyotard critiques the grand narrative as "incapable of describing that meaning adequately" (31). "The grand narrative," Lyotard proclaims, "has lost its credibility, regardless of what mode of unification it uses, regardless of whether it is a speculative narrative or a narrative of emancipation" (37). Grand narratives, Lyotard notes, become recitations rather than factual encounters or historical points of reference. "The narrative's reference may seem to belong to the past, but in reality it is always contemporaneous with the act of recitation" (22). Those grand narratives disciplines, including composition studies, recite repeatedly include ones that involve Democracy, Capitalism, Marxism, or some other sweeping tale of success or plight. In education, we have our own grand narratives, some of which revolve around literacy, others that revolve around pedagogy, others that deal with a variety of issues extending from student learning to investments in technology. My interest is in how certain 1963 narratives have been recited (often without being questioned) and why others haven't been recited as much or at all. Such narratives, or lack of narratives, constitute what we come to accept as knowledge.

It is a point Michel Foucault makes as well in the beginning pages of *The Archeology of Knowledge*. Knowledge, Foucault writes, and the history of any specific knowledge system, depends too much on the question of maintaining a tradition, what Lyotard later refers to as the grand narrative. But, Foucault notes, "the problem is no longer one of tradition, of tracing a line, but one of division, of limits; it is no longer one of lasting foundations, but one of transformations that serve as new foundations, the rebuilding of foundations" (5). Foucault continues: "In short, the history of thought, of knowledge, of philosophy, of literature seems to be seeking, and discovering, more and more discontinuities, whereas history itself appears to be abandoning the irruption of events in favour of stable structures" (Foucault 6). To Foucault's list of stable structures, we can add composition studies' own sense of stability. It is my contention that a great part of the rebirth narrative composition studies embraces has resisted discontinuities in favor of stability. Yet division, not tradition, shapes Havelock's initial juxtaposition of isolated moments in 1963. Havelock juxtaposes for insight ("what do these different moments have to do with one another"), not to deliver a "stable structure" nor an emancipation narrative ("here is where we were reborn"). North, on the other hand, and those who have followed his thinking, seems to depend too much on the emancipative narrative. The 1963 emancipation of composition has made the field feel very stable about its origins, its practices, and its present makeup. When Havelock drew attention to 1963, however, he did so not to praise the overlap of interests in writing and literacy (as North implies rebirth did for the field of composition studies) but to note how this overlap was missed by a number of academic queries, that these moments that overlap are "events that in retrospect take on the lineaments of a single phenomenon unperceived at the time, but marking a crisis in the slow realization of the oral problem" (*The Muse Learns to Write* 25). What Havelock calls "the oral problem" (the importance of orality and its history to literacy and meaning making), I call the digital problem, the understanding that rhetorics of digital culture have been circulating and discussed since the field's rebirth even if composition studies has not paid attention to these rhetorics in a significant way.

In making that point, I am curious as to how "meaningful" or "emancipative" North's recited breakdown of 1963 is because it describes a shift in thinking that excludes the important discontinuity and digital relevance of cool. As much as North attempts to expand upon his premise by categorizing composition into various theoretical practices (practitioners, experimenters, philosophers), he doesn't refer to these other moments relevant to writing studies that don't fit neatly into the typical composition curriculum, what we might call, following the title of Lyotard's text, the "postmodern" presence in composition studies prompted by cultural studies, technology, and writing. That postmodern presence hints at the divisions Foucault emphasizes in his own approach to historical reflection, what he refers to as "points of choice" in defining knowledge.

> Rather than seeking the permanence of themes, images, and opinions through time, rather than retracing the dialectic of their conflicts in order to individualize groups of statements, could one not rather mark out the dispersion of the points of choice, and define prior to any option, to any thematic preference, a field of strategic possibilities? (37)

Instead of the postmodern move that would seem more capable of marking various points of choice, North creates, intentionally or not, a modernist grand narrative regarding the field (a permanent theme), one that stresses more or less a moment centered on a unified theory of empirical (or scientific-oriented) research, one that has found a home in many subsequent discussions and publications on composition studies history.

We hear that narrative in the first Watson Conference in Rhetoric and Composition, held at the University of Louisville, whose published proceedings begin by repeating the significant ramifications of 1963 to the field:

> For the first Watson Conference, we focused on the period between 1963 and 1983, a time often referred to as the "Birth of Composition" (with a capital "C"). In those 20 years, composition changed in a number of crucial ways, including the development of theoretical warrants and research methodologies, the transformation of pedagogical assumptions and practices, as well as a growth in professionalism. (Journet et al. xii)

We hear the date's importance in James Berlin's "The Renaissance of Rhetoric" chapter in his important historical treatise of composition history *Rhetoric and Reality*. Berlin tells us that the time period surrounding 1963 led to "the emergence of rhetoric as a discipline in the English department and has simultaneously [led to] the complementary professionalization of writing instruction" (137). And we hear mirrored claims in Robert Connors, Andrea Lunsford, and Lisa Ede's tribute-collection to Edward P. J. Corbett in *Essays on Classical Rhetoric and Modern Discourse*: "All who attended that convention [CCCC 1963] felt the galvanic charge in the air, the exciting sense of intellectual rebirth. Within the next five years the spirit which had been born at that convention began to transform the teaching of writing" (10). And we hear the same claim in Lester Faigley's *Fragments of Rationality*, which employs the date in order to trace composition's disciplinary identity and "beginnings of a research community" (Faigley 14). Thus, I'm not critiquing North when I problematize the grand narrative; I am critiquing how that narrative remains unchallenged and accepted as de facto history, how its recitation continues to be sounded out in our conferences, journals, and work, how it has become, in Foucault's language, the permanence of a theme. That a handful of publications centered on classroom practice and empirical study have come to dominate and mold our perceptions of what writing entails makes me wonder if we have not erred in the choice to ignore what Havelock calls "startled recognitions." The repetition of the composition grand narrative has done little to startle us, to provoke us, to cause us to wonder what else could have shaped our current writing pedagogies, theories, and practices. Following Faigley's own desire to include the postmodern in composition studies, I ask why hasn't composition studies refocused its narrative for the postmodern, the multiple narratives, the differing stories, the unrecognized moments, the idea of, of all things, cool?

This book, then, marks my attempt to highlight these kinds of questions, to echo Lester Faigley's challenge regarding composition studies' relationship to 1963 and postmodern studies in general.

> But if composition studies coincides with the era of postmodernity, there is seemingly little in the short history of composition studies that suggests a postmodern view of heterogeneity and differences as liberating forces, and there are very few calls to celebrate the fragmentary and chaotic currents of change. (Faigley 14)

In this book, I will celebrate the different, as Faigley argues. I will celebrate a difference so great that it proposes *cool*, a term that, at first glance, may seem the most distant to composition practices and teaching, as itself the basis of electronic writing. And I will celebrate cool in such a manner as to suggest that its presence as a writing practice is neither novel nor fleeting but rather a part of composition studies history not yet explored. To make this celebration explicit, I want to foreground a heterogeneous composition studies history, one that sheds light on how cool's impact on communication, or what Diane George and John Trimbur have named the missing "Fourth C" in composition, needs to be recognized for its rhetorical influence and, specifically, for how it generates a new kind of electronic rhetoric. Specifically, George and Trimbur identify the 1962/3 period as the defining moment when composition abandoned communication studies. "From the time Ken Macrorie took over as *CCC* editor in 1962," George and Trimbur write, "articles on the 'communication approach,' on mass media, propaganda analysis, and general semantics virtually disappeared from the journal" (685). The missing Fourth C is not just communication, as George and Trimbur argue, but it is cool as well. To be even more pronounced in my declaration, I borrow a comment from Ken Macrorie (who George and Trimbur critique) in 1963. In *Uptaught*, Macrorie's influential text divided up as journal entries and thoughts on composition instruction, a November 1963 entry reads, "Mr. Rice wasn't kidding; he's not a kidding man. Many professors who had given their lives for this effort felt insulted. But I didn't hear of one who came forward with a batch of lively student papers to prove Mr. Rice wrong" (18). Unlike the (fellow Michigander) Warren Rice whom Macrorie mentions, I am not coming forward with a batch of student papers. I am coming forward, however, with a batch of untold composition studies-related history. The story of cool, I claim, doesn't begin, but becomes meaningful, in 1963.

## 1963

When I draw attention to 1963, I don't feel I'm exaggerating its representation in composition studies' history, for this very history has had profound implications on how composition studies sees itself today. In addition to my own recognition of significant events and publications of that year, Robert Connors, Andrea Lunsford, Lester Faigley, Geoffrey Sirc,[1] and others have written to some extent about this date's role in composition studies' rebirth. These writers have used the date to further various pedagogical theories and practices as a response or continuation of what occurred in 1963. Unmentioned in any of these narratives is what interests me: The coincidental overlap between those forces that drive composition studies to emphasize 1963 as fundamental and what I have come to recognize as the rhetoric of cool. Central to this overlap is the question of historical representation, of pedagogy, and of disciplinary identity. That one dominant representation and, consequently, one dominant pedagogy can be traced to this date disturbs James Berlin's observation that rhetoric and composition comprises "a diverse discipline that historically has included a variety of incompatible systems" (*Rhetoric and Reality* 3). Berlin cannot be entirely correct in his assumption that incompatible systems operate within our discipline because the continuance of a grand narrative persists, one that has paid little—if any—attention to the technological, visual, and cultural studies moments paralleling the field's rebirth. My overriding question is how I can enter into the historical and pedagogical conversations regarding composition so that cool challenges how the field represents itself in specific ways, why it does so, and how it allows for incompatible systems or re-presentations of this very history, what Victor Vitanza calls a "critical sub/version" of the history of rhetoric. Vitanza has argued that rhetoric allow for the historical re-presentation, which is always a subversive act for how it undermines dominant thinking and encourages "breaking with the encrusted ideology of the tradition" (Vitanza 45).[2] Vitanza's sub/version is not just a rereading; however, it is a call for a completely different kind of rhetoric, one that draws from the very specific rhetorical lessons poststructuralism generates, what Vitanza calls The Antibody Rhetoric. A major feature of The Antibody Rhetoric, borrowed from Lyotard, is the characteristic of "paralogism," the undermining of agreement and assumptions.

> It will not be "persuasion" or "identification" (consubstantiality") that will inform our "newer" histories of Rhetoric. (We will, for example, have another option and consequently no longer repeatedly have to rediscover and reinvest in, as Perelman does, a tragic, Aristotelian Rhetoric.) Instead, it will be a Rhetorical/critical attitude and practice known as "paralogism," or what I have called "Sub/Version" (and possibly even sub-sub-versions) a kind of intellectual guerilla warfare conducted by marginals, that will function as a de/stabilizing principle (through paradox or irony) or as a dis/placing principle (through oxymoronic metonymy) in the writing of our "newer" histories. (Vitanza 52)

My re-presentation of a history (and not, necessarily, *the* history) of composition studies is meant as a sub/version, for who would think to associate composition studies and cool? And when I make that connection, how am I undermining an assumed history of composition studies? By arguing for a sub/version, I want to make composition studies uncomfortable about its history because we have agreed too quickly about what that history entails. But I don't yearn for uncomfortability merely for the sake of upsetting. By undermining an accepted history (and thus the consequences of that history), I want to disrupt composition's commonplace assumptions regarding cultural studies, technology, and writing, how they fit into a given curriculum, and how they mesh with one another. Out of this discomfort, I hope that composition studies will become more accepting of alternative approaches to the teaching and theorizing of writing. For it is only from preliminary discomfort that we eventually come to understand and work with new positions. What I pose, then, is *one* alternative, one re-presentation, one sub/version meant to draw us out of a dominant re-presentation in circulation today. Out of this alternative, I would hope others will follow as well.

By saying "composition studies," I am also referring to myself, my relationship to the field, my understanding of the field's theory, my disciplinary identity, my past work as a writing program administrator, and my own participation in the various practices influenced by North's accepted reading of 1963. I, too, am caught within these commonplace assumptions even as I try to resist and reshape them. I participate in the field's conferences, contribute to its journals, have served in administration, and have named myself a member of the rhetoric and composition community. Still, I feel little connection to the commonplace historical narrative disseminated among us. Vitanza writes, "Commonplaces have an insidious way of fostering, protecting, and maintaining only the status quo" (44). By denying cool a place within composition studies' history, I feel that we are fostering a status quo, a restriction regarding what terms and definitions become circulated in our disciplinary vocabulary. The consequences of that restriction are ideological as much as they are practical. The very act of restriction controls the field's perception of itself and ability to re-present itself in a variety of ways, especially if those ways conflict or disrupt our expectations. The restriction keeps one imaginary element in place (what we imagine ourselves to be doing or what we imagine ourselves to be) and shuts out another (what we imagine we might become). No truer has this claim I make been than with the role of technology in writing instruction.

In this alternative space I present, cool offers composition studies an opportunity to address the rhetorical demands electronic communication creates, if we can rethink our commonplace assumptions regarding what cool is, what electronic writing consists of, and what we need to know to engage with the electronic (instrumental learning or theoretical discovery). The best way to rethink assumptions is to revisit important historical moments in our field's imaginary history and create what Geoffrey Sirc has called "the ruptures in composition's history" (*English Composition* 269). What Sirc calls a "rupture" I understand as a move away from predetermined meanings and a beckoning of other possibilities, what Jacques Derrida identifies as "only contexts without any center of absolute anchoring" (*Limited Inc.* 12). This book is meant to provide the contexts of cool as electronic writing, not the specific situations, tools, or other devices we use to anchor meaning when we say computers and composition, new media, digital literacy, or any other disciplinary name for the work we do. We can imagine this book's rhetorical breakdown of cool as applicable to Weblogs, wikis, Web pages, Flash presentations, IM, or any other technology that has or will emerge.[3] The tool is not the issue; rhetoric is the focal point of discussion. As Stuart Selber writes, the danger of theorizing only toward instrumental application is that we will eventually reinforce a status quo (rather than invent a new practice or critical approach):

Needless to say, there are consequences associated with such conventional instructional approaches and misconceptions. In the context of computer literacy, for example, computers will be understood primarily in instrumental terms—as systems for supporting status quo, relatively hierarchical student-teacher relationships, or for automating repetitive and routine tasks, or for making difficult texts and concepts ostensibly more interesting to study. (9)

Along this line of thinking, and as a way to avoid reinstating the conventional, I am engaging with a "rupture" in terms of rhetorical perception and production, not with which tools we opt to use (pen vs. word processor/word processor vs. Weblog) nor which new media texts we encounter when we surf the Web or buy software. Thus, I am not surveying contemporary new media practices in detail nor offering critical readings of new media texts. These types of new media readings can be found elsewhere, such as in Katherine Hayles's provocative books *Writing Machines* and *My Mother Was a Computer,* Mark Hansen's fascinating survey of new media and affect in *New Philosophy for New Media,* or William J. T. Mitchell's speculation on the future of digital space in *City of Bits: Space, Place, and the Infobahn,* among other places. To do the kinds of readings Hayles and Hansen accomplish in their recently published texts is highly useful for understanding writing and new media. But for me to do that work in this book would mean that I avoid the historical and critical reflection I feel is still needed in order to understand an over-forty-year-old connection between technology and writing instruction, a connection I feel is missing in composition studies scholarship. Before composition studies eagerly absorbs contemporary media theory, it might benefit first to reflect on why it has come to media theory so late in the game.

By returning to 1963, my principle intention is to offer that reflection in order to draw out a rhetorical practice that will teach electronic writing as a rhetoric of cool. In doing so, I follow Marshall McLuhan's remark in *Understanding Media* that "[t]he 'message' of any medium or technology is the change of scale or pace or pattern that it introduces into human affairs" (24). Change motivates my project. As McLuhan noted in the early 1960s, we are in a time of communicative transition. Such transitions can be difficult to immediately notice because their effects are felt either sporadically or over extended time. The changes the nineteenth-century American educational system experienced regarding the assessment of print-based writings came about long after the introduction of the printing press. The changes brought on by new media are still being experienced and struggled with. Yet despite the difficulties involved in addressing communicative changes, absence of change has served the narrative of 1963 and composition studies for very relevant reasons. And it is the absence in the 1963 narrative of any significant mentioning of a change in how writers interact with and respond to cultural or technological moments that motivates my own interests in this time period. Even if such changes have not been recognized as relevant to the field's rebirth, that doesn't mean that they have not affected how we write.

My job is to bring these changes together into a rhetorical practice for electronic work. And because I anticipate critiques that I am not speaking enough about specific applications, I feel the point needs repeating: The practice I call the rhetoric of cool will not be instrumental; it will not identify how to use software or work with specific applications like Dreamweaver, Fireworks, Photoshop, or others. Instead, this book will define a rhetorical practice conducive and generalizable to digital culture. The rhetorical moves I identify as belonging to the rhetoric of cool are possible only because of digital culture; they challenge and disrupt print-oriented conventions and structural logic. Even if those texts and writers I draw upon to learn these practices don't actually work with technology, the rhetorical value I find and present as part of the rhetoric of cool is the result of post-World War II American culture, a culture largely shaped by an emerging electronic apparatus based on television, film, the transistor, radio, and, of course, the computer. The figures I draw upon could not have produced the rhetorical work they did within any other kind of apparatus; their work is technologically fashioned by implicit and explicit forces.

## Rhetoric and Writing

My contention is that 1963's importance to writing studies must now be understood as a technology-based moment, even if traditional readings of the date state otherwise. My rationale for focusing on 1963 in order to explain the rhetoric of cool stems from what composition studies imagines as this date's importance and legacy to how we define ourselves as compositionists, and how we define our teaching as composition today. Largely, composition studies concentrates on a number of issues central to a perceived rebirth in 1963, among them the rhetorical revival. Triumphed by Edward P. J. Corbett and his later textbook based on classical rhetoric, this revival stressed the return to classical rhetorical approaches to discourse construction. In a 1987 issue of *College Composition and Communication* (*CCC*), Corbett reflects on the early 1960s as a time of renewal when he remarks, "I have always dated the emergence of rhetoric as the rationale for the teaching of composition from the spring of 1963, when the Conference on College Composition and Communication held its annual convention in Los Angeles" ("Teaching Composition" 445).

The rhetorical revival intended to compensate a lost art of rhetoric. Thus, in 1963, Richard Weaver recognized this lack by expressing dissatisfaction with the state of rhetorical and compositional instruction, alluding to classical rhetoric as the lost model. "Our age has witnessed the decline of a number of subjects that once enjoyed prestige and general esteem, but no subject, I believe, has suffered more amazingly in this respect than rhetoric" (201). Weaver was not alone in his lament. "What does classical rhetoric have to offer composition teachers?" Corbett inquired in the October 1963 issue of *College Composition and Communication* ("The Usefulness of Classical Rhetoric" 162). Seeing classical rhetoric as a handbook that students can draw from in order to properly perform such rhetorical feats as *status, dispositio,* and *imitation,* Corbett answered his own question by responding, "a great deal." "What most of our students need, even the bright ones, is careful, systematized guidance at every step in the writing process. Classical rhetoric can provide that kind of positive guidance" ("The Usefulness of Classical Rhetoric" 164). Alongside Corbett's essay in the same issue of *CCC*, Wayne Booth's "The Rhetorical Stance" probed what rhetoric exactly entails: "Is there such an art? If so, what does it consist of? Does it have a content of its own? Can it be taught? Should it be taught? If it should how do we go about it, head on or obliquely?" (Booth 139). Booth's response, the rhetorical stance, appears less as the paradigm shift it promises to be and more as a return to classical rhetorical thought: knowledge of all available arguments, knowledge of one's audience, and establishment of speaker ethos. Booth argues for the Ciceronian breakdown of invention plus a few added elements. Combined with Booth's conception of rhetoric as the Aristotelian "art of persuasion," the rhetorical stance is a plea for a classical return as well. Academic figures like Weaver, Booth, and Corbett searched for ways to change the apparatus. They chose, though, to reinstate an old form in place of the emerging new. Corbett, for example, claimed that Greek orators or rhetoricians "made more provision for bringing 'the whole soul of man into activity' than do the authors of any modern textbooks that I know of" ("The Usefulness of Classical Rhetoric" 162). More specifically, Corbett declared that "[o]ur students might very well profit from the ancient discipline of imitation" ("The Usefulness of Classical Rhetoric" 163).

No doubt imitation is useful. Just as useful, at least useful for specific kinds of writing instruction, has been the general textbook approach that, too, often stresses imitation as a pedagogical tool for writing instruction. As Robert Connors and Lester Faigley have both written, James McCrimmon's 1963 textbook *Writing with a Purpose*[4] marks another vital moment in composition's rebirth, one as important as the rhetorical revival. McCrimmon's textbook, Connors writes, signifies a clear "picture of where composition teaching has been during the period 1950–1980 and of where it may be going" (Connors 209). According to this version of McCrimmon's influence, *Writing with a Purpose* introduced the concept of process to writing instruction, preempting Rohman and Wlecke's *Pre-Writing: The Construction and Application of Models for Concept Formation in Writing* by one year. *Writing with a Purpose*'s chapter "The Process of Composition," for instance, establishes various steps a writer should take when composing for school, a novel idea for a product-oriented pre-1960s discipline. Rohman and Wlecke may have created the concept of prewriting when they noted:

> That part of the entire activity called writing which occurs before words appear on the page, and that part after words on a page. The former we called "pre-writing," the latter "writing" and "re-writing." We concerned ourselves almost entirely with pre-writing both because we believed it to be the initial and crucial stage of the writing process, and because we believed it had not been given nearly enough of the theoretical attention it consequently deserved. (Rohman and Wlecke 12)

But McCrimmon's impact on how writers compose seems to have carried further. His interests in outlining and planning as well as his definition of the "four qualities" of good writing, "completeness, unity, order, and coherence," are easily recognizable to teachers and students working out of contemporary textbooks (McCrimmon 69). His teaching that "a good thesis is restricted, unified, precise" will elicit much agreement among many first year instructors who, too, strive to situate student writing within these parameters (McCrimmon 40).

These parameters for defining writing (precision, clarity, order, coherence) dominate the empirical research generated by Braddock and colleagues and Albert Kitzhaber in 1963 as well. Both *Research in Written Composition* and *Themes, Theories, and Therapy* understand the study of writing as the restricted empirical observation of behavior, performance, and expected results. Basing their studies on the concept of the student as variable, these texts, which have become two of the most influential 1963 theoretical works on composition pedagogy, attempt to transfer composition pedagogy from a hodgepodge collection of anecdotes and teaching stories to the clear and coherent reasoning of how classroom practice can best succeed. The keyword in this kind of research is *control,* control over who and what are being studied, and control over how these studies are employed to maintain some degree of standardized practice. In his critique of Braddock and colleagues' legacy of control, William Irmscher writes, "In their zeal to follow rigorous procedures, researchers frequently run counter to the act of composing or the act of teaching that they supposedly are studying" (83). That opposition, Irmscher argues, means that for a good deal of our discipline, "research in composition has become identified with one kind of research—controlled experimental studies producing statistical evidence" (82). Indeed, there is little difference between the precise and restricted notion of a thesis (how it controls idea development) in McCrimmon's textbook and the practices these two books outline (how to control the research process). Ordered observations produce ordered practice. Ordered practice produces ordered rhetoric, which, in turn, produces the ordered student. Such is what McCrimmon teaches students to perform in their own work, and such is what Braddock and colleagues and Kitzhaber ask of the field regarding its academic future.

The question I raise throughout this book, however, is if we have made the right choice by extending this principled method of teaching so that it remains a staple of current practice and a significant number of contemporary textbooks (as Connors, in particular, argued regarding McCrimmon) even though technological influence may prompt a different kind of writing and writing instruction than this method offers. As Cynthia Haynes notes, in our pedagogy, "Taking a stand, we teach, means adopting a critical stance. But we are unwilling to relinquish the *standardization* for the methods and means for doing so; and, we are not exactly eager to look into the *depths* of how this particularly pedagogy came about" (671). No truer is this claim than in the maintenance of specific ideologies and practices associated with technology and writing. What are the compositional ideological and practical depths associated with technology and writing? How do they owe their existence to 1963? Those contemporary textbooks that draw upon technology—like *Picturing Texts, Seeing and Writing, Writing in an Electronic World, Convergences, Writing in a Visual Age,* and *Beyond Words: Reading and Writing in a Visual Age*—often employ the same principles McCrimmon taught as essential to good writing. That these texts often assume the writing process in general as mostly unchanged is an indicator of how influential McCrimmon's text and its ideological approach has been. The challenge is to recognize how other texts in 1963 upset the conventions books like McCrimmon's set in place; sometimes that process involves a complete reevaluation of our work, and sometimes it means updating the work we do.

When McLuhan introduces cool, for instance, he mentions many of those characteristics we currently value as relevant to writing instruction, like process. With cool media, he writes, "Instead of the product the process." Yet McLuhan also challenges those traditions associated with print, like the outline. "In periods of new and rapid growth, there is a blurring of outlines" (*Understanding Media* 280). Which is it then? The adherence to process or to the outline? If outlines, the basis of print-oriented organization schemes (and thus symbolic of print in general), which process is largely based upon in

1963, are "blurred," where do we turn in order to organize, write, and express? That answer, I contend, can be found within 1963 itself. We built the wrong outline, I argue. In fact, we shouldn't have built an outline at all because the outline has kept us too structured and focused on an outdated (even for its time period) status quo.

In these three historical moments I briefly describe (the classical rhetorical revival, McCrimmon's textbook, and empirical research), I find the very status quo Vitanza argues against, and that has generated a disciplinary dilemma. Because these forty-year-old teaching instructions make so much sense today to the majority of the field's researchers and teachers, I am troubled. I am troubled because I fear that this kind of writing advice has been passed down and accepted without regard to various communicative changes spurred by technology, many of which also came out of 1963. My concern is not that a supposedly "old method" like classical rhetoric or textbook instruction becomes easily integrated into our teaching without thought or that either signifies faulty instruction to be avoided at all cost. Instead, I am curious as to how those individuals writing in 1963 could have missed the technological, visual, or cultural influences occurring around them *as they made their claims*. What are the consequences for not recognizing the important work done by the three figures I initially name in the beginning of this chapter, and other related moments that draw from their interests in cultural studies, technology, and visual writing?

Corbett's insistence on the unmitigated influence of an oral form of communication or McCrimmon's categorization of discourse as *only* clear and coherent pose serious consequences for how we imagine writing instruction today. These tropes circulate as truths, universal claims to how writing must be taught. If any trope is kept as truth (including those I project) without ever being questioned or re-presented, we encounter what Foucault named a privileging of knowledge production.

> If the history of thought could remain the locus of uninterrupted continuities, if it could endlessly forge connexions that no analysis could undo without abstraction, if it could weave, around everything that men say and do, obscure synthesis that anticipate for him, prepare him, and lead him endlessly towards his future, it would provide a privileged shelter for the sovereignty of consciousness. (12)

In my de-privileging, I examine a wide spectrum of writing, and I am not limited to the views put forth in the 1963 canonical texts. Yet, these three texts *(Research in Written Composition, Themes, Theories, and Therapy,* and *Writing with a Purpose)* as well as other related temporal texts, are essential focal points of my de-privileging. Because of how they have been easily accepted into our work, and because of how they have been seldom challenged for their viewpoints on writing, the doctrines they have put in place theoretically and pedagogically have masked new media related moments essential for contemporary teaching. Therefore, even though *Research in Written Composition* poses the question, "What forms of discourse have the greatest effect on other types of writing?" (Braddock *et al.* 53) as an open inquiry intended to make the field more inclusive, I have never discovered in 1963's "greatest hits" of rebirth any indication that cool might be one of those forms of discourse.

My argument, therefore, resembles (even if only slightly) Winston Weathers's call in *An Alternate Style: Options in Composition* for a "Grammar B." Drawing on what he felt were nonconventional rhetorical sources (like literature), Weathers's "Grammar B" was meant to disrupt "the characteristics of continuity, order, reasonable profession and sequence, consistency, unity, etc. We are familiar with these characteristics, for they are promoted in nearly every English textbook and taught by nearly every English teacher" (6). Weathers wanted to challenge specific assumptions regarding "good writing" (the "traditional" composition Weathers named Grammar A) by focusing attention on distinctive texts read outside the classroom, but seldom used as rhetorical models for "good" writing. Weathers writes:

> It is not just another style—way out of the periphery of our concerns—but is an altogether different "grammar" of style, an alternate grammar, Grammar B with characteristics of variegation, synchronicity, discontinuity, ambiguity, and the like. It is a mature and alternate (not experimental) style used by competent writers and offering students of writing a well-tested set of options that, added to the traditional grammar of style, will give them a much more flexible voice, a much greater communication capacity, a much greater opportunity to put into effective language all the things they have to say. (Weathers 8)

Cool belongs in this tradition of alternatives, a tradition, Weathers notes, that emerges out of digital culture. The innovative rhetorical moves twentieth-century literary production followed resulted from electronic influence. "The influence of radio, television, and movies on the evolution of Grammar B is tremendously important," Weathers argues. "Many of the stylistic devices that finally became a part of Grammar B are based on cinematic techniques as well as on the audio techniques found in radio and stereo systems. More important, it was electronic media that used an alternative style so frequently and so powerfully that its grammar could no longer be ignored" (Weathers 10–11). I want to push Weathers's interest in the rhetoric of literature even further so that we draw on a variety of media forms for rhetorical instruction and not just novels and poetry. But like Weathers, I want it to be understood that this rhetoric—even as it comes from literature, film, music, and elsewhere—is the result of electronic culture.

I recognize that it's too easy to critique a field for missing what I, the writer, believe to be an important moment. After all, many moments must have been ignored, passed over, or considered insignificant within each year deemed significant to composition's past and future. But because cool in 1963 draws attention to issues of increasing concern to writing pedagogy, we must question its absence in the 1963 paradigm shift as well as inquire as to how its rhetorical contributions can finally be interwoven into current curricula and theoretical work. This book works to establish the rhetorical foundations from which cool operates. It can be read as a resalvaging of the alternative theoretical (not classical rhetoric) and practical (not McCrimmon) moments in 1963. This book can be read as sub/versive as well. In addition, the following chapters can be read as a guide, a how-to, regarding the various rhetorical moves at stake in a rhetoric of cool, how they come about in 1963, and how they can be applied to current teaching and writing. Each chapter introduces models the rhetoric of cool draws upon in order to function. From these models, I generalize rhetorical moves that I have come to understand as necessary for any kind of writing that will be placed within a digital/electronic context.

The chapters also can be read in conjunction with the textbook I have written for Longman Publishers, *Writing about Cool: Hypertext and Cultural Studies in the Computer Classroom* (2004), if readers desire a more systematic application of each rhetorical strategy marketed to students. The textbook, of course, has its own audience and focus whose needs do not demand theoretical explication as to why the rhetoric of cool requires a rethinking of composition studies in general. This book, on the other hand, is meant to serve the practitioners, the instructors, the theorists among us who want to understand how diverse rhetorical systems are created, and how such systems can be applied to electronic writing. That I conclude each chapter with a pedagogical nod to my own textbook, though, is deliberative (and not egocentric). The unification of theory and practice is a widely circulated trope seldom acted upon in the manner I am attempting: to write both a textbook and a theoretical book on the same subject. All of the theoretical work I propose here I have engaged with pedagogically as well (although I recognize that my pedagogy may not be the best approach or the test case; it serves as a general example). And because I expect some readers to ask, "How do I teach this theory you propose?" I also include these references to relevant assignments outlined in the textbook so that others may begin from where I have started—and where I hope they will expand upon what

I have proposed. Thus, what I would like is that readers will work from the various rhetorical strategies I associate with the rhetoric of cool, consider my own usages both theoretically and within my pedagogy, and then attempt to reshape these ideas for new work, both in the classroom and in other theoretical and practical spaces.

How each strategy operates in hypertext, on a Weblog, in Flash, or any other new media-oriented platform depends on the user and the situation the user encounters. The focus is not meant to be with the tools but in the practices that often result from the various kinds of electronic media we either work with or are shaped by. Gregory Ulmer writes regarding his own nontool-based experiment in electronic rhetoric, "My interest is not only in the technology itself but also in the problem of inventing the practices that may institutionalize electronics in terms of schooling" (*Heuretics* 17). Whatever tool one chooses for electronic writing, what is apparent to me is that these rhetorical applications I will discuss in the next six chapters—chora, appropriation, juxtaposition, commutation, nonlinearity, and imagery—do function in electronic work as the basis of the intellectual work we perform today. Like Lev Manovich in his influential text *The Language of New Media*, I want to draw attention to specific rhetorical features conducive to new media, what Manovich calls the "general tendencies of a culture undergoing computerization" (27). In place of Manovich's interests in databases, variability, transcoding, and other applications, I discuss these six rhetorical principles I have found conducive to cool. In this way, I am explicitly writing against the kinds of negative positions taken up regarding new media and rhetoric like that espoused by Alan Liu in *The Laws of Cool*. "Whether it is expressed as appropriation, sampling, defacement, or hacking," Liu comments, "there will be nothing more cool—to use the term of the nascent, everyday aesthetics of knowledge work—than committing acts of destruction against what is most valued in knowledge work—the content, form, or control of information" (8). Liu, as this book shows, is mistaken in his assessment of technology and cool, for these very acts of electronic rhetoric he dismisses as destructive are central to the information system he hopes to return to the Humanities. "Cool feeling may be everywhere on the Web (cool, after all, ranks among the most totalitarian aesthetics ever created)," Liu writes, "Yet there is so little feeling in cool feeling" (237). Unlike my project, Liu finds cool to be counterintuitive to digital work. His premise is based on an accepted topos of cool as a superficial meaning system ("cool feeling" equates being cold). The topos, which I show in the next chapter, no longer apply—as they have applied—to how we construct new rhetorical systems, like the rhetoric I construct with cool. And while I don't want to make a straw man out of Liu's argument, I do draw attention to its continuation of a topos of cool as popularity or feeling. What Liu foregrounds is, I contend, the reason why areas of study, like composition studies, have yet to notice the potential for an alternative kind of new media writing. To produce knowledge in what McLuhan names "The Gutenberg Galaxy," we are obligated to learn the rhetoric of a newly emerging electronic apparatus centered in acts of appropriation, sampling, hacking, and other related moves. *The Rhetoric of Cool* is meant to give context for how that functionality currently is situated, as well as how it may change yet again in the not too distant future. And because what I describe emphasizes change over fixity, I turn in the next chapter to chora, the principle that rhetorical meaning is not stable but instead fluid and moving. Cool, as I will show, indicates a very specific choral moment in new media writing.

# 2

## Chora

Cool has a history, and cool has a meaning. We all know cool when we see it, and now, more than at any other time in American history, when mainstream America looks for cool we look to black culture. Black cool is imperialistic and ubiquitous.
—Donnell Alexander, "Are Black People Cooler Than White People?"


Mr. Rice wasn't kidding; he's not a kidding man. Many professors who had given their lives to this effort felt insulted, but I didn't hear of one who came forward with a batch of lively student papers to prove Mr. Rice wrong.
—Ken Macrorie, *Uptaught* (1963 entry)


In his 1963 essay "The Usefulness of Classical Rhetoric," Edward P. J. Corbett dramatizes the importance of audience awareness in rhetorical production. "The classical rhetoricians kept constantly in mind the audience toward which the discourse was directed" (162). Audience expectation is defined by writerly knowledge of a given topos. Cool is one well-known topos. Its popular meaning reflects the commonplace assumptions we typically make regarding youth culture, fashion, music, or anything else deemed worth having or being in popular culture. We employ the *topoi* for purposes of familiarity, to speak to those assumptions and beliefs we imagine an audience relating to and recognizing quickly. Popular advertisements like Levi's "Be Cool. It's Strange Out There" or Gap's "Cool Khakis" utilize the familiar meaning of cool as status, social standing, or popularity. The Levi's ad replicates the well-known cool images of James Dean and John Lennon (the ad is an appropriation of John Lennon's album cover for *Rock 'N' Roll;* Lennon appropriated the image of James Dean for the album cover). The Gap ad appropriates imagery from *West Side Story,* replacing the film's street toughs with khaki wearing teenagers dancing against a sanitized prison backdrop to Leonard Bernstein's song from the film, "Cool." These appropriations capture a familiarity. Other familiar meanings of cool circulate around individuality or individual taste.

Following this tradition of cool as topos, "Be Cool," Keds 2004/2005 campaign for its tennis shoe states, "Cool Is You, Pure and Simple."[1] If cool is "me," as an ad like this professes, it is because I am an "individual"; it is because of the tastes I carry into a conversation, event, moment, or other activity. Polly Esther, editor of the now defunct Web site Suck.com, describes cool accordingly as a level of personal taste that dictates consumer spending and fashionable lifestyle:[2] "Go to one of those used furniture stores, the ones with the shitty furniture from the '70s that's marked up to '90s prices! Pick out the ugliest, most outrageous stuff, preferably in powder blue or avocado, and pay way, way, way too much for it! Voila! Instant cool!" (Esther). Such rhetorical gestures are often aimed at teenagers. VH1's series of shows *My Coolest Years* fuses the familiar tropes of youth, social status, and individuality through the eyes of celebrity culture in the series' episode titles: "My First Time," "Bad Girls," "Summer Vacation," and "Jocks and Cheerleaders."

> *My Coolest Years* is the series that gives us the fun look back at a time we all remember so well. High School. Being cool never mattered as much as it did in high school, right?! Image was everything! What you wore (jellies, concert t's, braces head gear, etc.), what you listened to (Judas Priest and A HA, etc.), who you hung out with (other freaks & geeks, etc.), where you lived, what you could do. We thought it all mattered so much—and it kinda did. High school was where you learned that achieving "coolness" meant possibly surviving the hormone-soaked, acne-faced battles for acceptance in the face of guaranteed ridicule from peers and classmates. (My Coolest Years)

In his discussion of adolescent behavior, *Cool: The Signs and Meanings of Adolescence*, Marcel Danesi echoes this vision of cool. He presents a topos of cool most of us readily understand because of how it situates all cool activities as relevant to teenage behavior.

> *Being cool* for the denizens of the contemporary social territory that I have called *teenagerhood* entails knowing how to dress for a peer audience, how to carve out an appropriate body image for that same audience, what kind of rock music is fashionable, which peers to hang out with, how to smoke, what parties to attend, how to speak in strategic ways, and so on. (Danesi 125)

This is the topos driven image of cool always fixated on youth and fashion and often carried out by advertising. Cool is represented by a "kid" or "youth figure" who is emotional and trend oriented. "Joe Cool says 'No Way' to everything," Charles Schultz's character Snoopy declares; Joe Cool is the perfect example of this type of figure whose basis is structured after the peer group (37). It is an image easily carried over into popular rhetorical expression.

Two commercial advertisements for the web hosting service .TV make Danesi's point more explicit. .TV capitalizes on the topos of cool by using James Dean's image in order to promote its products. One ad presents a series of "cool" and "not cool" images over the soundtrack of Richard Strauss's "Blue Danube"; only instead of being an instrumental, the song's rhythm is replaced by the persistent repetition of the word *cool*. Another .TV advertisement features a shirtless James Dean promoting the company's product to a young audience. "James Dean was cool," the ad declares. "There was no cooler name than James Dean." After several images of Dean posing, the commercial concludes with the statement, "This moment of cool was brought to you by .TV." Dean the figure is replaced by Dean the name, the symbol of rebellious youth, the cultural marker indicating the too fast to live/too young to die motif that teenage consumption buys into. Through the image of Dean, consumers easily recognize the type of associations .TV wants to equate with its products: hipness, rebellion, and popularity. These kind of associations are what Stuart Hall and Paddy Whannel recognized in their 1964 *The Popular Arts* as the focal point of a commonplace recognition of cool.

> James Dean portrayed the ideal of blue-jean innocence, tough and vulnerable in the same moment, a scowl of disbelief struggling with frankness for mastery in his face and eyes, continual changes of mood and expression on his features that mark that style of "cool" indifference—a kind of bland knowingness about the ways of the world, even, at times, a disenchantment, an assumed world-weariness. (Hall and Whannel 283–84)

The James Dean audience is assumed to consist mostly of teenagers, moody adolescents, or those who relate to the widely disseminated image of worldly detachment and occasional aloofness that Dean projects. One doesn't need to have seen a Dean film to be included in this audience. One only has to be familiar with the circulated meanings.

The topoi, Aristotle tells us, establish common meanings and assumptions so that audience expectation can be anticipated and met with ease. The topoi, as Aristotle indicates in *The Rhetoric*, are the "places or lines of argument from which to draw enthymemes" (15). Topoi function as rhetorical building blocks; they provide communicators with common ideas from which to create discourse. For Aristotle, the topoi instruct orators what to say when speaking to specific audiences ("Another topoi depends on the fact that men do not always make the same choice on a later as on an earlier occasion"), when confronted with specific situations ("Another topoi is from the accidental"), or when faced with complex language choices ("Another topoi is from the various senses of a word"), among other items (168, 175, 163). All of the topoi are context dependent; how and why one chooses among the selections depends on what one is saying and to whom. In contemporary culture, when students (as well as instructors) are faced with entertainment culture at home, school, and work, popular culture tends to dictate the contexts of our understandings and absorption of the commonplace topics. Popular culture also alters what we perceive as commonplace. We find ourselves dependent on popular culture to make meaning, whether we appreciate popular culture's dominant role in our lives or not.

The topoi have served print-based writing instruction by allowing students (and often instructors) the ability to work from a common repository of ideas. This legacy is found in numerous first-year writing textbooks that pose the question of argumentation in terms of audience, purpose, and invention. First-year composition students, the theory goes, need set places of argumentation to draw upon in order to construct positions. There exists, however, a limitation to rhetorical work when we focus entirely on how to utilize topoi for purposes of persuasive, informative, or any other discursive activity. Because expectation is situated as the norm of rhetorical output in this kind of system, writers often face obstacles regarding how they engage language innovatively, how they fashion new ways of expression, or even how they adjust to formats and structures that don't accommodate topoi well. David Bartholomae calls innovation over convention and the commonplace "dangerous" and "counterproductive" in first-year writing (81). But, as I will show, the danger might be more with our dependence on the topoi in the age of new media. The topoi situate writers and their ideas within a fixed place of discussion, and thus, they create a problem when we begin to work in the digital.

I realize that the nonexpected meanings of cool I draw from in order to invent the rhetoric of cool come from a strategy different than Aristotelian topoi. Cool as cultural studies, cool as technology, and cool as visual writing all individually operate from different topos-based positions. My usage of all these positions at once is associative, not categorical or permanent, as the Aristotelian method demands. Gregory Ulmer names this strategy I employ *chora*, a hyper-rhetoric practice that updates the topoi for new media. In *Heuretics: The Logic of Invention,* Ulmer notes that the Aristotelian topoi are a literate method for structuring argumentation. The topoi serve print culture by providing a fixed method for categorizing information in anticipated ways. The nature of print to refer back to specific "things" (via the notion of referentiality) works by expectation. We expect a specific word to refer back to a specific idea, activity, or thing, so that understanding may be achieved easily (as writer and receiver of a given message). In many ways, print upholds expectation by creating fixed "places" of argumentation; paragraphs, lists, tables, and other print-based writing features locate ideas spatially (and, thus, conceptually) apart from one another. In the digital, Ulmer writes, the topoi are replaced with Plato's forgotten concept of chora, the open receptacle of meaning. Chora, when updated for digital culture, functions as an argumentative/narrative strategy "by means of pattern making, pattern recognition, pattern generation. It is not that memory is no longer thought of as 'place,' but that the notion itself of spatiality has changed" (*Heuretics* 36). Ulmer states that "choral writing organizes any manner of information by means of the writer's specific position in the time and space of a culture" (*Heuretics* 33). The ability to link information, manipulate information easily, morph information, and so on lends itself to choral practices. Ulmer names this electronic writing practice "chorography" and offers a set of instructions for how to be a chorographer: "do not choose between the different meanings of key terms, but compose by using all the meanings" (*Heuretics* 48).

I, too, am interested in more than one meaning of cool as well as how these multiple meanings produce discourse. Ulmer notes that cool is one of many ways to make sense of the world. Cool emerges from the institution of entertainment. Family, church, and school are other institutions that produce discourse. Ulmer names the framework that ties together these areas "the popcycle." The popcycle demands that scholastic practices include attitudes like cool within their curriculums.

> School may no more stop the spread of funky reason than could the Church suppress science by threat of torture. Funk as a metaphysics is not yet in the Schools but its circulation through the popcycle is well underway from its origins in the Street (a fifth institution of the popcycle, with the bar as its site of appearance) through Entertainment, where it has merged with technology and capitalism. The younger generation is assimilating aesthetically the atmosphere of Funk through a taste for being "cool." Perhaps the hybrid predicted by this riddle will produce a new institution called Chool, whose methodology will promote a kind of objective fashion. ("I Untied the Camera of Tastes [Who Am I?]" 588)

The institution of Chool (the juxtaposition of cool and school) Ulmer calls for needs its own rhetoric. In composition studies, rhetorical practice is often defined as acknowledgment of audience, purpose, and, even as many in the profession dispute its influence, ability to engage with one of the so-called modes: compare and contrast, definition, classification, narrative, or argument. None of these points prevents writing from being taught in constructive ways. These points' dominant position within our pedagogical apparatus, however, is a topos of instruction in need of updating. We can no longer assume that the modes (or any variation of the modes) are appropriate for the sake of being appropriate. Chora, in particular, challenges each point's relevance to digital writing because its focus shifts to a hyper-rhetorical method that displaces much of the conventions of print logic. Chora does so because its logic is not based on the fixity we currently associate with print culture. As Edward Casey argues, with chora, "Place is definitely not precedent if by 'place' is meant something like a particular locale or spot: anything of this order of specificity, that is, of the order of *topos* or of *thesis* (position), misses the mark" (43). One of chora's "essential properties is its connectivity—its power to link up, from within, diversely situated entities or events" (47–48) . Casey notes chora's Platonic origins as well. "From Plato we learn that receptivity is connectivity" (48) . Chora, I learn, teaches me to bring together disparate events and texts from 1963. It teaches me how to make connections.

My choral move is to begin with McLuhan's notion of cool as a highly interactive system of pattern making that foregrounds connectivity. In *Understanding Media,* McLuhan defines cool accordingly: "There is a basic principle that distinguishes a hot medium like radio from a cool one like the telephone . . . hot media are, therefore, low in participation, and cool media are high in participation" (36). Cool media operate by a choral logic: Users of a given term's various meanings must actively engage with those meanings in rhetorical ways, discovering unfamiliar and unexpected juxtapositions of these meanings as they compose. Readers, too, respond to chora in a participatory manner unlike typical definitions of meaning or analytical understandings. While all reading and writing practices demand participation to some extent, writing multiple meanings simultaneously generates a method more conducive to digital culture, which itself (through the Web, film, video, and other media) is constructed out of multiple texts and meanings that often overlap and interlink. "The past mechanical time was hot, and we of the TV age are cool" (*Understanding Media* 40). As McLuhan writes, the task is to transfer choral practices into pedagogy so that we not only understand what a cool medium is but that we write cool as well. "Our new concern with education follows upon the changeover to an interrelation in knowledge, where before the separate subjects of the curriculum had stood apart from each other (*Understanding Media* 47).

The best demonstration of choral moves on the Web can be seen (but not only found) in the hypertextual link that allows writers the capability of developing threads around single words or ideas, and that requires readers to navigate these threads in various ways. The link is indicative of a new media push to reorganize space in terms of meaning construction. Through new media applications, like the hyperlink, chora displaces how a given topos represents one idea for one situation. Chora challenges the representational nature of the topos ("X means Y"). "What would a writing be that produces understanding without representation," Ulmer asks regarding chora (*Heu-*

*retics* 66). Indeed, how can writing generate ideas without representation or referentiality? Wouldn't such a writing deny composition studies at least some of the tools it has found useful for pedagogy, tools like the topic sentence or thesis? Ulmer offers a general response to these kinds of questions by describing choral writing accordingly: "How to practice choral writing? It must be in the order neither of the sensible nor the intelligible but in the order of making, of generating. And it must be transferable, exchangeable, without generalization, conducted from one particular to another" (*Heuretics* 67). For me to demonstrate how chora functions in the rhetoric of cool, I must do so in terms of "making" and generating"; that is, I need to present my ideas not in a representative manner but as a series of exchangeable patterns. As the popular saying goes, the proof is in the pudding. I raise that proof throughout this book as a series of generalizable lessons for writers who want to engage with the rhetoric of cool. If I am to insist that chora is one part of the rhetoric of cool, therefore, I need to show how it works. This chapter, then, will begin with a meta-demonstration, and each chapter, in turn, will also establish some degree of meta-oriented discussion of its contents, some chapters more so than others. My rationale is both explanatory (this is what chora means) and example (this is how to do it). The performative nature of the rhetoric of cool demands that I, too, enact some portion of that activity throughout my own theorization. The performative nature of cool also requires that I explain my method as I also show its results (i.e., the content of the rest of this book). In what follows, I show my own chorography of cool so that my invention process is revealed and so that the rhetorical moves I make are more readily understood. I then will present briefly a pedagogical example of writing with chora as it pertains to the rhetoric of cool's application to electronic writing.

## A Choral Introduction to Cool

My discovery of more than one meaning of cool came by way of accident. Reading through Eric Havelock's description of 1963 as an important moment in writing instruction (which I note in chapter 1), I found myself focusing on his comment that "startled recognitions of a host of related facts" can be located within any given moment deemed consequential for one reason or another. Regarding my own initial interests in composition studies and 1963, the remark allowed me to question the narrative of composition studies' rebirth as restricted for its insular breakdown of the year's important moments. Related facts don't appear to be within North's list of practices, if by "related" we mean writing-oriented activities not specific to composition studies. The question of information's "relations" or "related facts" Havelock alludes to in his own temporal juxtaposition is one that asks that readers and writers consider less obvious rhetorical, conceptual, and historical connections that might be made for a given moment. With this in mind, I understood Havelock's remark as an instruction for getting around such restricted gestures: Expand upon the date's other, unmentioned moments in order to find your own startled recognition. Note and map the less obvious relationships. If successful, the result of this process will lead to a moment of awareness, a key point in the invention process when the writer realizes that an idea is about to be formed because of how unlikely ideas have been brought together or suddenly have been made "likely."

Surveying various moments that I knew to be related to 1963—John F. Kennedy's assassination and Martin Luther King Jr.'s "I Have a Dream" speech—at first revealed little that "startled" me into imagining something beyond the composition paradigm. These moments merely extended my own already established topos-structured reading of 1963 (popular representations of the date immediately converge on these two events). To repeat these moments would mean to repeat the already known. It wasn't until I realized, however, that George Lucas's film *American Graffiti* takes place at the end of 1962 and the beginning of 1963 that I began to think about popular culture in relationship to this date. The iconic imagery that dominates *American Graffiti*'s mise-en-scène speaks to the attitude displayed by the film's main character, tough guy and cool figure John Milner. The film's imagery of souped-up automobiles, cruising, and hanging out are all systems of meaning circulated through the motif of what we commonly know as cool. These are material items whose rhetorical value connects to so-called cool individuals, like the Milner character. Even more so, the iconic presentation of these images, I appreciated, reflects a type of writing meant to elicit a general feeling that captures the spirit of early 1960s American culture, or at least a spirit we have come to identify with the 1960s. Unlike Fredric Jameson's critique in *Postmodernism: Or the Logic of Capitalism,* that *American Graffiti*'s pastiche of signifiers without meaning produces an empty gesture devoid of content or historical significance, I found these iconic markers indicative of an alternative writing applicable to film, but possibly worth studying for their value in other media outlets. From this moment, I became aware of a potential choral move that would allow me to explore other meanings patterned after those found within the film's narrative.

Those other patterns emerged out of *American Graffiti*'s soundtrack. While the film's soundtrack does not entirely reflect early 1960s attitudes regarding cool, the one song on the soundtrack that best exemplifies cool is Booker T and The MGs "Green Onions." The racially mixed house band at Stax records, Booker T and The MGs were comprised of two African-Americans (Booker T and Al Jackson) and two whites (Steve Cropper and Donald Dunn). The racial makeup of the band reflects the popular African-American association with cool that contemporary writers like Donnell Alexander identify as "synthesis," and the film characterizes in thirteen-year-old Carol's comment regarding African-American culture as marginal. "I just love listening to Wolfman Jack," Carol remarks while driving with Milner. "My mom won't let me because he's a Negro." The outcast-marginal-bad-boy status Carol attributes to black males is often the synthesis of 1960s popular cultural attitudes for both black and white audiences. This status surfaces in other popular songs from the time period surrounding 1963. 1960s hits like The Crystals' "He's a Rebel" (1962), Elvis Presley's "The Devil in Disguise" (1963), and The Shangri-Las' "Leader of the Pack" (1964) all speak to the definitive attitude we acknowledge as cool by repeating the bad-boy image in some fashion. Like *American Graffiti,* these types of songs construct the feeling of cool through writing; they are compositions. The connection between composition and composing (another choral move among terms) is one I will develop as well when I discuss the issue of appropriation. For now, it is sufficient to point out how songs like "Leader of the Pack" present the easily recognizable situation of the innocent school girl falling for the bad motorcycle boy. The rhetorical formula might be as follows: The girl's parents put the boy down; the boy comes from the wrong side of town; the boy is bad, but in that badness the girl sees something valuable; and, in the end, despite his tough demeanor and lack of public acceptability, the girl falls for the boy. The leader of the pack signifies the cool, masculine body, the bad boy who seduces the nuclear-family raised adolescent (much like Marlon Brando's Johnny in *The Wild One*). He is cool for being a rebel, moody, and (even though he is most likely white in 1960s mainstream media representations) from the wrong side of town. The meaning is familiar; it, like my initial impressions of 1963 regarding Kennedy and King, represents an already defined topos.

Missing from *American Graffiti*'s soundtrack, however, is the other side of 1963 race and music, James Brown. Brown's 1963 release of *Live at the Apollo Vol. I,* recorded the previous year at the famous Apollo Theater in Harlem, became the first soul record to significantly chart on the white-dominated Billboard sales charts. Brown's entrance into the segregated music divisions of popular music (rhythm and blues for African-Americans, pop music for whites) indicates an economic and political shift in popular musical reception. Traditional musical segregation, which paralleled social segregation, broke down through widespread acceptance of Brown's song*writing. Live at the Apollo* creates an iconic identification of African-American cultural production through the crossover celebrity but does so by identifying black musical production with social concerns and values, not marginality and outcast status. Amiri Baraka writes:

James Brown's form and content identify an entire group of people in America. However these may be transmuted and reused, reappear in other areas, in other musics for different purposes in the society, the initial energy and image are about a specific grouping of people, Black People. (*Black Music* 185)

Brown, Baraka argues, typifies the cultural move from cool (political detachment) to soul (political involvement). The early love songs on *Live at the Apollo* eventually become manifestos for black empowerment when juxtaposed with Brown's late 1960s work. *Live at the Apollo*'s "Please, Please, Please" and "Try Me" read in the light of 1960s black power become entreaties for equal rights and self-awareness. They become the building blocks of later hits like "Say It Loud—I'm Black and I'm Proud Pt. 1," "Soul Power," and "I Don't Want Nobody to Give Me Nothing (Open Up the Door I'll Get It Myself)." In *Blues People*, Baraka fleshes out this cultural move.

The step from cool to soul is a form of social aggression. It is an attempt to place upon a meaningless social order, an order which would give value to terms of existence that were once considered not only valueless but shameful. Cool meant non participation; soul means a "new" establishment. It is an attempt to reverse the social roles within the society by redefining the canons of value. (*Blues People* 219)

This initial recognition, that cool can be situated in 1963 in a manner unlike the tough guy or stereotypical African-American (or even white) male image, prompted me to identify its rhetorical potential as chora. Brown's music understood as cool is not the same as the lingering figure of The Crystals' rebel who will "never ever be any good" and "never ever does what he should." Nevertheless, I cannot deny either as indicative of cool. Both meanings are relevant. The larger implication of this discovery is the awareness of how an idea crosses several genres (film, music, popular beliefs) while maintaining its overall meaning structure. One could draw an imaginary thread through these unlike moments and find a concept. And, indeed, that is what I have begun here to do and will eventually accomplish as I expand upon these early observations in the rest of this book.

Here, then, was my watershed. The initial insight into this choral move is not what cool means (though that may be explicated, or it may be discovered with more work) but rather a suggestion regarding what would happen if the imaginary thread extended outward into other definitions of cool. A writing experiment would be formed, one that would obviously make the thread very real, for it would add new ways of producing knowledge and offer a method of writing outside of composition's recognizable trajectories. This experiment would be choral, not topos-bound. The challenge is to run that thread through academic writing as well; the juxtaposition of the popular and the academic will yield a new term whose meaning will pose significance to our work.

Such an idea influenced Raymond Williams's well-known breakdown of the word *culture*. Encountering usage of the word *culture* in everyday conversation as well as in the university in late 1940s England, Williams saw discrepancies in its usage, differences that at times emphasized the word's multiple meanings or ignored them. "The very fact that [culture] was important in two areas that are often thought of as separate posed new questions and suggested new kinds of connection," Williams writes (14). His answer to dealing with the differences in meaning eventually became the text *Keywords*, an important work for cultural studies that provides etymological, historical, and social meanings to widely used terms. To create a chorography of cool, I realize, is in many ways to create a modified keywords for new media. It is to write a word through its connections and meanings, and not necessarily to only write *about* that word.

## Chorography

The thread I find forms the basis of my own chorography. I still, of course, need to flesh out the initial patterns that allow me to use chorography to structure the rest of this book and the major premises regarding how the rhetoric of cool relates to composition studies' history as well as informs a new, electronic practice. My initial work demonstrated so far, however, sets me up to proceed in that direction. My associative moves motivate my project as a digital-oriented one; I am not endorsing a platform or electronic system but rather foregrounding the invention practice central to a digital rhetoric like cool. Ulmer explains the need to generate new inventive practices for the digital as a recognition that these practices stem from different kinds of logics than we have traditionally employed within print culture: "This difference in 'logics' is the point of departure for imagining what a new rhetoric will do that does not argue but that replaces the logic governing argumentative writing with associational networks" (*Heuretics* 18). As I tease out associations that network *American Graffiti* with *Blues People,* I find myself performing a rhetoric that is not entirely argumentative in nature but rather one which reveals information in unfamiliar ways. This rhetoric connects my writing to cultural studies.

Baraka's identification of James Brown with cool could be initially understood as the simple fixation of status onto a celebrity (and thus a repetition of the Milner character in *American Graffiti*): James Brown is a cool singer.

Baraka's identification, however, does not do that but instead contextualizes Brown's writing in terms of political and social response, thus evoking the project of cultural studies at the same time the Center for Contemporary Cultural Studies was establishing itself in Birmingham, England, as a site of cultural analysis and pedagogical practice. The Birmingham project set out to legitimize the study of popular culture in order to recognize "a growing recognition that the media of mass communication play such a significant role in society, and especially in the lives of young people" (Hall and Whannel 21). As Walter Ong writes around the time period the Birmingham School is founded, "Teachers and students of language and literature must cultivate sensitivity to the more profound significance of the media of popular culture" ("Wired for Sound" 229). The relationship between media and society is prominent in Baraka's definition of cool. Cool, Baraka writes, includes the specific kind of early 1960s African-American inability to control political and cultural oppression.

> To be cool was, in its most accessible meaning, to be calm, even unimpressed by what horror the world might daily propose. As a term used by Negroes, the horror, etc., might be simply the deadeningly predictable mind of white America . . . It is perhaps the flexibility of the Negro that has let him survive; his ability to "be cool"—to be calm unimpressed, detached, perhaps to make failure as secret a phenomenon as possible. (*Blues People* 213)

This choral move within media further allows me to connect Baraka to McLuhan at the level of participation. Baraka's description of cool as nonparticipatory contrasts with McLuhan's notion of cool as a highly participatory media form. "Any hot medium allows of less participation than a cool one" (*Understanding Media* 37). That Baraka appropriates cool from "cool jazz" (a point I will return to in the next chapter) in order to demonstrate the nonparticipatory response forced upon African-Americans should not be lost on McLuhan's equivocation of jazz as a cool medium. "Cool jazz came in quite naturally after the first impact of radio and movie had been absorbed" (*Understanding Media* 40). These conflicts in meaning regarding participation are not obstacles but rather potential moments for invention. "An important aspect of chorography," Ulmer writes, "is learning how to *write* an intuition" (*Heuretics* 37). My intuition is that this pattern is important. I don't need to clarify the contradiction; I should use the discrepancies in meaning to motivate further exploration of the questions that guide my project. What do I do when I encounter opposing meanings of the same term? How can these meanings be combined in order to generate a new idea? Why should I desire difference and conflict rather than the "comparison of one method of instruction to another" where "all variables other than the method should be controlled," as Braddock and colleagues argue writing research should entail (25)? In other words, I am choosing a lack of control (discrepancy) over control (method comparison) as the principle of my research.

Complicating this situation, I must chorally introduce a third meaning of cool also found in 1963. Doing field work in West Africa during that year, anthropologist Robert Farris Thompson discovered that the modern notion of cool has its origins in indigenous Yoruban practices. Cool, or *itutu*, indicates a form of visual writing employed in order to express in art and aesthetics a lifestyle characteristic of appeasement, conciliation, and calmness. Yoruban culture articulated cool as a visual aesthetic in sculpture, weaving, and dance.

> The equilibrium and poetic structure of traditional dances of the Yoruba in western Nigeria, as well as the frozen facial expressions worn by those who perform these dances, express a philosophy of the cool, an ancient, indigenous ideal: patience, and collectedness of mind. ("An Aesthetic of the Cool" 73)

Yoruban discourse, Farris Thompson writes, embraces a visual mode of communication based on iconic and emblematic representation, indicating that my initial interest (i.e., my intuition) in *American Graffiti*'s iconic displays was anything but accidental. Moreover, cool representations are based on religious iconicity. "The coming of the icons of the Yoruba to the black New World accompanied an affirmation of philosophical continuities" we currently understand as cool (*Flash of the Spirit* 93). Iconic representations are important to electronic writing. Any kind of computer-oriented rhetoric must account for the iconic display of information, either through the complex patterns of os and 1s that comprise all digital writing or the visual displays on desktops, in software, or on the Web. In the digital, the look of a text becomes as important as the text itself. "Whether the material comes to our eyes as light shining through a screen," Anne Wysocki writes regarding electronic visual displays, "or as light reflecting off paper or stone or the flesh of a tattoo—, we open possibilities for new arrangements, new articulations with other of our material practices" (14–15 Wysocki). Even as I introduce the visual—a point I will return to in more detail by the final chapter—I note that I am already following Wysocki's understanding of visuality. My visualization of cool, which I start to map out in this chapter, opens up a new arrangement for me to compose with, one that is chora-based and not topos-based. I began this chapter with a moment of iconicity (James Dean), followed it through my early interest in 1963 (Jameson's critique of iconic display in *American Graffiti*), recognized it in 1963 music (iconic representation of the bad boy), and encountered it again in James Brown (iconic celebrity). Those principles understood by Farris Thompson as cool, therefore, still are relevant for the kind of rhetoric I will develop in the following chapters. They are also the basis of my chorography.

## The Handbook

In a sense, the choral moves I demonstrate briefly here suggest the presence of a handbook, or collection of meanings as the medieval definition of *Ars* demonstrates. The handbook's legacy in writing pedagogy is extensive. The *Ars*, or as Walter Ong translates the term, "Art," played a role in the invention of the pedagogical curriculum. In the early university tradition to which Peter Ramus contributed, Ong notes that the role of the *Ars* was to teach rhetorical production. "Art refers to a habit or acquired skill of the practical intellect when this latter is concerned with doing or making something" (*Ramus* 156). Handbooks currently serve the majority of students enrolled in first-year writing classes; most courses assign handbooks like *A Writer's Reference, Keys for Writers,* or *The Scott-Foresman Handbook* so that students will have reference material to consult regarding grammar, punctuation, citation, and organization. These handbooks are, however, limited in that they propose the known and expected, the single meanings already in disciplinary and cultural transmission. They are meant for reference, not for pedagogy, and not for production, as one aspect of the traditional sense of the *Ars* proposes. That is, these contemporary handbooks are not to be used for further teaching by students; they are only to be read by students looking for advice.

The pedagogical relevance of the handbook to chora is how it serves as a teaching device for displaying multiple meanings at once, yet allowing for those meanings to be read and written concurrently and in juxtaposition, rather than separate. The Ramist tradition found in handbooks, Ong writes, is limiting for how it "protests in principle if not in actuality, that invention is restricted to a dialectical world where there is no voice but only a kind of vision" (*Ramus* 288). Too concerned with the division and arrangement of separate and distinct categories to study (which we can today recognize as modes, process, punctuation, or types of grammatical error), the Ramist tradition hinders the handbook's potential to voice inventive rhetorical moves and gestures. Still, my usage of cool reflects the handbook in spirit and in production while it also diverts itself from part of the tradition: I gather a number of meanings and put them to use in order to generate an approach to new media writing. McLuhan's *Understanding Media* represents an earlier media-oriented handbook that functions likewise; its chapters pose as "some general aspects of media" to be read in conjunction with one another and as a guide for how media shapes "man" over (21). Readers of *Understanding Media* juxtapose the chapters on money, roads, the printed word, and movies in order to "understand" media as well as to be able to apply such understanding to further exploration of media and writing.

> The new electric structuring and configuring of life more and more encounters the old lineal and fragmentary procedures and tools of analysis from the mechanical age. More and more we turn from the content of messages to study total effect. (*Understanding Media* 39)

Media is the choral thread (the preliminary handbook) that unites these sections I have initially laid out as relevant to the rhetoric of cool. As I will describe in the next chapter, other writers the rhetoric of cool learns from, like William Burroughs, present their work as handbooks and not just as texts to be understood for critical commentary; they pose writing and media as pedagogically applicable for its "total effect." Both McLuhan and Burroughs situate the handbook as a new media collection whose role is to demonstrate and teach rhetorical production.

My own experience with chora demonstrates a handbooklike approach for how it exhibits the basic aspects of invention in regards to cool. Likewise, this approach has served as a writing assignment in many courses I have taught.[3] The focus of these assignments is the exploration of a given term (which is up to the student's discretion) relevant to the student's area of study (Nursing, Education, Accounting, Biology, etc.). Following the principle of chora, students locate and research other meanings associated with that term from other disciplines, events, moments, and media. These meanings will differ greatly and, at times, contrast with one another. Those differences, however, are important, for the purpose of the handbook is to work with all meanings at once. The key to such work is identifying patterns, moments of overlap among the original definition and those other definitions that appear throughout the research. A found pattern evokes the eureka principle of insight, the aha moment when knowledge is suddenly discovered (like Havelock's concept of the "watershed"). Based on this found pattern, the final collection of meanings can then be combined in a handbook in order to reveal a new application of the term for the student's area of study. The purpose of the handbook is not to reinforce an already accepted definition but instead to present the unfamiliar usages of the term and how such approaches can change the initial area of study. Another version of the assignment is to have students limit their chorography to those subjects they are studying in a given semester (four or five courses) and construct the handbook around the one term common to each course. In this project, a point of connection is discovered where one would not be expected (English, Statistics, Biology, and French all unite?), and that point may then be developed into a principle or moment of insight.

Placed on the Web, students can further explore the choral moves they discover through hyperlinks and image placement. Images and hyperlinks offer students the opportunity to present various connections whose overlap is meant to produce new meaning. Images and hyperlinks also replicate a hyper-rhetorical expression that is more participatory (readers and writers must actively engage with the conflicting meanings; they must assemble the meanings in both expected and unexpected ways) and associative (I will encounter links and images in more detail in later chapters as well). Besides the commonplace advice to compose via a Web site, another place the handbook can be written is in the wiki. Wikis pose the potential to do more than a static Web site can because, conceptually, wikis are based on the notion of open meaning. The popular Web encyclopedia Wikipedia[4] represents an early attempt to write the handbook in electronic form. Wikipedia, however, still operates from a traditional encyclopedic perspective. While it is "open" in the sense that it encourages readers to contribute to its development, Wikipedia's entries, layout, and organization do not convey multiple meanings and choral possibilities. Instead, entries replicate the fixed meanings (conceptually and formally) a print-encyclopedia might offer. Because anyone can edit, add to, or delete from a wiki, however, the wiki, in general, should be considered as another space where a choral handbook might be engaged.[5] The open nature of composing that wikis support allows for meanings to always be developing and growing in what media theorist Matthew Fuller calls the "compositional fragment" that "opens up into other permutation fields" (16). As meanings interact with other meanings in complimentary, conflicting, obvious, and not obvious ways in media spaces, Fuller argues, new compositional forms emerge. This process of interlinking, which I contend can be performed on a Web site or wiki for new media writing, is not individualized but "composed in part by the necessity of relations" (Fuller 96). Cool is one such form that already shows me relations (the idea of the handbook foregrounds the process in my work). Other forms and meanings, of course, can and will emerge as well as writers consider the viability of relations they discover among texts and ideas.

Just as the assignment I have described uses chora pedagogically, I want to evoke the handbook sense of cool more fully throughout the remaining chapters of this book. Each chapter signifies a rhetorical dimension of cool but also stands for another choral move I make. In other words, *The Rhetoric of Cool* is itself a handbook. The significance, therefore, is twofold: to demonstrate the rhetoric of cool (and thus to evoke the performative nature of writing) and to pose a model that can be appropriated for other kinds of hyper-rhetorical work (the writing itself). That I want this method to be appropriated for other terms and concepts is important; thus, in the next chapter, I move from chora to another area of interest to the rhetoric of cool: appropriation.

# 3

## Appropriation

And Meester William in Tétuan and said: "I have gimmick is cool and all very technical."

       —William Burroughs, *Nova Express*

Keep cool, keep cool, but care. It's a watchword.

       —Thomas Pynchon, *V*

"When I think back over the experiences which have had any actual effect on my writing," Wayne Booth notes in the October 1963 issue of *College Composition and Communication*, "I find the great good fortune of a splendid freshmen course, taught by a man who believed in what he was doing, but I also find a collection of other experiences quite unconnected with a specific writing course" ("Rhetorical Stance" 140). In this 1963 composition moment, Booth suggests that writing is shaped by forces outside of the writing course. Experience is the focus of Booth's remarks. We might imagine those "unconnected" experiences Booth alludes to as being cultural: films, books, music, art, television, and so forth. Our daily interactions with such media shape, implicitly or explicitly, our understandings of rhetorical production. We appropriate from such interactions in order to gather ideas and insight from a variety of issues and situations, and in order to reflect those gatherings in writing. Although it hints at this process I describe, Booth's example of where writing influences come from eventually draws only from other university courses. Booth's "collection" of experiences are, in essence, insular; they are situated only in the university. In the previous chapter, I described how my own writing became shaped by a number of factors either within English Studies (critical theory/film) or *outside* of English Studies (music, popular culture). That willingness to look also outside of the university for an understanding of writing is what intrigues me. Where else, I ask, is my writing about cool being shaped? How do I balance out those areas that generate my understandings of cool and composition studies? How do I appropriate non-university interactions for my writing? "The common ingredient that I find in all of the writing I admire," Booth continues,

> is something that I shall reluctantly call the rhetorical stance, a stance which depends on discovering and maintaining in any writing situation a proper balance among the three elements that are at work in any communicative effort: the available arguments about the subject itself, the interests and peculiarities of the audience, and the voice, the implied character of the speaker. I should like to suggest that it is this balance, this rhetorical stance, difficult as it is to describe, that is our main goal as teachers of rhetoric. ("Rhetorical Stance" 141)

I find this balance Booth highlights in many of the models the rhetoric of cool draws from. But because interactions vary, because interactions may or may not be in the university, I also find several important elements missing in Booth's breakdown, elements not associated directly with balance. These elements I identify are not associated with recognizing both sides of an argument nor with audience expectation, nor with a particular ethos-stand. Among these elements is the very specific rhetorical act of appropriation.

My own appropriation of cool for composition studies suggests something, at first, off balance: cool and writing instruction? How do these two items go together? How can you appropriate a popular term for pedagogical purposes? *Cool* is a term whose origins are not in the university. Cool, as I've already realized, can be found in Yoruban practices, music, or media definitions. Together, these items may not feel in balance with one another because of how their interactions do not fit with a typical university expectation regarding a term's meaning and usage. Thus, there exists a different type of rhetorical stance I am seeking to create, one dependent not on balance but on how terms or ideas are appropriated (cool as appropriated from media, from music, from Yoruban visuality). But like Booth, I notice that the place I work in (which for Booth is only the university) is relevant to the work I do. That place is Detroit. Because appropriation is an obvious feature of Detroit (Detroit's design and layout appropriated the look of Paris), and because Detroit is where *my place* of employment (Wayne State University) is located and where I am in charge of the Department of English's Digital Literacy Initiative's quest to integrate technology into first-year writing, I look locally first (as opposed to looking only at the university) in order to explore appropriation's role in electronic writing.

## Cool Cities

At the May 2003 Detroit Regional Chamber of Commerce's Leadership Policy Council conference held at Mackinac Island, Michigan's Governor Jennifer

Granholm sported a pair of dark sunglasses and introduced her public relations campaign designed to encourage suburban Detroit-Metro residents to move back into the city. "Bright Future/Cool Cities," she informed the waiting crowd, will make Detroit and its suburbs cool once again. The city's "coolness," supposedly embodied in its now mythic past of music (Motown, early 1970s rock and roll, and techno) has been lost, general opinion seems to declare. Granholm's plan is to bring back that feeling, not so much the musical tradition. *The Detroit Free Press* described the event accordingly:

> Granholm said Michigan cannot prosper if its cities, especially Detroit, fail. And the key to success is making those cities places where young people want to live, not leave. Young people are moving out of Michigan at a higher rate than all but three other states, she said. To reverse that trend, Michigan needs to get cool. (Bell)

"Cool Cities" attempts to lure young residents into those neighborhoods and metro communities no longer deemed attractive to young professionals by offering various communities $100,000 grants for development. Followed up by the 2004 conference "Tipping to Cool: Next Steps in Linking Culture, Community and the Economy," held at the Lansing Center in East Lansing and featuring guest speaker Malcolm Gladwell (author of the popular *New Yorker* essay "The Coolhunt"), "Cool Cities" is a rhetorical project that fuses the spirit of technology with urban affairs. Inspired largely by Richard Florida's concept of the creative class (the theory that creative people drive urban renewal), "Cool Cities" identifies youth culture attitudes and social interests as community building blocks for the ways they circulate around a general conception of coolness. Bring back young people, the idea professes; bring back cool individuals with creative energy and provocative ideas, and their presence will allow blighted urban environments to prosper once again. The proposal has since been put online at the Cool Cities Web site (http://www. coolcities.com/), which frames the project as the reclaiming of urban space for young people.

> What makes a city "cool?" Is it a leafy, green park and an inviting public square? Or is it a sidewalk bistro and an internet café? Maybe it's a jazz club or a coffee house that invites office workers to linger in your downtown well past 5:00 P.M. Maybe it's nothing more extravagant—or more important—than a quality neighborhood school, a job within walking distance and a safe path for getting to both. Whatever your vision of a cool city, we are working to make that vision a reality. (Cool Cities)

Those who are interested in the project can visit the Michigan Cool Cities Web site (http://www.michigancoolcities.com/) and fill out an online survey regarding the kinds of places in which they would like to live. The results of this continuing survey, we can assume, will form the basis of the imaginary "cool" locales the city's planners and public relations staff envision. Based on online user input, the city will more accurately be able to apply cool to its living spaces. That the plan's organizers connect it to the Web is a point worth mentioning, for the city's urban residents without Internet or computers seem to be the ones not included in the city's "cool" plan. In a typical (and by now unfortunately accepted) trope of access, the city's largely African-American population's input is not directly solicited. Cool Cities' focus is not the African-American population of the city, after all, but the largely suburban white population. The success of Cool Cities is still debatable; Michigan Metropolitan Information Center's Kurt Metzger told the *Detroit Free Press* in 2005 that despite the anticipated influx of new people resulting from the equation of cool with Detroit, the city continues to lose residents to nearby communities. "When you talk about cool cities, we're becoming less and less cool all the time," Metzger noted (Gray). Metzger's comment is meaningful. The city's rhetorical stance feels lacking, and the local population seems to feel that lack. People are not moving back to Detroit. This stance, however, did not arrive out of nowhere. It belongs within a larger rhetorical appropriation, part of which deals with technology.

The technology connection Detroit makes with the Cool Cities plan through its web site is not lost on those of us who came to the Internet early in its popular inception and recall the fascination many Web portals had with making Web sites "cool." Michigan's Cool Cities definition of "what makes a city 'cool'" echoes Netscape's once popular What's Cool listings: "Someday we'll all agree on what's cool on the Net. In the meantime, the Netscape cool team will continue to bring you a list of select sites that catch our eyes, make us laugh, help us work, quench our thirst . . . you get the idea." Before being completely eliminated from its Web portal, the browser's categorization of cool shifted from the above general claim to the following, more specific, statement:

*What Makes Us the Arbiters of Cool?*
It takes a willingness on our part to apply well-honed skills of judgment, together with a certain savoir faire. Of course, no one can claim to be the definitive source of cool even though we're trying. Meanwhile, we refuse to hoard cool URLs solely for our own enjoyment.[1]

I read into Michigan's Cool Cities plan an appropriation of Netscape's and similar Web sites' usage of *cool* as a general system of popular meaning that applies this word as a method of categorizing tastes, interests, and future activities. When Michigan appropriates cool, it does so in a way similar to Netscape. It appropriates a generic meaning for a purpose of categorization

(Detroit now fitting the category of cool). Indeed, the criteria Netscape once used to determine what's cool ("well-honed skills of judgment together with a certain savoir faire) are mirrored in Michigan's "Listening," "Planning," "Acting," and "Measuring" standards, all of which sound like, if anything, Netscape's savoir faire.

> We specifically want to focus efforts on embracing innovation, encouraging talent, welcoming diversity and enhancing the quality of life by creating environments that recognize the impact these characteristics have on ideas, events, places, organizations and people. (Cool Cities)

In addition to language and categorization, I find another kind of appropriation occurring as well, one that speaks more broadly to race, technology, and writing in ways that issues of access (as I noted previously) don't account for but that are extremely meaningful nevertheless. Because both Detroit and Netscape appropriate cool to perform these tasks, I will use this chapter to include appropriation within the rhetoric of cool. The overlap of my work on cool, my own move to Metro-Detroit, and the initiation of Detroit's urban renewal plan mark a focal point for thinking about how the rhetoric of cool functions through the city's appropriation of the word. This appropriation also allows me to consider what the pedagogical implications of this moment might be for composition studies—how we appropriate and apply appropriations rhetorically to make meaning in technology-rich environments.

## The Cool City

Most of the local newspapers recognize the "Cool Cities" proposal as a rhetorical ploy with little significance beyond its catchy name, even if its intent is a welcome effort to solve the many problems Detroit strains to overcome. Once a prosperous, industrial city, Detroit currently struggles to attract investment, new residents, and solutions to its decaying infrastructure. Granholm's response has been to make the city "cool" through targeted investment and marketing opportunities. As one newspaper article noted:

> It would be too easy to criticize Granholm's idea and even easier to mock her delivery of it. Much like a recent Pepsi commercial, where a kid discovers his parents in a mosh pit, it is often painfully embarrassing when one of "them" tries to act like one of "us." What Granholm is trying to do, however, is long overdue as her predecessor, the un-hip and out of touch former Gov. John Engler, ignored these vital issues for far too long. ("Team Cool")

The real issues "ignored" for so long concern the city's large African-American community, those mostly shut off from technology access. That point, however, is not central to the "Cool Cities" program. And yet at the same time, two major components of the governor's plan include technological display (usage of the Web site) as well as recognition of the city's long standing black identity. Labeling Detroit "cool" elevates the city's image as a black city. Cool, as Norman Mailer interpreted it in his 1957 essay "The White Negro," often becomes confused with stereotypical (and typically racist) characteristics associated with African-American figures and culture. When Granholm named the mayor of Detroit, Kwame Kilpatrick, the "Prime Minister of Cool," she solidified her own appropriation of the term and continuance of cool's generalization of black culture. The decision to name Detroit's various neighborhoods as well as its African-American mayor as "cool" represents an effort to rhetorically equate the city with those perceived aspects of black culture that white American has come to admire: hipness, fashion, and marginality. The city already has a black majority; Granholm merely romanticizes blackness to encompass imaginary, exotic characteristics and not those less-ideal issues that often find their way into newspaper headlines and the nightly news (murder, crime, rape, arson). By focusing only on a supposed "exciting" meaning, the governor's plan is meant to lure in the largely white suburbanites who, possibly bored with their mundane existence north of 8 Mile, desire the attractive elements of coolness, what Richard Florida calls "the Creative Class lifestyle." "On many fronts, the Creative Class lifestyle comes down to a passionate quest for experience," Florida writes. "The ideal, as a number of my subjects succinctly put it, is to 'live the life'—a creative life packed full of intense, high-quality, multidimensional experiences" (166). Granholm's appropriation of cool reduces those experiences to an imaginary African-American experience. In doing so, Granholm localizes the city's significant African-American population within one essentialized meaning. If Detroit-Metro residents fled in 1967 because of race, as the city's mythology claims, surely they will return for the same reason: to become as cool as the black residents who remained.

Granholm's usage of the word *cool* signifies the rhetorical act of appropriation. Even as this moment appropriates African-American characteristics, it is not alone in its eventual juxtaposition of African-American culture, the urban and cool. There exists a history of such juxtapositions in literary or cultural texts. Granholm's vision of the cool, urban city purposefully differs from (yet belongs in the same tradition of) less complimentary cityscape portraits like that exposed in Warren Miller's novel *The Cool World*. Miller poses the urban environment as a demoralized and illiterate African-American experience where drugs and violence are the norm. In Miller's description, the cool city is a city of industrial, emotional, and language collapse.

People in an out of the street all the time. An at the end of the street loomin up is the projeck. Man when they tore down the bildings to make room for the projeck you could see all the crap them old bildings was made of. They just go whamo with the iron ball an a whole bilding come crashing down. Maybe ony the back wall standin an then you could see green walls pink walls all the colors people painted their walls. (Miller 69)

Miller's urban image of the cool city mirrors the ways popular media (i.e., the nightly news, talk radio, and talk shows) often rhetorically construct the African-American city as a place of despair and destruction. His appropriation of language, behavior, and attitude is meant not to romanticize or denigrate but rather to critique through imagery and suggestion. His rhetoric mirrors Gwendolyn Brooks's canonical poem "We Real Cool," published in her 1963 collection *Selected Poems*. Brooks takes to task the cool city where education is lacking, alcoholism dominates day-to-day affairs, and violence rules.

We real cool. We
Left school. We
Lurk late. We
Strike straight.

(Brooks 73)

Instead of adopting this view of desperation, a view intended to force public response by foregrounding real problems of urban blight, a view intended to situate a political balance in various political and social issues, Granholm's appropriation more closely resembles Mailer's seductive notion of cool, his description of white teenagers appropriating black culture in order to get their "Saturday Night kicks." In this scenario, African-Americans signify a source of thrill seeking and not despondency. For Mailer, white suburban teenagers (i.e., hipsters) dissatisfied with post-World War II lifestyles "drifted out at night looking for action with a black man's code to fit [their] facts. The hipster had absorbed the existentialist synopses of the Negro, and for practical purposes could be considered a white Negro" (Mailer 273). The hipster appropriates black culture as a fantasy for living out sexual recklessness. This act of appropriation is what Mailer imagines as cool: a distortion of one ethnic group so that another can justify its behavior. "To be cool is to be equipped," Mailer writes (284), implying sexual pleasure as its core. Mailer plays off of stereotypes (tropes) so that he can structure a dominant white vision of American cultural relationships: white equals civilized; black equals primitive; whites enjoy pleasures of the mind; blacks enjoy the body. The equations form a commanding breakdown of meaning for how they tap into both white fear (the primitive) and attraction (the body).

I can hear a diluted but nevertheless similar appropriative strategy operating in Granholm's proposal. That Granholm's appropriation can serve urban planning by distinguishing abandoned neighborhoods as suddenly worthwhile places to live again interests me less for its negative value and more for how it reconfigures meaning through an attempt to write the city in new ways. Detroit is a cool city not because of anything specific it has done (or not done) but rather because of how one individual appropriates imagery and ideas in order to construct a new place of meaning. I'm particularly interested in how Granholm's appropriation of cool marks an extension of what Amiri Baraka critiqued in 1963 as the consequence of white cultural appropriation. Baraka's recognition that the African-American cultural experience is tied to cool because of damaging appropriative strategies carried out by dominant culture marks a rhetorical gesture I want to investigate further for how it challenges the very specific image of a rhetorical stance popularized by Booth, one that has become ingrained in how we teach writing. My point is not that we identify these appropriative gestures in order to condemn them as unfair or unjust (as Baraka does with music or many of Granholm's critics have done with her plan) but that we identify them in order to learn how appropriations create new types of meaning in general. In particular, I want to situate Baraka's identification of appropriation as cool within a rhetorical strategy suitable for electronic writing.

## Baraka

Baraka challenges how the appropriation of black culture becomes legitimized when used for commercial purposes (like consuming music or, in the Granholm example, urban planning). The rhetorical value of appropriation is cool for its recontextualization of previous forms and meanings, but also for the ways specific groups respond to the appropriation itself. In the context Baraka lays out, cool is a political response to an inability to become involved in white America or counter an illegitimate writing. Cool lends itself to cultural production as the direct result of this lack of empowerment. Even a lack of response, Baraka notes, may be cool for it specific political orientation.

Baraka asks how white production appropriates the representation of African-American culture in popular music on a consistent basis. For Baraka, twentieth-century African-American music finds itself appropriated by not only white performers but by white commercial interests who isolate African-American cultural artifacts from their original musical context and recontextualize them in nonhistorical manners. Baraka argues that appropriation begins with minstrel adaptations of black face, waters down jazz stylistics through the popularity of white performers such as Paul Whiteman, and transforms the look of musicians, in particular Dizzy Gillespie, into a commodity representative of a growing 1950s white "hip" movement.

> The goatee, beret, and window-pane glasses were no accidents; they were, in the oblique significance that social history demands, as usefully symbolic as had been the Hebrew nomenclature in the spirituals. That is, they pointed toward a way of thinking, an emotional and psychological resolution of some not so obscure social need or attitude. (*Blues People* 201)

Baraka describes the popular need to commodify cultural representation. Within this commodification, Baraka writes, there exists a sense of detachment, for power structures (that which creates the commodification) alienate the original producer of the look, fashion, music, or some other form. Drawing from the short lived 1950s musical genre cool jazz, Baraka finds a composition analogy between this process and African-American experience centered around the term *cool*. Cool jazz took its name as a reaction to the "hot" style of first swing and later bebop, the fast, tension driven East Coast sound of musicians like Dizzy Gillespie and Charlie Parker. Cool formed on the West Coast after the release of Miles Davis's 1948 *Birth of the Cool* album. Quickly abandoned by Davis, the sound was picked up by white musicians such as Chet Baker, Stan Getz, and Gerry Mulligan and tended to emphasize a restraint and modesty in expression as well as a lack of challenge to structural forms. This restrained and detached nature of cool jazz, opposed to the later emerging free jazz sound of 1960s performers like Ornette Coleman and John Coltrane, led Baraka to comment on similar attitudes within black culture. Shut out from mainstream society at the cultural level (music and artifacts often taken over by white culture as commodities—but frequently done so in ways that seem natural to the white majority) and at the political level (denied access to the institutional order because of segregation), African-American culture created its own aesthetic called cool.

Baraka's understanding of cool as detachment explains African-American culture as a failed rhetorical experience, much like the bemoaning of cool that Richard Majors and Janet Mancini Billson contextualize as black failure in their book *Cool Pose*.

> We believe that cool pose helps to explain the fact that African-American males die earlier and faster than white males from suicide, homicide, accidents, and stress-related illnesses; that black males are more deeply involved in criminal and delinquent activities; that they drop out of school and are suspended more often than white children; and that they have more volatile relationships with women. (Mancini Billson and Majors 2)

This explanation is also a question for writing, for it suggests both how African-Americans are *written* into the culture either by themselves or out-side forces ("criminal," "delinquent") as well as how one may *write* about African-Americans (or any other group be it ethnic, political, gendered, etc.). Baraka's importance to 1963 includes how he foregrounds appropriation as a rhetorical gesture based on race. The absence of racial issues among any of the main figures noted in composition's 1963 narrative is suspicious enough, but what I find even more suspicious is the lack of attention to how race and popular culture generate a rhetorical situation far more extensive than that originally outlined by 1963 notables like Wayne Booth. This rhetorical situation is not balanced on all kinds of levels (fairness, of course, prominent among them). Nevertheless, it is quite effective in its force.

By breaking down the cultural construction of African-American identity, Baraka argues that various signifiers of cultural experience eventually inscribe a social status on a given group, whether that group concedes to the signification or not. How such signifiers reference African-American culture is what troubles Baraka most, and it is the problem he engages throughout his text. Baraka's thesis is not a particularly revolutionary one in light of the last thirty years of cultural studies work, but it is a useful concept for both 1963 writing and for reimagining discourse so that we shift from a referential system of meaning whose focus is purely on representation (print) to a flexible system of signifier placement whose focus allows for representations to be borrowed, altered, and remade for different purposes (electronic). What Granholm identifies as attractive to white professionals, for instance (potential for development; quaint, unspoiled neighborhoods; cheap housing), the culture writes negatively on the current black residents (urban blight, drugs, dilapidated housing). The different and flexible usages of appropriation for negative or positive response interest me less than the power of appropriation itself. As I noted in the previous chapter regarding chora, moments of dual meanings serve inventive strategies in new media writing. Through Baraka's work, I am imagining how such appropriative moves take place in the digital. I, therefore, use Granholm's appropriation of black culture as a catalyst to more fully understand how appropriation fits overall in the rhetoric of cool.

## Appropriation

My intent is to extend appropriation into a generalizable method that will comprise part of the rhetoric of cool. What I learn from both Granholm and Baraka is how we employ cultural signifiers for various, often conflicting, moments of writing (as I already have seen with chora, and will see with many other parts of the rhetoric of cool). *Blues People* argues against a writing whose basis is in the cultural theft of signifiers. "To understand you are black in a society where black is an extreme liability is one thing," Baraka writes, "but to understand that it is the society that is lacking and is impossibly deformed because of this lack, *and not yourself,* isolates you even more from that society (*Blues People* 185). And yet, despite Baraka's fears, all writing involves some degree of theft, particularly when writing is introduced into the digital, an area that relies to a great extent on the "borrowing" logic associated with appropriation. Such was William S. Burroughs's contention: The theft of language, image, and text is the basis of an emerging new media structure. In his 1962–1964 trilogy of *The Soft Machine, The Ticket That Exploded*, and *Nova Express*, Burroughs introduces appropriation as a mechanism for survival in digital culture. A more explicitly pronounced writing strategy than Baraka's definition of cool, Burroughs's cut-ups appropriate language, text, image, and ideas in order to fashion critiques of media and ideology (and not to spur consumerism, as Granholm and Baraka contend appropriation does). Burroughs situates the cut-up as a new media method shaped by various emergent technologies: film, tape recorders, and, of course, computers. Whether one resists or engages with new media, Burroughs argues, one must understand its logic of appropriation. "So i press a button and record all sounds and voices of the city—So i press a button to feed back those sounds with cut ins a few seconds later" (*Ticket That Exploded* 169). The move from Baraka to Burroughs, then, indicates a move within cultural and technological appropriations for purposes of digital writing.

Both Baraka and Burroughs indicate an acknowledgment of the power of appropriation as rhetorical move. Yet nowhere in 1963 composition studies do we find appropriation presented as exemplary of good writing, or, for that matter, writing in general. Imagine Burroughs's appropriation of language (e.g., "Photo falling—Word Falling—Break Through in Grey Room—Towers open fire" [*Ticket that Exploded* 110]) in a textbook anthology required of first-year students like John Gardner and Lennis Dunlap's 1963 *Forms of Fiction*. A 1963 Random House advertisement for the book in the *English Record* quotes Richard Carpenter praising the text for "its organization" and analysis that "seem intelligent and far from esoteric, while the questions seem answerable by students" (Random House). Another ad in the journal for David Conlin and George Herman's *Modern Grammar and Composition* promises that the text will be "largely traditional" with "a method and emphasis that are sensibly structural. In composition, structural skills are applied to all kinds of writing situations" (Modern Program). I cannot visualize Burroughs's rhetorical understanding of appropriation fitting anywhere in these or similar texts' pedagogical agendas. I cannot imagine it because writing like "Photo falling—Word Falling—Break Through in Grey Room—Towers open fire" is not "sensibly structured" nor easily "answerable by students." Burroughs's appropriative gestures pulled from other texts, speeches, audio tapes, and his own writings bear little resemblance to the "balance" (particularly at the levels of language and sentence structure) that Wayne Booth demands in order to enact the rhetorical stance these advertised textbooks seem to convey. And when I make the choral move from Baraka to Burroughs in order to explore appropriation (and when I, in part, appropriate these writers' terms), I find the conventions of structure and answerability questionable. I find the "balance" unsettled. I find "Towers open fire" to more accurately reflect my own process of writing than *Modern Grammar and Composition*'s pedagogical promise.

Appropriation, as Burroughs demonstrates, is based on the rhetorical premise of parataxis, that items can be arranged and positioned in a variety of ways and each time generate meaning even if the organization is not clear. Consequently, structure and organizational principles that emphasize logic and order are challenged as ideological positions and not as given rules of writing. Thus, when working with appropriation, it's not enough to simply cut and rearrange words or images. Writers also must reimagine the logic of structure as well; they must appropriate structure itself so as to discover how digital culture engages more than one kind of structuring principle. For that to happen, in 1963 and since, composition studies would have to recognize an organizing principle different than it currently does. In doing so, composition would almost have to accept a lack of order as one type of pedagogical directive for writing.

Since 1963, composition has shown some interest in cut-ups and appropriation, but that interest is tempered by the legacy of "structural skills" and "organization" noted in the ads above. Those texts or writers who do point to appropriation serve only to reinforce the ideological preference for structural and ordered systems. When the *St. Martin's Guide for Writing* provides, for instance, instructions regarding a version of the cut-up, it still supports the notion of structure and clarity: "Use your word processor's cut-and-paste or block-and-move functions to shift material around. Make sure that you revise transitions so that material fits *smoothly* in its new spot" (Axelrod and Cooper 53, my emphasis). Similarly, Peter Elbow's freewriting-oriented "cut-and-paste" method instructs writers to eventually "put your pieces in their best order" (*Writing with Power* 147) in order to create writing that is a "complete and coherent whole" (148). Elbow's version of the cut-up teaches writers to avoid *initial* coherence so that they may achieve it *later* in the writing process: "But the odd thing is that when you stop trying for unity and connectedness and put all your effort into just getting rid of what doesn't work, you often discover a surprising coherence lurking in your pile of good pieces" (149). And even those new media texts that have the most influence on composition studies like Nancy Kaplan's provocative "E-literacies: Politexts, Hypertexts, and Other Cultural Formations in the Late Age of Print"[2] still foreground structure and order. Kaplan's hypertextual quest to complicate literacy through hypertextual linking is structurally sound and easy to navigate through a pronounced hierarchical order made prominent in the text's makeup and pushed to the reader's immediate attention through its front-page setup. If anything, texts like "E-literacies" (and many other notable academic hypertexts found either on independent Web sites or in Web journals like *Kairos*) don't appropriate the media-directed cut-up extensively, if at all, but instead opt for the print-driven mechanism of hierarchy, making their structures transparent so readers can achieve coherent readings. To say that is not to dismiss these texts but to note an ideology still present in many new media writings, even if those writings present their structure otherwise.

One recognizable problem worth foregrounding, however, is that these kinds of print and hypertextual appropriations' preference for some semblance of clarity prevents the needed lack of clarity evident in Baraka's critique (the complex ways cultural groups write or are written) or in Burroughs's work (the power of cutting and reusing texts so that organized thought is undermined). They do, however, echo Governor Granholm's efforts to appropriate Detroit's racial background in order to create an ordered city, to turn the eccentricity and oddness of Detroit into a structured, economic success where whites reclaim the living spaces of the city's African-American population. Granholm's appropriation works to make the solution for urban renewal *clear* despite the complexity such acts generate. In other words, these examples I present favor clarity over initial disruption, assuming that appropriation must always settle in a clear presentation. The preference for clarity via organization, I contend, weakens appropriation's rhetorical power. The disciplinary preference for clarity in writing instruction minimizes appropriation in general.

These kinds of discrepancies regarding appropriation in popular culture are detailed by Thomas Frank in *The Conquest of Cool*, Malcolm Gladwell in "The Coolhunt," and Douglas Rushkoff in his PBS documentary *Merchants of Cool*. These writers note how the rhetoric of cool is often transformed into a complacent discursive strategy when coherence is the ultimate goal. As Frank writes regarding the appropriation of youth culture for consumer purposes:

> Rebel youth culture remains the cultural mode of the corporate moment, used to promote not only specific products but the general idea of life in the cyber-revolution. Commercial fantasies of rebellion, liberation, and outright "revolution" against the stultifying demands of mass society are commonplace almost to the point of invisibility in advertising, movies, and television programming. (4)

Gladwell makes a similar observation, noting how supposedly "subversive" styles are merely commercial appropriations recirculated in any number of ways.

> Ask a coolhunter where the baggy-jeans look came from, for example, and you might get any number of answers: urban black kids mimicking the jailhouse look, skateboarders trying not to look like skiers, or alternatively, all three at once, in some grand concordance. (80)

When the spirit of appropriation is reduced to another corporate slogan or commercial strategy, its rhetorical value is as minimal as Elbow asking students to utilize collage for coherent meaning or Web texts always emphasizing their hierarchical order. In these kinds of scenarios, appropriation serves only to reinstitutionalize the already accepted form of discourse. Appropriation is not applied in order to make a new rhetorical turn; it is used to keep the same rhetoric already in place. My interests are in thinking about appropriation differently. Thus, my initial thinking about appropriation borrows from practices that stress rhetorical turns, like William Burroughs's work as well as the practices outlined in Francis Brow's 1963 text *Collage*. The metaphor appropriation borrows is not coherence, as Elbow eventually suggests, but rather collage. Brow defines collage as the "pasting or gluing; specifically pasting paper, cloth, etc. into pictures or objects; the artistic product of this process" (5). With a nod towards collage's tendency to disrupt and alter expectation, she notes that "the best way to learn the art of collage is by experimentation" (Brow 16). That sense of experimentation can be seen in Burroughs's writing as well as contemporary new media production.

Even as dominant systems of thinking (corporate and education) work to utilize appropriation in order to maintain status quos, it is still possible to locate examples of appropriation as a cool writing strategy for digital work, and, consequently, to apply (i.e., appropriate) these lessons for our own pedagogies. Media critic outlet Adbusters provides one obvious example not because of its ideological positions regarding advertising and consumer culture but rather because of how it employs appropriation in noncomplacent manners for digital display. Even though I name their practice as part of the rhetoric of cool, Adbusters' founder Kalle Lasn, sounding much like Alan Liu, dismisses cool by making it the source, not the solution, of the problems consumerism creates.

> A heavily manipulative corporate ethos drives our culture. Cool is indispensable—and readily, endlessly, dispensed. You can get it on every corner (for the right price), though it's highly addictive and its effects are short-lived. If you're here for cool today, you'll almost certainly be back for more

tomorrow. American cool is a global pandemic. Communities, traditions, cultural heritages, sovereignties, whole histories are being replaced by a barren American monoculture. (xiii–xiv)

Lasn rightly notes the rhetorical power of corporate advertising that, as Frank has described aptly, appropriates cool iconology for purposes of extending consumer culture. But if the point is to reject cool as a response to this power, I disagree. Just as cool works as a topos for advertising, it can, as Burroughs demonstrates, serve as a way to resist corporate influence (if such a move is, in fact, a writer's desire, a point I will not specify as preferable but rather as one type of application). Lasn's notion of cool reflects American culture's promotion of consumer products as a dominate lifestyle.

> "Cool" used to mean unique, spontaneous, compelling. The coolest kid was the one everyone wanted to be like but no one quite could, because her individuality was utterly distinct. Then "cool" changed. Marketers got hold of it and reversed its meaning. Now you're cool if you are not unique—if you have the look and feel that bear the unmistakable stamp of America™. Hair by Paul Mitchell. Khakis by The Gap.[3] Car by BMW. Attitude by Nike. Pet phrases by Letterman. Politics by Bill Maher. Cool is the opiate of our time, and over a couple of generations, we have grown dependent on it to maintain our identities of inclusion. (113)

Unlike Lasn, I do not see cool as entirely a reinscription of corporate drive nor as an opiate. In consumer culture, cool involves the appropriative logic that Frank describes as the strategy of recontextualizing counterculture attitudes for commercial purposes *as well as* the Burroughs inspired cut-up. In the rhetoric of cool, even if cool contributes to corporate appropriation, it still functions as a lesson for electronic writing (it thus enacts its choral functionality). Academic scholarship turns to appropriation not to sell products but rather to learn the methods of persuasion conducive to new media. Appropriation and recontextualization reveal powerful tools for composition. Much like the French Situationists' 1963 calls for *détournement*, a method of recontextualizing past artistic works for new, political purposes, appropriation is a form of composition. The Situationists, Greil Marcus writes, "practiced intellectual terrorism, and inseparable from that practice was the theft of intellectual property" (*Lipstick Traces* 178). This "theft," like Burroughs's notion of appropriation as theft, Gregory Ulmer has since identified as the rhetoric of postcriticism, critical writing based on collage where copyright indicates the right to copy ("Object of Post-Criticism" 96).

Practicing "the right to copy," Adbusters, in the spirit of what Mark Dery terms *cultural jamming*, recontextualize print ads (like Obsession) and re-present them (Obsession Fetish) as critique. Another Adbusters' image shows a patient lying on an operating table; his EKG reveals not the typical patterns associated with heart movements but rather a McDonald's iconic M. The appropriation of McDonald's imagery attempts to critically assess the company's health value. In yet another example, Adbusters attacks cigarette companies for using cool as a marketing ploy by producing an ad with two generic-like boxes of Marlboro and Camel cigarettes followed by the heading "Losing Their Cool."[4] The word *cool* attracts attention to both the original product, the ideology cool carries (youthful trends), and the critique. Adbusters' method is cool not because of content but because of form and method. Cool is, as well, the practice that appropriates Marlboro and Camel as a way of turning marketing upon itself.

These examples of appropriation demonstrate writing that does not return to the coherence narrative Elbow stresses and that also dominates much of contemporary thinking regarding writing, with and without technology. Instead, these examples problematize messages, how messages are constructed and reconstructed for a variety of purposes. We don't have to agree with the message in order to apply the strategy. This strategy asks digital writers to cut up and reapply the messages, images, and ideas they are exposed to in contemporary discourse. The purpose is not, as Alan Liu writes, to continue the postmodern project of destruction but instead to foster new ways of re-structuring language and thought. These kinds of acts are both ideological (resistance to dominant thinking) and rhetorical (generating new thought). And, in turn, new media texts are produced that often challenge perceptions of clarity and order. Throughout the rest of this chapter, I will outline and apply appropriation as a specific new media practice relevant to the rhetoric of cool that cannot be explained through traditional notions of clarity or coherence. I begin with a more detailed description of the cut-up, and then I discuss how it plays out in digital practices like sampling.

### The How-To

In *Naked Lunch*'s "Atrophied Preface," Burroughs draws attention to 1963. "Hair, shit and blood spurt out 1963 on the wall . . . 'Yes sir, boys, the shit really hit the fan in '63,' said the tiresome old prophet can bore the piss out of you in any space-time direction . . ." (*Naked Lunch* 226). Burroughs's mention of 1963 is situated around a set of instructions for how *Naked Lunch* should be read, and for how it was (and could be again) written: "You can cut into *Naked Lunch* at any intersection point . . . I have written many prefaces . . . *Naked Lunch* is a blueprint, a How-To Book" (*Naked Lunch* 224). Burroughs's instructions for reading his work are instructions for how new media utilizes appropriation. Texts are cut into, written many times, in many variations, in many versions. When Elizabeth Kerr and Ralph Aderman write in their 1963 textbook *Aspects of American English* that students in need of "Suggestions for Long Papers" "analyze the slang vocabulary of a specialized group, such as Beatniks, to show language processes and principles at work" (265), they ignore the rhetorical issues raised by the Beats regarding textual (and today we can say "digital") production. To mimic "hip" language (exemplified in early 1960s slang with Beat novels) is not the same as to employ a general rhetorical strategy in order to produce new texts. The Beats don't teach us how to talk; they teach us how to compose digital texts.

My naming of Beat writing, exemplified momentarily in Burroughs's work, is not an indication of Burroughs working with new media but rather a recognition that rhetorical production may be shaped by technology regardless of the media we encounter it in. Burroughs's novels, therefore, offer rhetorical instruction for media composing, not for how to use a computer. The rhetorical method Burroughs uses is the "cut-up." The cut-up involves cutting and pasting together separately pieces of writing in order to construct narrative. The cut-up method entails taking a page and cutting it down the middle twice so that four sections remain. One then rearranges the sections in random order to create a new page. Variations of the four section cut are permissible and can lead to even more juxtapositions. The cut-up derives from understandings of the power of technology to create association by pointing to the relationship between technology and collage. "The cut-up method brings to writers the collage, which has been used by painters for fifty years. And used by the moving and still camera. In fact all street shots from movie or still cameras are by the unpredictable factors of passersby and juxtaposition cut-ups" (Burroughs and Gysin 29). The cut-up can be applied to any text, any sound recording, and any filmic representation. As a writing strategy, its purpose is to undermine the dominant ideology of a given text, to reduce "control symbols pounded to word and image dust; crumpled cloth bodies of the vast control machine" (*Ticket That Exploded* 31). Its logic stems from that of juxtaposition and parataxis. "The simplest variety of cut up on tape can be carried out with one machine . . . creating arbitrary juxtapositions you will notice that the arbitrary cuts in are appropriate" (*Ticket That Exploded* 207).

In digital culture, the cut-up is best exemplified in practices ranging from Web site construction (appropriating images and HTML code from other sites to create new sites) to Weblogs (cutting and pasting links) to hip-hop and DJ culture (appropriating sounds and music, remixing them, and generating new compositions). We find the cut-up as new media in Burroughs's definition of The Subliminal Kid, one of many collagist Burroughs creations who either search out modes of resistance to technology or succumb to technology.

Like other Burroughs characters, The Subliminal Kid formulates rhetorical responses by using technology in media intensive ways. The Subliminal Kid "had recorder in tracks and moving film mixing arbitrary intervals and agents moving with the word and image of tape recorders" (*Nova Express* 148).

> "The Subliminal Kid" moved in and took over bars cafés and juke boxes of the world cities and installed radio transmitters and microphones in each bar so that the music and talk of any bar could be heard in all his bards and he had tape recorders in each bar that played and recorded at arbitrary intervals and his agents moved back and forth with portable tape recorders and brought back street sound and talk and music and poured it into his recorder array so he set waves and eddies and tornadoes of sound down all your streets and by the river of all language. (*Nova Express* 147)

Burroughs produces a lesson not just for how to appropriate for purposes of writing (gather various influences, juxtapose them, play them back) but for how media-based writing transforms writers into media beings. As a media being, the contemporary writer is always attune to sound, imagery, words, ideas; she appropriates these items and mixes them for innovative purposes, either on a Web site, as a podcast, for a Flash presentation, or for another kind of digitally motivated project. The Burroughs writer isn't a student writer, nor is she a placement test taker, nor is she a variable to be studied as Braddock and colleagues in *Research in Written Composition* contend. She is a *writer;* and the connotation of that word means one who engages with rhetoric in order to enact, counter, uphold, or resist social change and policy. It's not hard to imagine this writer today working with an iPod, a browser, a digital mixer, Flash, a word processing program, a video recorder, an HTML editor, or any other new media tool for discursive purposes. It's not hard for us to imagine this writer appropriating texts and ideas from various We blogs in order to reinscribe them on her own Weblog space; nor is it hard to imagine this writer appropriating other texts as links embedded in a wiki. The Subliminal Kid today seems everyday to many of us because of the dominant images of cutting, pasting, sampling, and mixing that inundate most new media practices we take for granted. "Rip, Mix, Burn," a popular Apple advertisement states. "Start something sonic," a Windows XP ad requests. "Start recording your own mixing and mashing." These practices are quotidian when it comes to computing. "A mix," DJ Spooky writes, "is a way of providing a rare and intimate glimpse into the process of cultural production in the late 20th century" ("Algorithms" 351). I've partly identified that process in Governor Granholm's appropriation of cool in order to enact a mix of identity and urban planning; and I've noted how cool's 1963 connection to the mix stems from Amiri Baraka's concerns with appropriation as cultural production. Overall, the mix reveals this type of composing in most twentieth- and twenty-first-century new media writings. The one place the mix as appropriative rhetoric is missing is in writing pedagogy.

## The Sampler

It's not hard for us, contemporary writing instructors, to imagine a writer who, at the computer, appropriates and mixes. And yet in our teaching we don't imagine such writers. Even though there exists an important theoretical point regarding media-based writing in 1963, and even though that point is demonstrated throughout a number of Burroughs's writings, composition studies does not learn from writers like Burroughs how to include appropriation within a broad definition of what writing entails. Lest we cast Burroughs's Subliminal Kid as an aberration of 1963 sampling and mixing, I note that 1963 also marks the invention of the digital sampler, the composing tool that structures almost all of contemporary hip-hop and DJ-oriented music. The simultaneous invention of the sampler and Burroughs's thoughts regarding sampling generates a heuristic that allows me to follow this choral line a bit further.

Often cited as the first real sampler, the 350-pound Mellotron synthesizer came with eighteen prerecorded rhythms and eighteen different instrumental sounds. Constructed out of seventy tape machines, the Mellotron could play back prerecorded rhythms and instruments in a number of ways, depending on user input. The Mellotron signifies an early interest among composers to convert topics of discourse (topos) into digital expression. The sounds loaded into the Mellotron represented commonplace sounds that listeners would be familiar with (popular songs, street sounds, voices). A Mellotron composer, like Aristotle's imagined rhetorician, could pick and choose popular topics (prerecorded sounds) for various discursive purposes and audience expectations.

The Mellotron demonstrates the relevance of discursive interchangeability in electronic rhetorical production. The question for the composer working at the Mellotron (and its current manifestation in digital samplers like the Pioneer 1200 and CDJ-1000) is, in essence, the same question the modern writer faces: How do I synthesize vast amounts of information already circulating in discourse? Composition studies attempts to answer this question by creating anthology-based textbooks or by proposing students write the term paper with its required bibliography of texts consulted. These models for research, though, don't account for the synthesis sampling teaches through appropriation, nor do they account for the specific role a sampler, or DJ, plays as writer. Instead, these models for research maintain a specific, nonmedia status quo regarding writing. Instead of identifying writers as nonmedia beings, as the 1963 history requires, we need to construct images of writers from media oriented beings, like that of the DJ.

## The DJ

What does it mean to identify the DJ as a new media writer who utilizes some aspect of cool for rhetorical production? Since I am describing appropriation as a sampling practice, I turn to the DJ as a model for one type of digital writer who negotiates a variety of unlike texts and ideas by juxtaposing them, mixing them, and producing new meaning. "DJ-ing is writing, writing is DJ-ing" Paul Miller (DJ Spooky) notes in *Rhythm Science* (57). "I think the combination of the dj and the writer makes a lot of sense," Kodwo Eshun states. "I think that both are different kinds of remixology at work, and that all we're really doing is bringing writing and putting it onto the second deck and just accelerating it as much as a record" (189). The DJ as writer revises Walter Benjamin's concept of the *flaneur,* the inheritor of a new poetics in which cultural artifacts guide the composition process. The *flaneur,* Benjamin writes, acts as a collector; his writings stem from collected findings repositioned for new purposes. In Benjamin's *Arcades Project,* writings are collections of moments, places, things (i.e., samplings) that become juxtaposed and recontextualized in order to evoke alternative understandings of cultural history. "The collector was the true inhabitant of the interior" (*Charles Baudelaire* 168), Benjamin writes, adding that "poets find their refuse on the street" (79).

Behaving like contemporary *flaneurs,* early DJs of the 1970s and 1980s, like Grandmaster Flash and Afrika Bambaataa, built record collections from bargain street sales. These record collections functioned as the basis for future compositions, a point stressed by Kodwo Eshun. "Your record collection now becomes an ongoing memory bank in which every historical sound exists as a potential break in the present tense" (Eshun 20). S. H. Fernando Jr. writes about Bambaataa's introduction to hip-hop as a *flaneurist*-writing experience, describing how Bambaataa's mother's record collection influenced the young artist's own roaming for new items to gather:

> She had already bestowed upon him a love of music and a record collection that ran the gamut from James Brown and Sly Stone to Miriam Makeba and Fela Kuti, from the Who and Led Zeppelin to Latin soul and calypso. Bam [Bambaataa] picked up from there, scouring furniture stores in the Bronx and used record stores in Greenwich Village for obscure vinyl to play on his set. (18)

DJs like Bambaataa isolated sounds and tracks from their collections, remixing them into new compositions. "A lot of what I do is acting like a refraction point of my record collection," DJ Spooky states. "I collect all sorts of stuff" ("Watch That Man: The Many Phases of Paul D. Miller"). What Burroughs theorizes through the character of The Subliminal Kid, digital samplers actualize in electronic writing. The cut-and-paste logic of electronic writing is captured in the sampler (which I oppose to the essay), making it an alternative space for digital composing.

> A recording device that captures sound as digital information, which is then saved in computer memory instead of on magnetic tape, the sampler made it possible to create intricate soundscapes with virtually any source material, including already recorded music and live instruments. (McElfresh 170)

I see the digital sampler as an important tool for writers who appropriate in order to work with the rhetoric of cool. The basic principles integral to digital sampling suggest a model for digital composing in general; we are not required to use digital samplers in a given classroom, but we can apply its logic for a variety of new media writing. Sampling overturns the foundations of traditional research, which asks writers to use research in order to narrow down a topic or idea (and, of course, to produce coherent narratives). Sampling does not fit with McCrimmon's summarization of linear research: "Because of the importance of the research paper, the composition should usually be done in three stages: writing the rough draft, preparing the final revision, and proofreading the finished paper" (262). Sampling instead appeals to the definition of critique Joseph Harris poses in "Revision as Critical Practice": "writing that responds to and makes use of the work of others" (578). That processes of response, which many of the examples in this chapter show, may result in fair representations or unfair and manipulative stances. Whichever results, research is complicated. Whereas Peter Elbow advises writers doing research to "throw away more" (*Writing with Power* 76), Cecil B. Williams and Allan Stevenson write in their 1963 textbook *A Research Manual* that students doing research "sample some passages to see what experience, penetration, and logic the writer seems to be endowed with. Sampling will also help you determine whether a work is more on the periphery of a particular study than at the center" (30). The importance of this passage is not that Williams and Stevens are speaking to contemporary understandings of digital sampling. Instead, the mere mention of sampling as a research method tells me to explore hip-hop's usage of digital sampling (inspired by the role DJs play in hip-hop) in order to learn more about how this practice informs the rhetoric I am constructing. And it doesn't hurt that I sample this passage from *A Research Manual* to emphasize my point.

## The Mix

In Public Enemy's "Caught, Can We Get A Witness," Chuck D challenges charges that appropriation (via sampling) equates plagiarism or copyright violations. Chuck D raps that the courts have accused Public Enemy of stealing beats for their albums. Chuck D's response is to call for a witness, someone who will testify that the composition that incorporates previously found material is the product not of theft but of rhetorical innovation. The witness—the audience, other artists, those who understand the changes new media prompts—will see the emerging value of the new composition, a value that does not reduce or deny previous compositional values (where the borrowed material comes from). At least that is how I read Chuck D. That is how I read Chuck D and Public Enemy, because the equation of sampling, mixing, and appropriation with theft is a limited gesture regarding new media production, yet it is a gesture all too familiar to composition studies.

> If the research paper is to have the educational value it is intended to have, it must be an honest job. Any student who perverts the assignment by deliberately plagiarizing the paper not only convicts himself of dishonesty but raises the question whether the money and effort being expended for his education are justified. (McCrimmon 239)

Crying plagiarism has done little to teach writing how appropriation works for various purposes. Governor Granholm appropriates black identity for urban renewal. William Burroughs appropriates previously written and recorded material for critique. I appropriate one term's meanings for a new definition and pedagogical practice. To cry theft is to refuse to recognize the mix's role in new media-based expression and how that role may destabilize rhetorical and pedagogical expectations.

Chuck D underscores what I've been drawing attention to in this chapter: how digital writing undermines established belief systems regarding authorial production. Chuck D extends the appropriative strategies belonging to hip-hop's cultural origins, like those found in early sampling (and now canonical) efforts like Grand Master Flash's *The Adventures on the Wheels of Steel*. Indeed, Public Enemy's usage of "Flash Gordon" in "Terminator X to the Edge of Panic" echoes Grandmaster Flash's major hit from the album, "Adventures of Grand Master Flash on the Wheels of Steel." Grandmaster Flash samples the original Flash Gordon serial, among a number of other songs and sounds, to critique copyright.

> With Chic's "Good Times" supplying the main beat, Flash manages to mix into this central rhythm the Sugarhill Gang's "8th Wonder," Flash and the Five's "Birthday Party," Spoonie Gee's "Monster Jam," Queen's "Another

One Bites the Dust," Blondie's "Rapture," the narrated title of Flash Gordon (without the "Gordon," i.e., "The official adventures of . . . Flash"), and other assorted spoken words. (Boyer 7)

The appropriations establish connections among disparate texts, and in Public Enemy's text, the appropriations work with these connections to persuade. Persuasion, in this case, relies on recognizable material, texts and ideas that are already in circulation. "Every past commodification—of blues, of rock-n-roll, or jazz, and of hip-hop itself—haunts the musical mix," Russell Potter writes. "Sometimes in person (a digital sample), sometimes only as a "ghost" or trace (a passing act of Signifyin(g) on some past text)" (Potter 110).[5]

To teach the mix through appropriation, we have to reject the disciplinary fixation on theft (represented in the general fear of plagiarism—whether that fear is posed as an economic one or a pedagogical one) and recognize that appropriation as mix signifies more than just borrowing text. "The mix gets inside us," Erik Davis proclaims, "and changes the way the world arises before us" (Davis). The new media being that Burroughs defines and I am pushing composition studies to identify understands that the mix is inside of her shaping perception in a variety of ways. She sees the dominance of the mix in her sense of selfhood, one that contextualizes digital identity as a series of appropriations and not as the authorial student writer identity she is asked to adhere to in the classroom, the role, too, already in circulation in most disciplinary conversations. "As the most technologically sophisticated form of writing," Jay David Bolter writes, "electronic writing should be the farthest removed from human nature" (217). It *should,* as Bolter notes, be removed from human nature, but it's not. We become as mixed and appropriated as the compositions we write. As Ulf Poschardt argues, "The remixer isn't concerned with salvaging authenticity, but with creating a new authenticity" (34). The appropriation-motivated mix is not recognized as human nature in the average writing course because the emphasis is often on salvaging an assumed authorial authenticity; students are asked to maintain singular identities distinct from their writings. Yet in popular culture, where other recognizable roles are circulated, appropriative identities are commonplace. They can be found among the early days of Hollywood film that asked actors and actresses to appropriate new names as well as in the alter egos and personalities hip-hop performers take on so that they can construct a variety of composition practices.[6]

In the mix, writing involves more than merely appropriating text and image; it involves a complete appropriation of the various structures we inhabit and that inhabit us. As DJ Spooky writes, "The mix speaks to you of the bricolage of place where the 'self' exists as a deployed network of personae"

("Algorithms 351). In the mix, networks of meaning are generated through a variety of appropriations. In that sense, Public Enemy's declaration "They say that I stole this" extends beyond the sampled sounds the group uses in order to record all of *It Takes a Nation of Millions to Hold Us Back* or *Fear of a Black Planet*. What has been "stolen" includes the composition process, which, in turn, includes the various interconnected identities involved in composing, the so-called cyborg personalities popularized in science fiction and digital studies but actualized in the appropriative gestures found in digital sampling. When we compose through appropriation, we often appropriate new identities and alter egos to parallel the rhetorical moves we make, a move quite different from Kitzhaber's insistence that composing includes "an impression of a consistent point of view and distinct personality behind the composition" (*Themes, Theories, and Therapy* 90) or McCrimmon's instruction to "restrict that subject so as to deal with it from a particular point of view" (47). The consistent point of view emphasized in these positions, McLuhan notes, in *Understanding Media* and *The Media Is the Message,* collapses in a media-oriented culture of involvement and participation. The hip-hop magazine *Re:UP* foregrounds this perception shift in its 2005 *Manual 07* issue, an issue devoted to the alter ego. Interviews with some of hip-hop's more dynamic alter ego personalities are featured: Quasimoto (a.k.a. Madlib), Humpty Hump (a.k.a. Shock-G), and Prefuse 73 (a.k.a. Scott Herren). To treat these appropriative gestures as an anomaly, it seems, would be an error. They suggest a shift in the relationship between composing, identity, and digital media at the level of appropriation.

Eminem's alternative D12 band is one of the more popular examples of how the alter ego functions,[7] but we can find other appropriations in the identity labels of the MC and DJ that preempt one's name (DJ Kool, DJ Kool Herc, etc), in the activity names that absorb DJ culture into one's name (as in rap singers and DJs Busta Rhymes, Cut Chemist, and Method Man), or in those names that associate themselves generally with cool (Kool Herc, Kool Keith, Kool Moe D, DJ Kool, L.L Cool J, and Coolio). The rap group Wu-Tang Clan foregrounds all of their work in terms of identity and appropriation. The name Wu-Tang is itself appropriated from a series of kung-fu movies of the same name. Each member of the group goes by a number of alter egos; RZA is also Bobby Digital and Prince Rakeem; the late Old Dirty Bastard was also Big Baby Jesus and Osiris; Method Man goes by Ghost Rider and Iron Lung. In the *Wu-Tang Manual*, group leader RZA's account of the philosophy behind the Wu-Tang, alter egos are noted for their importance to *the writing* the group does. RZA explains his own alter ego as a rhetoric of appropriation: "So Bobby Digital is about what molded me: comic books, video games, the arcade scene, break dancing, hip-hop clothes, MCing, DJing, human beatboxing, graffiti plus Mathematics and the gods" (91). These acts of appropriation extend beyond the writings themselves; they indicate an apparatus shift in the construction of personality where composition juxtaposes with the ideas and the being of the one who produces writing.

But to employ appropriation via identity and composing simultaneously, one does not have to work solely with hip-hop. A significant portion of digital culture in general functions in similar ways—from popular culture to politics. In my textbook *Writing about Cool,* students are asked to extend appropriative gestures into their own work by developing their own alter egos through an assignment patterned after *The Autobiography of Malcolm X.* The process of renaming oneself is not, of course, an action only found in hip-hop culture; it represents a very political application of appropriation not unlike the critical gestures Adbusters makes. In the 1960s, both Malcolm X and Muhammad Ali appropriated other names in order to write themselves into the culture on their own terms (or what they perceived their own terms to be as the civil rights movement gained momentum). These new names were construed from a variety of cultural influences whose meanings are only fully understood when juxtaposed together. Thus, Malcolm X erases the name he was born into, "Little," by replacing it with X. His decision is made after discovering a pattern of racism in various moments of his life (his father's death, drug dealing, imprisonment). He appropriates both these moments as well as the X in order to compose ideas regarding black empowerment and civil rights.

In order to apply this cool method of writing, students are asked to identify specific cultural influences from their own lives. These influences may come from background, school, history, politics, music, objects they've owned, anecdotes, and a variety of other sources. In a series of Web assignments, students appropriate these influences from their original contexts (i.e., don't write a narrative about the church you attended; appropriate the church and its relevant imagery for its placement in a new composition). Students then present and juxtapose these influences in order to find a pattern. That pattern, which is also a mark of appropriation, becomes the student's new name and alter ego. Demonstrated on a Web site through hyperlinks and images, the student engages appropriation as a new media method of composition aligned with her own name.

The principle methods of this writing are appropriation and juxaposition. These rhetorical moves challenge writers to rethink their relationship to electronic writing in ways David Bartholomae's canonical appeal for student appropriation doesn't. Bartholomae describes the student writer as one who "continually audits and pushes against a language that would render him "like everyone else" and mimics the language and interpretive systems of the privileged community" (474). Mimicking *may* occur in an assignment like the one I describe above. Unlike Bartholomae's image of the student as appropriator, however, the alter ego appropriation does not ask writers to be *student writers* in the end, or to appropriate the university for the goal of being a student. To appropriate only to remain a student is not to fully engage the challenge appropriative gestures pose for writing. The only writing that can emerge from the student as appropriator is student writing.

Using appropriation within the rhetoric of cool allows writers to write outside of the limitations of student writing and, therefore, to fully enjoy other forms of writing that occupy their media lives; in other words, writers juxtapose these other forms to their lives. Because juxtaposition, too, plays a role in this process, I turn to it more completely in the next chapter.

# 4

## Juxtaposition

The basic law of association and conditioning is known to college students even in America: Any object, feeling, odor, word, image in juxtaposition with any other object, feeling, word or image will be associated with it.

—William Burroughs, *Nova Express*

"There," I said, pointing to the elongated letters painted in yellow on the macadam street: SHCOOL. "The Sh-cools have gone to pot." I said.

—Ken Macrorie, "Writing's Dying"

In his 1963 essay "A Conceptual Framework for Augmenting Man's Intellect," Douglas Engelbart proposed that juxtaposition be the focal point of writing with computers. In contrast to the linear, ordered logic of mainframe computing—entering data to be processed by a machine without continuous writerly input—Engelbart envisioned computer applications for purposes other than numerical calculation, notably for that of writing. Imagining an environment comprised of what we now recognize as personal computing, Engelbart noted that

> [t]he category of "more radical innovations" includes the digital computer as a tool for the personal use of an individual. Here there is not only promise of great flexibility in the composing and rearranging of text and diagrams before the individual's eyes, but also promise of many other process capabilities. (9)

Engelbart developed his idea of "composing and rearranging text" into a series of window-like boxes meant to resemble the size of actual paper, which, projected onto a display, a user could juxtapose and overlap. In turn, users could augment the strategy of comparing and manipulating texts through juxtaposition, a process difficult to do in a print-based environment that supports the separation of text and image by unconnected paper as well as by logic. The potential of this juxtaposing-windows system, Engelbart argued, would allow writers the ability to work simultaneously with a variety of versions of the same text, each version contributing differently to the learning and discovery process writing evokes. Juxtaposition, therefore, would be central to a computing-based heuretics.

I call this method of writing Engelbart proposed *cool* for how it replicates the same logic behind Marshall McLuhan's 1963 insistence that cool media involve the rhetorical act of juxtaposition because of the "promise of depth involvement and integral expression" (*Understanding Media* 40). The juxtapositions McLuhan employed to write both the 1962 *The Gutenberg Galaxy* and 1964 *Understanding Media* (as well as later visual texts) are cool for how they manage to force reader interaction at levels traditional scholarly prose often cannot. Juxtapositions among ideas as well as word and image prompt assumptions and inferences absent in most argumentative or narrative writing. At the meta-level, this method, McLuhan writes, generates "a series of historical observations of the new cultural completions ensuing upon the 'disturbances,' first of literacy, and then of printing" (*Gutenberg* 13). In a 1963 *College Composition and Communication* review of *The Gutenberg Galaxy*, John Freund comments on these disturbances when he remarks that the book "strikes us as a hybrid species, disquieting rather than beautiful, and as we do with almost every pioneering effort, we tend to note its departures from the ways of the past without discerning the new path it is pursuing" (112). Freund poignantly observes 1960s composition's inability to discern "the new path" new media logics like juxtaposition generate, whether they compliment or disturb our expectations. McLuhan's text was mostly considered an anomaly (a "departure" as Freund notes) and not the indication of an emerging writing practice. As I will note shortly, the idea that disturbances motivate new media writing (or new thoughts regarding writing and media) speaks greatly to the kinds of juxtaposition strategies central to Engelbart's windows-based system as well as its theoretical cousin, the cool-oriented writing machines suggested by William Burroughs. Engelbart's windows system echoes the hypothetical new media writing machines outlined in much of Burroughs's writings: "The Burroughs machine, systematic and repetitive, simultaneously disconnecting and reconnecting—it disconnects the concept of reality that has been imposed on us and then plugs normally dissociated zones into the same sector—eventually escapes from the control of its manipulator" (Burroughs and Gysin 17). In *The Ticket that Exploded*, Burroughs describes this machine in detail, noting how it brings together unlike text and image for rhetorical output: "A writing machine that shifts one half one text and half the other through a page frame on conveyor belts—(The proportion of half one text half the other is important corresponding as it does to the two halves of the human organism)" (*Ticket That Exploded* 65). Like McLuhan's observation, this juxtaposing writing machine reflects the broader cultural shifts that arise out of technological innovations. The tradition of literacy studies, McLuhan notes, often cannot fully grasp how such shifts lead to cultural juxtapositions. Instead, McLuhan argues, literacy studies frequently focus on individual acquirements of literacy or literate methods like linear organization. Such positions are out of place within a digital apparatus that promotes juxtaposition in compositional, cultural, and technological ways.

The Burroughs writing machine (or what McLuhan calls the "kaleidoscope" approach) mirrors the types of cultural, social, and technological juxtapositions writers engage with in the digital world. From the emerging satellite-based culture of the early 1960s to the hyperlinked Web familiar to contemporary computing, ideas and discourse juxtapose within and through compositional and rhetorical exchanges. Even a Web service as simplistically designed as Google News (http://news.google.com) speaks to what early 1960s writers recognized as juxtaposition. The "many other process capabilities" Engelbart identified with juxtaposition can be encountered through the algorithms Google News runs to gather and display a variety of news headlines in one visual space. What Burroughs claims of the new media writing machine—that it "shifts one half one text and half the other through a page frame"—Google News (and other "feed" services generated through RSS or related applications) accomplish online. These "shifts" Google News creates merge global perspectives, popular press headlines and stories, and legitimate and nonlegitimate sources of information amid a variety of topical issues covering a number of informational categories (Entertainment, Sports, Health, World, U.S.). Burroughs names this process the "Juxtaposition Formulae" and situates it within the merging worlds of print and digital culture, the place where media culture appropriates the strategy for controlling purposes, and individuals struggle to learn it as a rhetoric of resistance to political and economic structures.

> Our technicians learn to read newspapers and magazines for juxtaposition statements rather than alleged content—We express these statements in Juxtaposition Formulae—The Formulae of course control populations of the world—Yes it is fairly easy to predict what people will think see feel and hear a thousand years from now if you write the Juxtaposition Formulae to be used in that period—But the technical details you understand and the machines—all of which contain basic flaws and must be continually overhauled, checked, altered whole blocks of computing machines purged and disconnected from one minute to the next—fast our mind waves and long counts. (*Nova Express* 85–86)

That Burroughs poses the Juxtaposition Formulae as teachable and computer based is important for how this process reimagines both literacy and pedagogy in nonprint terms. "We express these statements" is a directive to learn to recognize and compose with juxtapositions. "We appear content pretty much to go as we have been," Kitzhaber critiques composition studies in 1963, "changing textbooks and prerequisites and switching course numbers, but not seeing the curriculum steadily or seeing it whole. And yet, to those that have eyes to see, it is obvious that changes are not far off" ("4C, Freshmen English, and the Future" 131). Changes were not far off from Kitzhaber's appeal; indeed, as my introduction of Engelbart, McLuhan, and Burroughs begins to demonstrate, the desire to combine the curriculum as a whole through the method of juxtaposition had been put into circulation. There already exists a literacy of juxtaposition around us, Burroughs says. Our challenge is to work within that space and invent applications suitable for its placement within new media.

My own interest in creating a rhetoric of cool reflects the Burroughs/McLuhan method of composing; the meanings of cool that direct my thinking all stem from an initial temporal juxtaposition. The very process of juxtaposition, McLuhan felt, is a cool one for how it forges readers (and writers) to interact with the unexpected textual and visual associations juxtapositions force us to encounter. "Previous technologies were partial and fragmentary," McLuhan notes, "the electric is total and inclusive" (*Understanding Media* 64). Based on its own historical narrative, composition studies in 1963 neglects not only the power of juxtaposition for rhetorical purposes but also the need to juxtapose composition studies with other interests in writing, like computing (Engelbart) or media (McLuhan). The 1963 composition narrative remains partial and exclusive in place of being total and inclusive.

We can currently recognize the juxtaposition-based windows system Engelbart hypothesized in the operating systems of contemporary computing and in the interfaces of many Web browsers. That we accept juxtaposition today as the basis of electronic writing is not as obvious, though, as it may seem. The nature of new media composition represented on the Web, TV, film, iPods, digital sampling, and elsewhere is the result of the complex juxtaposition of ideas, images, texts, and sounds. In this data-rich environment, Johndan Johnson-Eilola writes, "we are not looking for simplicity, but interesting juxtapositions and commentaries" (*Datacloud* 4). While Google News demonstrates how popular news Web sites and portals demonstrate juxtaposition, other forces contribute to this type of composition. Tabbed browser pages can be read at once; Weblog news feeds bring together in one site an assortment of ideas; CNN headlines present multiple stories and facts simultaneously on a television screen; online mashups merge various songs into one new composition; Flickr image sets combine text and image through annotation and hyperlinks; and even online meet-up sites like MySpace ask writers to juxtapose music, image, and text in innovative ways.[1]

To read these new media applications as distinct from the research and compositional work done in the field is to deny the ways media shapes composition practically as well as ideologically. When I read Braddock and colleagues' warning that "it is impossible to construct mutually exclusive categories of research studies," I want to interpret this moment as an initial nod toward juxtaposition and how it might alter overall understandings of research and composing. Research studies, the authors contend, must deal "with environmental factors, but not to the exclusion of instructional factors" (Braddock *et al.* 33). And yet the dominant composition narrative that extends from this call maintains a division, rather than juxtaposition, of writing interests; North's categories of composition practitioners and theorists are separate entities whose overlap is little speculated on and whose interests are restricted to distinct classroom and research-driven writing practices. In addition, in North and Kitzhaber, as well as Braddock and colleagues, writing that exists outside the classroom is never mentioned nor, of course, juxtaposed with the work students (and the various "practitioners" and "experimenters" who teach the students) are expected to do (a point I used to introduce appropriation in chapter 2). While I want to imagine Braddock and colleagues' call as one for juxtaposition, I realize that the kinds of juxtapositions media evokes—both through the environmental and the instructional—were not the focus of the authors' writing.[2]

This lapse can be somewhat traced to the split between composition and communication studies, as it is loosely represented by McLuhan's presence in my own theoretical juxtaposition. Because some 1960s theorists like McLuhan express concern with media (McLuhan specifically noting the role media environments play in composing), their work often is studied in communication studies or related areas of interest and seldom in composition studies. John Trimbur and Diane George note that composition studies abandoned communication studies as "the fourth C" sometime around 1962 in order to forge a unique identity. Quoting outgoing 1963 Conference on College Composition and Communication chair Francis Bowman as saying that communication studies had failed to prove itself to composition, Trimbur and George proceed to highlight the field's declining interest in those elements that comprise communications studies, like media studies. A lack of interest in media studies, no doubt, prompted much of the anti-juxtaposition ideology I see in various 1963 composition writings or pedagogical innovations. Film and television, the most easily identifiable media studies areas of investigation of the early 1960s, consist of juxtaposed and spliced images and sound. They also form the basis of much of McLuhan's and Burroughs's observations regarding media and writing. Film, however, is not taken seriously by Braddock and colleagues as relevant to composition pedagogy.

> One wonders if a series of professionally prepared and mature teaching films on composition would not prove even more effective with freshmen than kinescopes or television. The problem is to find teaching films which are well done and which cover the particular matters emphasized in the individual school or college. (47–48)

A media directed approach would not try to find films that teach writing points (how to conjugate verbs/how to outline/the difference between independent and dependent clauses) as Braddock and colleagues appear to require but would instead pose media as an applicable rhetoric to writing studies. It would view film as another source of rhetorical expression for study and output. "Film," McLuhan writes, "both in its reel form and in its scenario or script form, is completely involved with book culture" (*Understanding Media* 250). This involvement is not the replication of print-based rhetorics but an expansion of the organizational methods print teaches. "In terms of other media such as the printed page, film has the power to store and to convey a great deal of information" (*Understanding Media* 252). I will return to this point in more detail in the next chapter when I discuss commutation as one kind of organizational method generated out of early 1960s cinema. For now, I pose film as emblematic of the lack of attention devoted to media-influenced rhetorics like juxtaposition.

The abandonment of the fourth C in composition studies can be found as well in reactions to the authors of the 1963 Conference on College Composition and Communication's report (published in *College Composition and Communication* that year), which encouraged "debate on the long research paper, its purpose, its place in the program" (*CCC* 182). Without the communication emphasis Trimbur and George find essential, the general followup to this report takes the shape of nonmedia approaches to writing. If we look for responses to the CCCC call in the year's most cited practical and theoretical writings, we find little in terms of media-based rhetorics such as juxtaposition. James McCrimmon's textbook *Writing with a Purpose*, with its lengthy teaching of the long research paper, can be imagined as one such response. Even though the general category of research supports the juxtaposition of unlike ideas that, when synthesized, generate new knowledge on a given topic, the research paper, McCrimmon explains, results from the very specific organization of information into linear argumentation, an organization where ideas are separated and categorized as distinct entities. How those ideas are combined is not entirely clear: "The writer of a thesis research paper is studying the facts to draw a conclusion from them; this conclusion becomes the thesis of this essay; and he selects and organizes his material to develop his thesis" (McCrimmon 240). The kind of organization McCrimmon lays out for students to work with contrasts with the juxtaposing machine Burroughs describes and Engelbart theorizes. The discrepancy in positions is not a matter of preference or viewpoints but an ideological positioning regarding the nature of composition. The ideology of the thesis—that writing (and thus research) depends on a single statement or idea—has led the initial CCCC call to not be fully answered. Indeed, the call for debate regarding composition pedagogy (generalized in the research paper issue) never has extended to include how writers juxtapose, or how writers organize ideas spatially, as Lev Manovich argues in *The Language of New Media*. Spatial composing, Manovich's term for multilayered new media composition, reflects how new media artifacts contain a "hierarchy of levels" (xxv). Manovich, like McLuhan, offers film as exemplary of this process, particularly for how film and computer-based writing overlap and shape one another. Manovich argues that the layering of processes, ideas, images, and texts into one space complicates any given composition. Layers, as in Photoshop layers, digital film compositing, or multimedia layers of text and image, may be removed and added to at any given moment within the composing process. Instead of a single idea or claim occupying a given space (topos), multiple ideas and positions are displayed. Spatial composing, as an update of Engelbart's windows, requires that "juxtapositions of elements should follow a particular system, and these juxtapositions should play a key role in how the work established its meaning, and its emotional and aesthetic effects" (Manovich 158). Spatial composing is a process—the ability to navigate and display disparate elements one encounters—as well as compositional—the writing one does. McCrimmon's pedagogy of the thesis, however, is not spatial; it directs writers to see each step of writing as a separate, distinct moment (first the facts, then the conclusion, then the organization).

Kitzhaber, too, when he considers the role technology may play in writing, and when he uses language similar to Burroughs's, does not recognize media as spatial. Instead, he promotes the separate stage process, in this case exemplified by an assessment system of error correction and fill in the blanks pedagogy. Kitzhaber describes his vision regarding what a teaching machine might generate for writing instruction.

> A teaching machine or a programmed text is a device that presents one item or frame at a time; that is, it allows students to see one sentence with a critical word left out or one statement followed by a question. The student writes the required answer on the program itself or on an answer tape or

booklet. If he has been using a typical teaching machine, it then activates a mechanism that moves his answer under a clear plastic window (where he cannot change it) at the same time that it reveals the correct answer. (*Themes, Theories, and Therapy* 85)

I'm caught between these two visions of writing machines: The Burroughs juxtaposing machine, which is spatial and layered, and the Kitzhaber drill and answer machine. How is it that one method dominates our disciplinary way of thinking about writing, and the other doesn't?[3] To more fully understand juxtaposition as a major feature of the rhetoric of cool, I choose to work with the Burroughs vision, to explore its power as a new media rhetorical device.[4] The most immediate place to explore a Burroughs-oriented writing machine for the rhetoric of cool is hypertext, for it allows writers to juxtapose ideas, texts, sounds, images, and animation in ways print cannot accommodate. While hypertext is not the only new media application worth studying, its dominance on the Web and in many computer-oriented classrooms today directs me to consider how it supports cool writing. Hypertext briefly caught composition's attention in the early and mid 1990s: John Slatin's "Reading Hypertext: Order and Coherence in a New Medium," Jane Yellowlees Douglas's "Gaps, Maps, and Perception: What Hypertext Readers (Don't Do)," Nancy Kaplan's "E-literacies: Politexts, Hypertexts and Other Cultural Formations in the Late Age of Print," Johndan Johnson-Eilola's *Nostalgic Angels: Rearticulating Hypertext Writing*, and George Landow's *Hypertext 2.0* mark a few of the more influential texts on hypertext that often are cited in composition studies scholarship. Hypertext, as well, generates the current rise of Weblogs and wikis as media for Web writing, applications receiving moderate attention within writing instruction. What I want to do, however, is not revisit that initial hypertext scholarship; nor do I want to critique current pedagogies of hypertext and writing. Instead, I want to understand how juxtaposition plays out as a rhetoric in hypertext in terms of the overall practice I am inventing (a thread I will continue in a later chapter as well). To do so, I turn to Ted Nelson who coined the term *hypertext* in 1963.[5]

## Hypertext

Hypertext is cool. Its coolness derives not from its supposed "hip" nature (as many popular Web sites tend to stress through cool sites or cool links lists) but rather from an interlinking, juxtaposed writing akin to the initial vision Nelson described in 1963. A Web site like Everything2.com resembles Nelson's concept best; its users "cool" topics by forging connections between disparate material.[6] When the site's writings are "cooled," they are juxtaposed with other writings at the point a pattern (word, concept, idea) appears. Particularly meaningful write-ups are pushed to Everything2.com's "Page of Cool" listings where they can be juxtaposed and connected to other writings. No single writing stands alone. Each writing always interacts and juxtaposes with another; each writing layers over another. The cool writing of Everything2.com actualizes much, though not all, of Nelson's initial concept of hypertext as a writing space outside of what Nelson calls "the paperdigm." The paperdigm limits technological integration into writing, for writers (and educators) expect writing machines to duplicate the familiar and ubiquitous writing practices we normally engage with in print culture (like Kitzhaber's fill in the blanks machine or, in general, thesis driven projects). Merely uploading print documents to the Web or engaging in file sharing does not allow writers the ability to rhetorically work with new media; instead such writing duplicates the logic of print in structure, content, and delivery. McLuhan raised similar concerns regarding computing and writing when he noted, "Programmers of computers are still using the old print technology—storage. Computers are being asked to do things that belong to the old technology. The real job of the computer is not retrieval but discovery. Like the human memory, the process of recall is an act of discovery" (*McLuhan Hot and Cool* 294). Instead of using computers to reinscribe the logic of print (linear narratives modeled after the essay), Nelson argued that writers composing with hypertext can combine their own material with an endless stream of quotations, essays, cartoons, reports, advertisements, sounds, images, and so forth, in order to generate an interconnecting network of knowledge, to practice discovery through this interlinking. Modern hypertext systems don't allow for the kinds of mutual linking and juxtapositions Nelson wanted, but the principle still remains relevant to the rhetoric of cool for how it allows me to translate juxtaposition to a new media environment.

While arguing against the paperdigm, Nelson did not initially have access to an appropriate medium in which he could demonstrate his theoretical assumptions. In *Computer Lib/Dream Machines,* he attempted to perform hypertext (long before the modern browser or the World Wide Web) within the limitations of the book format. With two interlinking sides (the book opens from both directions; therefore, it lacks a front or back), *Computer Lib/Dream Machines* juxtaposes a number of discursive threads on each page and across the two bound books. Readers must figure out on their own where to go, what to read, and how to interlink the different texts they encounter. That hypertext is originally performed in absence of its computerized medium is an important point, for it reminds us that immediate applicability is not always as essential as the theory that will eventually drive rhetorical production to its appropriate outlet. McLuhan actualized the point dramatically in his highly visual texts like the 1967 *The Medium Is the Massage,* where the combination of image, quotations, comics, and personal insight stand for how computing may be used to generate the process of discovery.

As a hypermedia rhetoric, juxtaposition, Nelson writes, comprises an intellectual challenge to writing studies. "The details of the hypermedia systems of the future are vital; for these will be the principle intellectual environments of the human race hereafter" (*Computer Lib* 7). One such intellectual trope is that of the individual writer. The notion of solitary thinking or individual authorship belongs more to premises native to print since print encourages individual directed thinking and composing. Wayne Booth described this type of writer in "The Scholar in Society": "What makes a scholar a scholar is the willingness to sit alone, for long periods, trying to learn something that cannot be learned 'in society,' something that cannot be learned except through sustained private inquiry" (15). Out of the premise of private inquiry, composition studies adheres to a belief in sequential thinking, to the "private point of view" McLuhan traces to the first century of printing, which was "united to the means of self-expression made possible by the typographic extension of man" (*Understanding Media* 157). "The typographic logic," McLuhan writes, "created the outsider, the alienated man" (*Gutenberg* 254). Nelson argues against private, solitary thought that encourages alienation or separation of ideas. New media extends writers' sense and observations outside of self; new media forces (whether wanted or not wanted) connections between the self and various levels of expression, what Matthew Fuller calls "*using* the Perspectivalism of particular approaches, materials and ideas as they intersect" (168). Within the barrage of information that new media generates, and that writers consequently absorb into their own compositions, thinking proceeds in a number of directions; some guided, some not; some productive, some not. In other words, following Manovich, the issue is not whether writers should choose to generate spatialized, juxtapositions; interaction with ideas is already a spatialized process. Hypertext foregrounds that process.

That said, composition studies still legitimizes the sequentiality of thought that structures much of McCrimmon's teaching regarding good writing. Emphasized in the concept of outlining (which is itself a print-based logic invented by Peter Ramus in order to accommodate the sixteenth-century new demands of print), sequentiality dictates organization (clear and in order) but also motivates the thinking process to be linear as well. "How easily you can shape your outline will depend on how clearly you have your purpose in mind . . . until you have done these things you are not ready to begin the final outline, since you do not yet know to what end you are trying to organize your material" (McCrimmon 57). Out of outlines arise ordered thought, McCrimmon argues. Organized thought stems from the very methods of organization writers employ *prior to writing*. That being so, we can imagine the kinds of thinking processes students are asked to engage with when they construct outlines: linear, sequential writings that place ideas in separation from other ideas either by organization (paragraphs) or by logic (disciplinarity or leveled structure of information where connections are not foregrounded). In an ordered system, everything has its place; that which cannot be classified or categorized does not belong in the writing. "If there is any doubt about the relation of any heading to the purpose statement," McCrimmon states regarding the parts of the outline, "that heading is either poorly stated or is a potential trouble spot in the organization. Whatever the reason, the difficulty should be removed before beginning to write" (59).

These are points relevant to the question of invention as much as to the production of writing. The outline's function is meant to situate invention as the following of reestablished thought and for that preestablished thought to be clear from the get-go. Preestablished thought reflects what McCrimmon and countless textbooks since have deemed "purpose." Purpose operates outside of the associations that motivate juxtapositions because it is predetermined; one first has "purpose" or identifies purpose through the outline. Further associations (i.e., juxtapositions) may arise as the outline is realized, but the outline is not designed to encourage such work. Once purpose is established, writing proceeds based on that initial vision or goal. Anything not initially conceived as relevant to one's purpose should be discarded.

Hypertext, as a cool form of writing, rejects the outline and functions by way of associations and juxtapositions, not purpose. In saying that, I am not speaking of hypertext tools like Storyspace or Tinderbox, which employ hierarchal tress to document how links connect, nor am I describing a published Web text that maps upfront paths users make take as they read. Instead, I am speaking of the process of hypertext, which, following Nelson, is a method meant to forge associations instead of only prescribing preplanned arrangements. Students who engage with hypertext, then, should be expected to produce writing far different than what results from an outline. Such expectations may not be situated entirely around purpose or predetermined meaning and should allow for the "discarded" moment to remain in case it does prove relevant in the mix of things. Whereas the nature of print is closed (the page can contain only one author at a time), hypertext was meant to generate open texts via the link's ability to join a variety of authorial positions. When Nelson or Engelbart stress juxtaposition or interconnectivity, they describe not just the final product one reads (like a series of hyperlinked Web pages) but also the thought processes that continue to evolve from and through the linking activity, both by writer and by reader. A hyperlinked thought process sees connections and associations where linear thinking may not because of its ability to interlink as well as to leave that interlinking open for further connections. The process is not utopist nor is it liberatory; it is open and, therefore, an entirely different kind of organizing logic.

What I note regarding purpose, I also can claim regarding the print-based emphasis on theses or topic sentences, two items central to contemporary writing pedagogy. Any critique of the thesis or topic sentence, no doubt, will irk a long-standing tradition within composition pedagogy that has depended on these items in order to teach first-year writing students how to order their ideas. Yet, to understand why a concept like juxtaposition can be easily passed over both in 1963 and today, we have to recognize the topic sentence legacy. "Many students," McCrimmon notes, "create trouble for themselves by trying to avoid the discipline that writing a thesis normally imposes."

> Faced with the task of expressing a controlling idea in a single sentence, they take one of two escapes: they write a thesis which is so general that it exerts no control over the development of the paper, or they write one which looks good but has no relation to the material in their notes and therefore does not represent the idea they intend to develop. (McCrimmon 258)

The thesis is, as McCrimmon also writes, restrictive. Its task is not to keep the text open for further invention or addition (like juxtaposing or layering new images, ideas, writings created over a period of time, outside writings) but to shut down the writer's scope quickly for reasons of narrowed interest. The student, obviously too scattered in thought and undisciplined in structure, needs the thesis to put everything quickly in its place (and, we might note, to be put, herself, in place). Indeed, McCrimmon's choice of words, like "controlling," reflects the controlled writing situations Braddock and colleagues and Kitzhaber impose on students when studying writing habits. "The attitudes of teachers and students should be controlled" (Braddock *et al.* 25). These compositionists create controlled environments via variables in order to study writing. Their studies reflect the control print directs and supports, limiting the ability to juxtapose new ideas, concepts, or texts as they are encountered (the "accident" or happenchance mistake is never explored positively in *Research in Written Composition*). And as these compositionists control the media within which they work (the classroom), the results of their work become similarly controlled, and thus, predictable. It is put in *its place* as well. That work reflects thesis driven writing.

Juxtaposition, no doubt, may also lead to control and predictability and thus should not be romanticized as an idealistic writerly alternative. Instead of idealizing juxtaposition, I am describing how it contributes to the rhetoric of cool. The potential of opening up writing to discovery and invention is what Nelson imagines in his musings on hypertext. In the hypertext system dramatized by Nelson, the environment within which writing is produced should not feel controlled, comfortable, nor safe, as the thesis demands of student writing or as *Research in Written Composition*'s scientific laboratory atmosphere demands of the teaching of writing. *Research in Written Composition*'s locale is a safe place where we never find out what students are writing about, just that they write nice papers in observed classrooms. If control means safety, discovery and invention become victimized, for in a controlled system thought becomes too narrowed to allow for the necessary conflicts and contradictions out of which ideas emerge. "The reality film has now become an instrument and weapon of monopoly," Burroughs writes regarding controlled writing situations (*Ticket That Exploded* 151). The central point of Nelson's initial 1963 vision was to work around that control by opening up connections within writing. When writers expand connections, when they begin to include a variety of material into the writing process (texts, images, fragments, sounds, quotes, figures, etc.), writers begin as well to move beyond immediate controlling situations. But as writers navigate through such distinct material, they often will encounter conflict as each connection comes into contact (i.e., juxtaposes) with differing positions. "When information is brushed against information," McLuhan notes, "the results are startling and effective" (*Medium* 77–79). The role of hypertext in cool, then, is not just a question of what appears on a screen or page (how links work) but how the medium shapes thought (encourages writers to search out conflicting viewpoints through connections). Controlled writing produces controlled beings. Interconnected writing produces interconnected beings. This is the nature of hypertext George Landow highlights when he writes that new media, like hypertext, shape educational outlooks and pedagogical positions: "I emphasize that this examination of the relationship between hypertext, an important form of digital information technology, and university education focuses chiefly upon hypertext as a paradigm, as a thought-form, rather than on the tails of hardware and software" ("The Paradigm Is More Important than the Purchase" 40–41).

When conflict is kept at bay, students—and what they have to say—are controlled. A student studying *Writing with a Purpose* in 1963, for instance, would not find conflict as a central tenet of the discovery process. And in turn, she also would fail to see the cultural conflicts juxtaposed around her: civil rights, Vietnam, the emerging counterculture, the rise in hallucinogenic drug usage, Stonewall and the gay rights movement, the themes of popular music, and so forth. After all, Martin Luther King's 1963 "Letter From Birmingham Jail" appears in the same year as *Writing with a Purpose* and has since become a canonical essay in many contemporary first-year rhetoric readers. Yet where do King's concerns with control or conflict surface in McCrimmon's examples of student writing like "The Abominable Snowman" (345) and the controversy surrounding Shakespeare's true name (348)? McCrimmon's writing situations do exemplify his pedagogical directive that writers learn that "whenever we have two statements so related that one is inferred as a conclusion from the other, we have an argument" (314). These examples don't, however, acknowledge that such sequential reasoning may not account for the ways conflicting information is delivered rapidly and at once in an information-overloaded society so that inference and argument are not easily, if at all, obtainable. Two statements may lead to a conclusion, but they don't teach how to deal with the kinds of racist conclusions King's work attempted to address and rectify. Two statements may also not account for the web of information one encounters in media where juxtapositions not only foreground conflict but make finding *one conclusion* to a situation conflicted as well (Which conclusion? The policy of King? The "By Any Means Necessary" of Malcolm X? The separationist policy of The Black Panthers? All? None?). As King himself writes in "Letter from Birmingham Jail," "The question is not whether we will be extremists, but what kind of extremists we will be" (King 773). What kind of extremists will we be if we reduce all positions to the least extreme rhetorical approach of all, the unified, coherent, and least worthwhile conclusion? Without juxtaposition, a McCrimmon-influenced pedagogy teaches a limited thinking processes.

While not hypertextual, Burroughs's juxtapositions are meant to introduce conflict as a response to information and cultural overloads via what he names the "nova technique": "The basic nova technique is very simple: Always as many insoluble conflicts as possible and always aggravate existing conflicts" (*Ticket That Exploded* 54–55). Media production and idea formation are too complex to avoid conflicting beliefs or positions. Rub out word, Burroughs demands, if we are to utilize juxtaposition for the complex and difficult task of invention. Word traps us into clarity, into making ourselves easily understood, into being complacent, into settling on one conclusion when many may simultaneously exist. Rub it out, and juxtapose in its place.

> Word evokes image does it not?—Try it—Put an image track on screen and accompany it with any sound track—Now play the sound track back alone and watch the image track fill in—So? What is word?—Maya—Maya—Illusion—Rub out the word and the image track goes with it . . . Image is trapped in word—Do you need words? (*Ticket That Exploded* 145)

There are few writers in 1963 more concerned with conflict and writing than William Burroughs. An important reason for me to juxtapose his work with the 1963 rebirth of composition studies is that Burroughs signifies the "nonsafe" aspect of writing composition studies, even in its own rebirth, denies. The radical innovations proposed by Engelbart or by Nelson don't approach the kinds of conflicts Burroughs suggests; nevertheless, combined they are all central to new media rhetorics. Burroughs provides composition with what Geoffrey Sic has since called "pedagogy as dare" (*English Composition* 18). Sirc explains this pedagogy as a challenge to those pedagogical principles composition studies holds dear.

> A pedagogy geared to clarification rather than disorientation will never yield to the sublime. To build a pedagogy on such a limited notion of titles dooms your curriculum (as well as the writing done with it) right from the start; it's no so much the *banking* as the *bankrupt* concept of education. Rather than even parodies of writing, then—let alone the full-blown possibilities of allegories–students are offered flat fictions: Horatio Alger narratives in which the moral is that if they just follow the neatly, ordered, representational program, they'll make it (to the authentic, the academic, the counter-hegemonic, etc.). (*English Composition* 215)

The orderly representational program Sirc critiques is historically and ideologically tied to the kinds of orderly organizational and rhetorical instructions found in *Research in Written Composition*'s control or McCrimmon's outline and thesis. To teach juxtaposition, composition studies has to put aside the fixation on order 1963 idealized composition practices stress at the expense of necessary rhetorical conflict. My interest is in using those points regarding juxtaposition I've raised above to theorize how juxtaposition can thus function "as dare" and teach students writing outside of "the neatly, ordered" systems believed to be the only authentic method. Another model for such work, and related to hypertext because of its ability to interconnect a wide variety of ideas and texts, are the DJ samples that comprise a great deal of hip-hop.

## The DJ (Remixed)

In the previous chapter, I noted how the DJ working within the rhetoric of cool appropriates found sounds for new compositions. I want to draw upon the model of the DJ again in order to demonstrate juxtaposition in a contemporary practice and to again integrate the pedagogical approach to this part of the rhetoric of cool. DJ created compositions work from the same kind of logic that hypertextual writing does: They strive to forge connections among disparate material through various types of appropriations and juxtapositions. Like all the elements of the rhetoric of cool, appropriation and juxtaposition overlap in their usage; they are not distinct but complementary moves. One does not necessarily juxtapose or appropriate but rather does both (while making other gestures as well) simultaneously. In fact, it may be difficult to engage with one aspect of the rhetoric of cool without engaging with at least one other. Hence, some of my examples may appear to be repetitive but are in fact mutual strategies that coexist in a given rhetorical move.

The DJ process of juxtaposition is exemplified in much of contemporary hip-hop, but I can single out a few examples in order to more fully understand its importance as part of the rhetoric of cool. In Digable Planets' song "Cool Like Dat," lead singer Butterfly raps about his juxtaposition of Blue Note records with other 1960s jazz labels in order to compose. After describing his search through various styles (Miles Davis and 1960s funk records) and his choice of each to add to his juxtaposition, Butterfly discovers a metaphor that describes this type of composing experience. What a key is to a lock, the metaphor explains, Digable Planets is to rap: cool like dat. To juxtapose is to find the right fit. In other words, to be cool like dat indicates the ability to appropriate "styles" as one is "Pullin' from the jazz stacks" ("Pacifics [NY is Red Hot]") and then to juxtapose those styles." When "pullin' from the stacks," cool writers juxtapose previous compositions (assembled as appropriations) in the spirit of the "found work" principle popularized in 1963 Situationist street compositions led by Guy Debord or the 1963 Happenings Alan Kaprow created, like *Words*. The idea of found work (art or writing) is to identify the right fit for a given discursive moment; a piece goes here, a piece goes there, but in any other kind of combination, the pieces might not work together.

Butterfly's remarks signify the importance of assemblages to the rhetoric of cool, a practice found in numerous DJ compositions like that of DJ Kid Koala. The various tracks included on Koala's *Some of My Best Friends are DJs* operate according to a McLuhanist logic of juxtaposition. Like the sampled passages that comprise most of *The Gutenberg Galaxy*, *Some of My Best Friends are DJs* offers overlapping juxtapositions of 1920s blues, spoken word recordings, jazz, and other assorted sounds. These samples are strung together as one composition. The same process can be found in Madlib's *Shades of Blue*, which remixes Blue Note records by juxtaposing early 1960s recordings from the label with new mixes Madlib has composed. Throughout the album, previously recorded Blue Note concert introductions and history are juxtaposed within Madlib's own versions of Blue Note recordings. Compositions like Ronnie Foster's "Mystic Brew" (remixed as "Mystic Bounce") and Wayne Shorter's "Footprints" (remixed as "Footprints—Yesterday's New Quintet") are pulled from the stacks and juxtaposed into this mix. In Madlib's *Unseen* (composed and performed under the alter ego Quasimoto), "Return of the Loop Digga" features Madlib in a record store "pullin' from the stacks" of old Blue Note and other jazz records, asking the store's owner for some "Grant

Green" or "Chick Corea" that he can later sample from. These collections will serve his ability to remix and juxtapose future compositions; they are the basis of his composition research and thus exemplify the new kinds of practices and logics generated by new media.

The topos of digital sampling emerges from the various figures and sounds produced over the last one hundred years (Grant Green/Chick Corea/Blue Note). Without the more immediate limitations of audience or purpose (first settle on an audience's expectation/first figure out why you want to say what you will say), digital sampling extends itself rhetorically so that the topos transforms into the remix. "I think the combination of the dj and the writer makes a lot of sense," Kodwo Eshun states. "I think that both are different kinds of remixology at work, and that all we're really doing is bringing writing and putting it onto the second deck and just accelerating it as much as a record" (189). Eshun's observation belongs within my own reimagining of writing and new media. I will discuss the remix in more detail when I introduce commutation as a rhetorical part of cool, but in general, the remix involves rethinking how writers compose with juxtapositions. The remix—motivated by juxtaposition—undermines the authorial presence I have already critiqued in this chapter via my discussion of hypertext, and which is stressed emphatically in McCrimmon's remarks regarding the research paper: "Writing a research paper, then, is not just stringing together statements from books and magazines. It is a complete reorganization and reworking of the source material into an original composition" (McCrimmon 260). Writing does reorganize and rework source material as McCrimmon claims; yet writing also strings together found compositions based on the intricate ways each connects or doesn't connect to the next. A brief examination of how DJs compose reveals the very "stringing together" of sounds, ideas, words, and other texts McCrimmon dismisses.

When Kid Koala or Madlib turn to the "stacks" for material, they are being "cool like dat" in the Digable Planets' definition because of how they string together other compositions in unexpected ways. Kid Koala's "Fender Bender" (from the album *Carpal Tunnel Syndrome* and remixed on *Some of My Best Friends Are DJs* as "On the Set of Fender Bender") strings together spoken voice recordings, car horns, scratching, a repetitive musical refrain, and someone giving directions ("left" "up" "right" "down"). "Are you sure you want to play bridge," a mixed in voice asks, "or you got another one of those fancy sound effects records you want to show off?" Those "fancy sound effects records," Kid Koala meta-reflects, are the basis of his own composition. They are the oddities, the cast offs, the throwaway points and ideas a "restricted" thesis (like McCrimmon's) would never consider as valuable. Whether in Koala's, Madlib's, or any other DJ's mix, restriction is antithetical to invention.

In the mix (and the remix), everything is valuable upon application (and not necessarily upon foresight).

DJs like Kid Koala or Madlib participate in the Gutenberg Galaxy McLuhan found central to electronic writing. This is not a galaxy removed from writing classrooms. This galaxy, McLuhan noted, depends, to a great extent, on how we reimagine literacy so that it acknowledges the aural dimensions of composing in the electronic age. Beyond its "listening" definition, aurality includes the associative combinations oral speech often generates. "The new physics is an auditory domain and long-literate society is not at home on the new physics, nor will it ever be" (*Gutenberg* 37). Walter Ong comments similarly when he notes in his 1962 collection of essays *The Barbarian Within* that "a new age is upon us, and its shift from sight-emphasis to increased sound-exploration spans this entire area from the diffusion of the word to the exploration of one's surroundings" ("Wired for Sound" 225). Literate society in 1963, represented in composition studies, no doubt felt at home with the auditory only in regards to the tradition of an oral-based Greek rhetoric. That system, however, structures our current understanding of literacy as framed by Aristotelian methods of logic and persuasion (how an oral delivery persuades an audience or compliments its expectations), and not as a "new physics," as McLuhan poetically describes new media. The new physics, like hip-hop's droppin' science, represents a nonliterate, or beyond literate, method of producing knowledge outside the parameters of argumentation[7] in which exploration, as Ong and McLuhan claim, involves a "sounding out" of sorts in the quest to combine information in unlikely manners. Sampling signifies one kind of digital writing that puts these ideas into a composition practice.

Recitation and imitation, staples of Corbett's ambitious return of classical rhetoric to composition studies and a major oral component of his contribution to literacy studies, show little commonality with nonliterate organizing patterns generated through sampling, a composing process Kodwo Eshun sums up as the funkengine, the juxtapositions behind much of what we name computer-based composing processes. "Grand Wizard Theodore, DJ Kool Herc, Grandmaster Flash are human samplers who isolate the Breakbeat by cutting right into their funkengine, discarding The Song, ignoring intention and tradition to capture its motion: the charge and pull of the beat and the bass, the gait motorized by the deck's direct drive" (Eshun 17). Eshun's description of DJ juxtapositions evokes a confusing whirlwind ("charge and pull" "ignoring intention and tradition") capable of inciting discomfort among even the best writing teachers currently employed in the field. The writer as human sampler? The writer who cuts "right into the funkengine"? What kind of writer is that exactly? Is this writer the same as Kitzhaber's Dartmouth student who is "noticeably superior both in intelligence and in preparation to his counterpart at less favored colleges and universities" (*Themes, Theories, and Therapy* 27)? What would Braddock and colleagues do with this kind of writer if they were to make her another variable in their calculations? How do you measure the funkengine scientifically? How do you assess it? I ask such questions not to find answers but to note the limitations they can pose when new media practices are being invented. Indeed, all of Eshun's book on sampling, *More Brilliant than the Sun,* can be read as an inventive response to such questions. Eshun performs the funkengine juxtapositions he locates in electronic writing in order to demonstrate their efficacy for persuasion. Eshun's lesson is that, in an age of new media rhetoric, the time has come to perform and not only to explain or assess. The performative nature of juxtaposition—exemplified in the music selections I highlight—is central to the Burroughs-based juxtapositions introduced earlier or the McLuhanist nod toward "understanding" media. In this sense, to engage with the rhetoric of cool at this level, writers must *perform* juxtapositions, not just offer critical analysis of juxtapositions' effects on a given readership. I, too, have strived for that performative writing throughout this book; my juxtapositions of 1963 are meant to show and not just critique.

## Hip-Hop Pedagogy

The challenge for composition studies is to translate the theoretical principles of juxtaposition to a pedagogy appropriate for digital writing. This kind of writing would not analyze juxtapositions found in either popular media or professional discourse and report on their rhetorical effectiveness but would produce a writing comprised of juxtapositions. It would be, therefore, performative. Previously, I have called this writing "hip-hop pedagogy"[8] not because it is dependent on hip-hop music but rather because of how it borrows the rhetorical strategies centered around juxtaposition, which are often found in digital sampling and which can be written within new media like hypertext. In hip-hop pedagogy, patterns motivate readers and writers to find unrealized connections among disparate events and material things. Hip-hop pedagogy favors discovery over the restricted topic sentence since writers composing with juxtapositions do not begin with an understanding of what they will write about. Nor do writers concern themselves with mastery of a given category (science), subject matter (film), or already established belief (topos). Instead, writers look for ways to juxtapose from a variety of categories and subjects (the sampling process of juxtaposition) in order to invent.

Using the temporal date as model (similar to how I enact a date as heuristic for this book), students search out distinct moments from a given year, identify a pattern among those moments, and juxtapose those items that comprise the pattern. Composed on a Web site, the patterns are realized through hyperlinks and fragmented pages. Writers construct their work through fragmented sections of explanation and exploration, each connecting to the next through a motivated or accidental overlap. Sometimes these fragments are textual; sometimes they are visual. Absent in this writing is a thesis or argumentative claim. Instead, association produces new knowledge for writer and reader regarding the chosen year. No one would have thought to join such distinct moments from science, popular culture, sports, politics, literature, film, or a number of other areas and find that something connects them all.

Hip-hop pedagogy also changes the meanings we would normally associate with each event chosen from a given year. Hip-hop pedagogy shifts the familiar into an unfamiliar space by joining unconnected familiar and unfamiliar positions. Using my own work in this book as example, we may have previously learned about McLuhan's theory of cool media, Baraka's writings on popular music, and Farris Thompson's anthropological research separately for each contribution to its respective field. "Separately" is key, for we have mostly viewed such distinct positions as pertinent to distinct categories of information organization and creation. The isolation of the pattern of cool found among all three authors, however, and my attempt to write that pattern in order to critique composition studies' grand narrative while performing an alternative practice, alters the meaning of each text, for I am not doing a music analysis, anthropological study, nor a media history. What I am doing is commutating these meanings as I juxtapose. And it is this final point I will use to begin the next chapter.

# 5

## Commutation

In the previous chapter, I opposed the thesis to juxtaposition in order to expand composition concerns with organization that more fully incorporate how the rhetoric of cool alters structure as well as invention. In this chapter, I extend this opposition in order to introduce the role of commutation to the rhetoric of cool. Commutation is the exchange of signifiers without concern for referentiality. In the 1964 English translation of *Elements of Semiology,* Roland Barthes defines commutation as an important writing strategy writers employ to make specific choices regarding meaning construction. Barthes explains commutation through Danish linguist Louis Hjelmslev's "commutation test": "The commutation test consists of artificially introducing a change in the plane of expression (signifiers) and in observing whether this change brings about a correlative modification on the plane of content (signification)" (*Elements of Semiology* 65). Barthes turns to commutation in order to understand how meaning systems can be altered for rhetorical purposes at the level of the individual signifier (or combination of more than one signifier), not the text's overall meaning. "In the ordinary commutation test, one calls into use the form of the signified (its oppositional value in relation to other signifieds), not its substance" (*Elements of Semiology* 66). Because of its role in shaping and navigating classification schemes, Barthes's semiology speaks to the ways media affect writing at the level of research (what to include) and at the level of delivery (how to organize and display what one has chosen): "In semiology, we may come across systems whose meaning is unknown or uncertain: who can be sure that in passing from household bread to fine wheaten bread, or from toque to bonnet, we pass from one signified to another?" (*Elements of Semiology* 66). Meaning systems in themselves are not stable entities, whether at the point of observation (like the objects that comprise a material existence—bread, wine, table for the home; the essay or the exam for the classroom) or at the level of writing about those objects (like a study of student work that discusses or is presented in any of these items). Composition studies has been less receptive to the kind of meaning alteration Barthes describes, opting instead to believe that meanings are located in fixed places (topoi) of argumentation.

Even though he offers the caveat that "Dartmouth cannot, it is true, be called a typical American college," Kitzhaber bases his research on the fixed place of the classroom and the institution (*Themes, Theories, and Therapy* 27). Kitzhaber's topos, Dartmouth, represents "a striking example of that particular variety that is centered on the study of standard literature, with writing assignments growing out of this study; an examination of the Dartmouth courses ought therefore to shed light on a significant philosophy of teaching Freshmen English, as well as provide an opportunity to consider problems that are common to all varieties of the course" (*Themes, Theories, and Therapy* 29). The fixed place, Kitzhaber contends, will demonstrate meaning of other places of discussion. In fixed places of argumentation, whether they be Dartmouth or some other object of study, composition studies argues that substance can be located and made permanent; these places' exchange is not warranted nor desired. Dartmouth will not be exchanged with the University of Oregon, for instance, in order to demonstrate an unstable meaning; instead, Dartmouth stands for the University of Oregon, and for other places of learning. The claim for Dartmouth is the thesis for the rest of higher education. A claim, therefore, signifies—whether in Kitzhaber's or a student's work—a permanent position a writer takes to make an argument. "In argumentative writing," Diana Hacker writes in her popular handbook *A Writer's Reference*, "your introduction should ordinarily end with a thesis sentence that states your position on the issue you have chosen to debate" (39). "A thesis," Christine Hult and Thomas Huckin write in their textbook *The New Century Handbook*, "should be *clearly stated*. It should leave no confusion in the mind of the reader as to what you are claiming" (113). Once positions are stated, this kind of pedagogy states, change is not encouraged. Ambiguity is unwanted. Permanence is the aim.

The thesis, as McCrimmon clarifies, has long been a focal point of the type of writing instruction associated with the topos; its purpose is to direct student writers to narrow down areas of interest into fixed places. The thesis also serves the central aims of literacy, for it allows writers to refer back to a specific idea or point worth expansion. Literacy, as Jack Goody has written, enforces referentiality because the basic conventions of literacy (naming, categorization, meaning) all depend on signification and, in particular, a signification dependent on referents. Commutation, Barthes notes, challenges our perceptions of the signifiers that generate signification (and one might assume, literacy conventions) by indicating that meaning is not a fixed notion; it is exchangeable. And while Barthes does not place his interests in commutation in relationship to digital culture,[1] the temporality of his work motivates me to juxtapose it with those digital moments I discussed in the previous chapter.

The digital, as I have been discussing via the 1963 writings of McLuhan, Engelbart, Nelson, and Burroughs, contests referentiality and the topos by engaging with rhetorical moves counter to how referentiality functions. These writers don't eliminate referentiality and signification as they theorize and perform nonreferential systems of writing, but they do argue for electronic writing that does not depend on either referentiality nor signification much in the way the literate methods of writing do. The cut-up, in particular, indicates a moment when writing becomes subjected to a nonpermanent or nonreferential status, or, as Vitanza argues, the cut-up stands for a writing in direct opposition to an "Aristotelian hierarchically arranged world" (57). Burroughs's theory is that writings can be cut and exchanged with other writings in order to produce new types of responses, which, in turn, may also be cut up and mixed. In that system, there is little room for Aristotelian hierarchies or topoi. Instead, the cut-up implements a logic of commutation.

In *Symbolic Exchange and Death*, Jean Baudrillard argues that electronic communication replaces signification with commutation as a system of exchange; the electronic age leads to the replacement of symbolic exchange (which is key to how we make meaning) with commutability. "From now on, signs are exchanged against each other rather than against the real," Baudrillard writes. Signs have become "totally indeterminate, in the structural or combinatory play which succeeds the previous rule of determinate equivalence" (*Symbolic Exchange and Death* 7). Borrowing from McLuhan's dichotomy of media forms, Baudrillard labels this system of commutation *cool*, a discourse that "is the pure play of the values of discourse and the commutations of writing."

> It is the ease and aloofness of what now only really plays with codes, signs, and words, the omnipotence of operational simulation. To whatever extent affects of systems of reference remain, they remain hot. Any "message" keeps us in the hot. We enter the cool era when the medium becomes the message. (*Symbolic Exchange and Death* 22)

Baudrillard asks readers to reconsider signification (the method of making meaning through signs and those items signs represent) as not a project to create referentiality but rather as one that recognizes the role simulation plays in the digital age. In commutation, referentiality is replaced by a system where signs are exchanged against each other instead of the real. Signs, then, become reversible, commutable, and exchangeable without dependence on referents. Determinate meanings yield to indeterminacy. "There has been an extermination (in the literal sense of the word) of the real of production and the real of signification" (*Symbolic Exchange and Death* 7).

Cool discourse, as Baudrillard defines it, challenges writing instruction to reimagine the notion of a permanent writing space based on a fixed (and real) experience. If all meaning is exchangeable, as Baudrillard claims, then composition practices that situate writing as authenticity conveyed from writer to reader, or what Peter Elbow names "that inner something—that makes readers *experience*," no longer maintain the same status the field has attributed to them (*Writing with Power* 4). Because cool depends on utilizing multiple meanings, what a term refers to (its referent) becomes dynamic and changeable. It also becomes indeterminate and less permanent than we traditionally expect writing to be.

Thus, to say that 1963 signifies an unchangeable historical moment centered on those moments or figures traditionally associated with a renewed way of thinking about writing instruction (Kitzhaber, McCrimmon, Corbett, Braddock, Lloyd-Jones, and Schoer) is to deny the possible historical moment that includes those commutated moments or figures not traditionally represented as relevant to composition studies within this time period (McLuhan, Baraka, Farris Thompson, and others). Engaging with the latter group allows me to commutate the signification of the field's history. By commutating these moments, I am challenging composition's sense of historical referentiality by openly calling for a history without referent, or at least without one defined referent. Even before I have explained commutation as a principle element of cool, I have already applied it in order to begin my project in the first chapter of this book.

Fredric Jameson claims that the abandonment of referentiality is at the center of postmodernism's dilemma and ultimate failure. As I noted briefly in chapter 2, Jameson bemoans postmodern history constructed "by way of our own pop images and simulacra of that history, which itself remains forever out of reach" (*Postmodernism* 71). Jameson dismisses commutative practices similar to collage, like pastiche, as nonhistorical, as a method of examining "the 'past' through stylistic connotation, conveying 'pastness' by the glossy qualities of the image" (*Postmodernism* 67). I am not convinced by Jameson's argument, for, as I will describe in this chapter, an important element of cool is its ability to generate a rhetoric of commutation, not one based on referentiality. And, as I will write, cool denotes much more than glossy images. In making that statement, however, I enter into a meta-level discussion regarding cool and commutation. As I try to explain how commutation functions in the rhetoric of cool, I also find myself commutating this very term. The glossy image Jameson critiques as central to postmodernism, of course, is often applied to the popular definition of cool. Cool, as I've previously noted, is easily identifiable by most people as a marker of popularity or stigma. Even that identification, however, often functions—either in popular media or everyday discourse—according to a commutative logic. In other words, even as its meaning is often fixed as "superficial," cool is still commutated into other discursive exchanges. Examples can be found in popular magazines and the legacy of the ever-present, Netscape inspired cool list. *Rolling Stone's* April 11, 2002 issue, titled "The Cool Issue," exemplifies the tendency to list an entire culture as nothing more than cool events, people, places, activities, and products. Preempting the issue's sixty pages devoted to cool, John Weir writes, "What's cool? It came out of mystery and is still mysterious. Some have it and some don't. Like the Supreme Court on pornography, we know it when we see it. Turn the page and see it" (67). The magazine's following pages include a hodgepodge of cool; the rationale for labeling these items cool seems as mysterious as the listed items' supposed makeup. Nestled amid the larger categories of Cool SUV, Cool Babe, and Cool TV are the subtle micro-sections entitled Permanent Cool (Sullen Stares, Muddy Waters, and *On the Road*), Pissed-Off Cool (Piercings, Adbusters, and Sniffing Glue), and Senior Cool (Jack Nicholson, IBM Selectric, and Never Reuniting). *Rolling Stone's* point is that cool is allusive and indefinable, yet even so, the magazine's arbitrary categories and ability to shift selections from one list to another indicates that cool is an exchangeable rhetorical act. Cool may mean Muddy Waters, and it may mean IBM. Shifting from one referent to another is also a cool gesture for how the signifiers' meanings are altered.

In a move preceding *Rolling Stone's* special issue, *Wired* magazine ran a "special advertising section" in its November 2001 issue called "The Phenomenon of Cool." The section highlights cool as a revolutionary force in the history of cultural and technological production. Although the section doesn't make clear what the advertisement promotes, amid a timeline of "cool" moments that include Miles Davis's *Birth of the Cool*, Jack Kerouac's image, and even cocktails, the advertisement concludes with an homage to technology.

> Media multiplied. Technology shifted gears. Cool could be beamed into 100 million homes, tracked and data-processed. Downloaded from across an ocean. Or bounced off a satellite on your wrist.
>
> Cool became remote, the opposite of mass. It morphed into the gadget, car, person, or party available to few but coveted by many.

The 21st century, long a sci-fi daydream, is here. Its slogan is simple: If your neighbors are in on it, it can't be cool. (9)

Cool signifies technology and cocktails; it can be morphed; it's twenty-first century and the 1950s. *Wired,* too, notes the exchangeability of cool. Knowingly or not, the two magazines apply Baudrillard's meaning of cool in order to commutate popular imagery. The point is not that cool is "anything you claim it to be" but instead that cool writing (the sum total of these magazines' lists) reflects a dynamic rhetoric not dependent on theses or topic sentence aligned structures. Substitute one signifier for another and you have cool regardless of your list's subject matter.

This type of rhetorical practice makes its way into many literary critiques focused on technology and contemporary culture. In terms of cool, one of the most recognizable is Alan Liu's bemoaning of a perceived relationship between cool and technology.

Certainly the technology that has been the necessary buzz of everything really cool (e.g. hot rods, reggae "sound systems," electric guitars, designer drugs, high-speed processors) plugs into the whole cargo cult of industrial age consumer leisure (stereos, DVD players, special-effects movies). (*Laws of Cool* 77)

Intentionally or not, Liu repeats the popular magazine trend of cool listings. While he may find these listed items to be indicative of "glossy images," Liu's signifiers are as easily exchangeable as are *Wired*'s or *Rolling Stone*'s. Like these magazines, however, Liu's lists never achieve anything beyond merely naming supposed cool things, moments, or activities he locates within an electronic-based information economy. Popularized on his initial Voice of the Shuttle Web site, which originally promoted the ultimate list called "Laws of Cool," Liu demonstrates the limitations these lists pose in terms of exchangeability. Once I swap DVD for special effects or designer drugs for high-speed processors, what do I do next? What emerges out of this swap? The Liu list does nothing but recognize that one might swap such items. Constructing these categories of cool, Liu repeats the very listings of cool/ not cool he belittles as "the rhetoric of unproducible knowledge." Using the Netscape "What's Cool" listings I noted in chapter 3, Liu calls the general cool list "knowledge that can never be known and shown simultaneously" (177). This notion that knowledge does not arise out of cool lists or the potential commutation proposes is somewhat extended in Dick Pountain and David Robbins's *Cool Rules,* a discussion of contemporary figures and practices they consider cool. Pountain and Robbins's set of rules for understanding cool includes as example all we might envision in the ever-expanding global society: homosexual culture, smoking, and even Avon market strategies in Latin America. "We can recognize [cool] when we see it" the authors contend in order to validate their examples (Pountain and Robbins 18). Their lists include social phenomenon (1920s avant-garde, the hippies), popular personalities (the images of James Dean and Marlon Brando), films (in particular those of Robert Mitchum), and gender (Billie Holiday, but also the odd mention of Hillary Rodham Clinton). Based on this kind of list, we discover an image of what cool may be (an actor, a moment in time) but not what these items together perform. These examples do little but perform yet another limited gesture of commutation. The lists are pleasant to read; they provide us with familiar names we can substitute for one another; they reach a level of personal affirmation ("oh right, James Dean *is* cool"). But like Liu's list, they contribute little more to rhetorical production than that basic gesture. How do I write with these commutations? How do I use them rhetorically to generate ideas beyond the list? Once I construct such a list, is that all there is for me to do?

These are questions I raise in order to return to Baudrillard. That Baudrillard locates commutation within electronic discourse is important, for it grants me a departure point regarding how cool as electronic writing involves exchangeability. I have already noted how that exchangeability is reflected in my own sub/version (borrowing Vitanza's term) of a specific composition studies history. My challenge throughout this chapter is to demonstrate it more completely in terms of its rhetorical application. Commutation generates more than list making. Commutation is a part of the rhetoric of cool. To explore this idea, I will commutate the writing space itself, using 1963 film (in place of a print-based writing) throughout most of the following sections as example and model.

## Commutation

Commutation involves more than just the swapping of signifiers (text, image, and sound). Commutation also positions rhetoric as a manipulative practice. The exchangeability Baudrillard triumphs, and that appears in many 1963 texts, is meant to persuade given audiences in a manipulative manner, not necessarily to construct arguments based on "common values and beliefs" or "reasoned arguments," as textbooks like *The St. Martin's Guide to Writing* claim (Axelrod and Cooper 202) or as Diana Hacker urges students to prove to readers they are "knowledgeable and fair minded" (39). *Research in Written Composition* and *Themes, Theories, and Therapy,* two studies I've identified as fundamental to composition's sense of identity, likewise situate themselves as nonmanipulative, scientific studies, and thus, they present their claims as reasoned arguments regarding student writing. Even though their structure depends, to a great extent, on the exchangeability of variables, these variables exploited for empirical study (the "student variable," the "rater variable," etc.) are discussed as fixed entities located in the specific place of a writing classroom, not as items that can be commutated and exchanged in order to produce different results. And these fixed positions are always presented as being nonmanipulative, and, thus, "true."

The desire for fixed meaning also promotes a vision of a fixed (i.e., uniform) writing program. Indeed, exchangeability is a focal point of Kitzhaber's critique of freshmen writing, an entity Kitzhaber imagines as too diverse in its willingness to commutate the meaning of first-year composition. Arguing against a heterogeneous composition pedagogy, Kitzhaber writes, "Most of the confusion in freshmen English stems from differing notions of how writing ought to be taught" (Kitzhaber 10). Kitzhaber's argument for one reasonable method of writing instruction is one that denies other approaches in the curriculum (like those that differ on the role of media in writing instruction). It also situates writing as a rational activity whose focus and agents must be rational and not commutable, for the unexpected moves commutation evokes often are not rational or reasonable (like Burroughs's writing on sex, racism, and homophobia, most of which is outlandish, hyperbolic, grotesque, and fantastic). All research is, therefore, reduced to rational speculation and analysis. Kitzhaber writes of his study's examination of student "error": "Though there may be a question whether a specific error should be called one in wordiness or one in jargon, there can be no doubt that it falls under the general head of errors in diction" (*Themes, Theories, and Therapy* 47). Distinction among signifiers (the so-called "errors") or factors that lead to these errors is not important. It is logical, Kitzhaber seems to say, that error and how error is assessed is a logical, rational process, one that is never manipulated. The plane of meaning, as Barthes might say, remains equal.

As appealing as Kitzhaber's critique may be, when we examine the impact of commutation on rhetoric in 1963, we find rhetorical approaches tied to media that work differently than this accepted system of meaning classification. Rhetorical output related to cool seems uninterested in rationality or reason, as it works to manipulate audiences to adopt positions outside of the status quo. My interest is in applying these approaches pedagogically so that differing notions of writing as well as *differing writings* can occur and influence how we compose electronically. In 1964, Barthes notes that outside of language, food and fashion systems can be studied for their relationship to commutation. Barthes's suggestion is to look for other commutative examples outside of obvious alphabetic-based writing. More recently, Lev Manovich writes that film (instead of fashion), and in particular the avant-garde's production of filmic texts, shapes digital writing in ways not fully explored yet. "One general effect of the digital revolution is that avant-garde aesthetic strategies came to be embedded in the commands and interface metaphors of computer software" (Manovich 15). Even more so, I add to Manovich's remarks, early 1960s avant-garde film has shaped digital writing rhetorically through the practice of commutation and through the teaching of manipulation.

## Scorpio Rising/Flaming Creatures

One place I discover an example of the rhetoric of commutation is in the opening sequence of Kenneth Anger's 1963 film *Scorpio Rising*. As the film begins, we see the Scorpio/scorpion image on the back of Scorpio's leather jacket. At another moment in the film, the image commutates into a scorpion coaster on Scorpio's desk; at another moment, Scorpio picks up a scorpion encased in amber; and finally, the scorpion encircled image juxtaposes within the montage of the concluding motorbike race sequence. The scorpio/ion commutation stands for an entire composition practice found throughout the film. As a composition, *Scorpio Rising* progresses through a series of commutated signifiers, each exchangeable against the other with no one signifier offering specific meaning. Thus, we see Marlon Brando's image, skulls, motorcycles, and Jesus all transferred into a variety of meanings depending on the sequence, not the signifier or its fixed placement. Viewers follow these exchanges as they would follow any other kind of narrative structure. Instead of plot or argument, however, changing meanings constitute the text. Barthes calls this type of meaning change "catalysis," the rhetorical moment when

> [i]t is possible to imagine a purely formal lexicon which would provide, instead of the meaning of each word, the set of other words which could catalyze it according to possibilities which are of course variable–the smallest degree of probability would correspond to a "poetic" zone of speech. (*Elements of Semiology* 70)

As poetic speech or as composition, commutation—like juxtaposition—provides layered meanings within a composition. The writer negotiates these layers as the composing process itself. Commenting on the commutation of Scorpio into Jesus in the film, P. Adams Sitney notes that the process allows readers of the film alternative meaning systems to choose from as they attempt to understand the text's narrative.

> Through the montage we learn what Scorpio would do if he were Christ, or perhaps what he thinks Christ really must have done: when Christ approaches the blind beggar, Scorpio would have kicked him, as he kicks the wheel of his motorcycle, and would have given him a ticket for loitering, as a cop places a parking violation on the bike; Christ touches the blind

man's eyes; through a very quick intercut we see that Scorpio would have shown him a "dirty picture"; and when the beggar goes down on his knees before Christ, Scorpio offers him his stiff penis. (Sitney 121)

A similar rhetorical usage of commutation can be found in Jack Smith's early 1960s films. Smith, like Anger a member of the so-called underground cinema of the early 1960s, utilizes commutation in the 1963 film *Flaming Creatures* in order to comment on gender. Susan Sontag writes that the film does not attempt to demonstrate meaning through rational argumentation or syllogistic logic. Instead, *Flaming Creatures* rewrites signifiers in order to provoke audiences' senses, even if comprehension is not a goal.

> There are no ideas, no symbols, no commentary on or critique of anything in *Flaming Creatures*. Smith's film is strictly a treat for the senses. In this it is the very opposite of a "literary" film (which is what so many French avant-garde films were). It is not in the knowing about, or being able to interpret, what one sees, that the pleasure of *Flaming Creatures* lies; but in the directness, the power, and the lavish quantity of the images themselves. ("Jack Smith's Flaming Creatures" 229)

In a 1962 *College English* essay, Morris Greenhunt argues differently than Sontag regarding the role narrative plays in meaning comprehension. Greenhunt, in what sounds like a temporal composition argument regarding ordered writing, points out that narrative always involves an understandable arrangement. "The order of [a text's] reading conveniently lends itself to an arrangement which begins with narration and description, proceeds to exposition, and ends in argumentation" (Greenhunt 137). Greenhunt describes what filmmaker Ken Kelman critiques in a 1964 *Nation* article as the cultural dependence on narratives that are "completely calculated, with believable characters, developed and motivated actions, clockwork time, everything to confirm to our belief—or hope?—that the universe is a casual, rational place" (24). Kelman critiques this type of "clear" narrative as a façade created to hide cultural inequities and various types of bias. That critique should not be lost on writing pedagogy. Rationality and predictability are the kinds of pedagogical points stressed in many first-year textbooks like *The St. Martin's Guide to Writing*: "Texts in a genre nonetheless follow a general pattern. This patterning allows for a certain amount of predictability, without which communication would be difficult, if not impossible" (Axelrod and Cooper 5). The predictability taught via either Greenhunt's work on narrative or *The St. Martin's* advice is the same predictability *Research in Written Composition* illustrates. Braddock and colleagues make a similar argument regarding rhetorical order; they identify meaning and rhetoric with the predictable discursive agreement that dictates organization and comprehension.

By "rhetorical" is meant there those aspects of writing which (to simplify somewhat) are larger than the unit of the sentence—in expository writing, for instance, the main idea and its analysis; the support of subordinate ideas with details, examples, statistics, and reasons, and the organization of the previous elements into an orderly and meaningful whole. (38)

Yet Smith's work, like Anger's, resists these pedagogical models of writing. The film is not "literary," as Sontag writes, nor "rhetorical" as Braddock and colleagues require, because it refutes the conventions of representation tied to the literary experience of analysis, interpretation, and orderly presentation, three items composition studies emphasizes repeatedly as important to writing instruction and central to any definition regarding what literacy acquisition entails. This filmic moment conflicts with the expectation of order and organization we have grown accustomed to. The reason is as much cultural as it is political; the 1960s avant-garde understood order and rationality as tools used by dominant powers to minimize dissent or to shut down alternative expression. In that dissent from predictability, in that transgression of a structural and compositional convention, a rhetorical lesson can be identified for new media writing. As Barthes writes of commutation's future potential, "[R]hetoric as a whole will no doubt be the domain of these creative transgressions" (*Elements of Semiology* 88). Anger and Smith do employ organization in order to "make" films (the films are not haphazard). But each film's organization depends on a logic quite different from Braddock and colleagues' "meaningful whole." That logic (whether deemed "creative" or something else), whose basis is in commutation, is essential to new media writing.

*Flaming Creatures* begins with the image of a drag queen applying lipstick while an advertisement for women's lipstick gives instructions for the application. Audiences anticipating a "woman" to be performing this act instead find a man behaving as if he were a woman. In this initial sequence, Smith alters the rhetoric of advertising whose particular focus in this case is to instruct beauty care for women. An expected "clear" position—women apply lipstick—is exchanged with a slightly unclear one—a man in drag applies lipstick. Similarly, the anticipated ordered structure of meaning (woman plus lipstick equals beauty) becomes displaced. Ordered explanation as well is displaced; the reason for this sequence is never explained. Not only does Smith resist supporting ideas with details or reason, but there is no "meaningful whole" to point to when the film is complete, no "conclusion" or literary "denouement." What have we seen, and why did we see it? Why is this man applying lipstick? What is it about drag that this film wants to convey? Is there a thesis within this form of electronic writing? Or are readers asked to more actively engage with the commutations and thus participate in the film's cool media meaning systems?[2] Reading this film's commutative rhetoric, "we may come across systems whose meaning is unknown or uncertain" (*Elements of Semiology* 66). The text cannot be rejected because of that uncertainty but instead can be employed to generate new perspectives and approaches. Without entering into an elaborate deconstruction of the film's narrative, I can note that a film like *Flaming Creatures* locates rhetorical value as an uncertainty. While predictability is rhetorically assuring, uncertainty is disturbing. In a 1963 interview, Barthes states that the montagist effect these kinds of commutative moves make have little to do with reaching a state of certainty: "The strength of the signifier [in montage] does not come from its clarity but from the fact that it is perceived as a signifier—I would say: whatever the resultant meaning may be, it is not things but the place of things which matters" ("On Film" 16). The uncertainty the commutations evoke is central to the text's rhetorical effectiveness. This uncertainty depends on the placement of signifiers, not their perceived meaning or structural relationships to other language or visual markers. For 1960s culture, this displacement of signifier placement is meant to disturb gender attitudes. The lesson can be generalized to contemporary issues and situations (gender or otherwise).

Writing like Smith's and Anger's poses consequences for computer-based compositions. Film represents one aspect of early 1960s electronic writing whose potential can be generalized to computing today because of how film utilized the medium itself to innovate upon print-based conventions. Anger's commutations destabilize the expectations of traditional Hollywood narrative, itself a print-oriented logic of continuity and sequentiality, much in the way we can imagine a composition assignment doing the same through its own application of commutation. Traditional composition instruction requires that print-directed assignments include what Donald Murray suggests as a checklist for evaluating a writing's overall approach to meaning construction. Murray's checklist has writers ask themselves, and each other, "what does the writing mean?" "does the reader need more information," and "does the piece of writing deliver on the promise made in the title and in the lead?" (Murray 168–69) The electronic suggests that meaning may not rely entirely on "promise" nor on recognized intention. When electronic compositions can be easily manipulated in order to refigure ideology (as Anger's and Smith's films do with gender), structure (the films' commutated items are composed from a series of "found" and new items spliced together without linear order), and intent (what is the change of Scorpio to Jesus or the scorpion image from jacket to skull actually about?), Murray's advice becomes counterproductive or not even applicable. To write the commutation, the traditional questions regarding expectation and writerly intent have to be reimagined.

## The Mix

The legacy of cotemporary digital writing, then, is not found in thesis driven instruction or even in the generic request for meaning but rather in the remix mentality commutation evokes through films like Smith's and Anger's. Smith and Anger mix and remix signifiers typically associated or not associated with masculinity, like bikers or cosmetics, and what an audience decides such commutations mean is intentionally ambiguous. The fixed topoi appeal to an audience's expectations regarding content and structure, much as the highly visual *Seeing and Writing* teaches students to write for new media: "The paragraphs should proceed in a logical order, with appropriate transitions to help readers connect the points you are making" (McQuade and McQuade16). Commutations, on the other hand, confuse and perplex expectations and generate unpredictable transitions. Like Pop artist Tom Wesselmann's collages *Still Life #20* (1962) and *Still Life #30* (1963), which remix the kitchen space with everyday life (kitchen appliances, TV sets, food) in order to challenge gendered cultural markers, Smith and Anger are composing without set claims but rather with shifting meanings and moving transitions: "The suburban kitchen in *Still Life #30* appropriated the visual codes developed in women's home and service magazines to display tasteful spaces of consumption managed and directed by the efficient middle-class female homemaker and consumer" (Whiting 57). Thus, in a typical biker film of the 1950s or 1960s, we would expect masculinity to be something akin to Marlon Brando's character Johnny in *The Wild One*. In the film's most remembered scene, a fellow biker asks Johnny, "Hey, Johnny, watchya rebelling against?" Johnny replies, "Watchya got?" The response is masculine and distant. It is cool in the traditional, topos sense, particularly for the way this meaning is gendered. We understand the transition from figure (Johnny) to response (apathy). We feel certain about the signifier of cool in this kind of writing; it demonstrates rebellion, male bikers, aloofness.

That sense of cool is made uncertain in Smith's and Anger's writings or Wesselmann's collages. One of *Scorpio*'s best known examples of this process is seen in the film's sequence featuring The Angels' 1963 hit "My Boyfriend's Back." The song plays over the camera's display of a man's motorcycle; the boyfriend signifier is unclear (boy or bike?). In the film's very next sequence, the song commutates into Bobby Vinton's 1963 "Blue Velvet." The bike remains, but the sexualized song lyrics—directed initially towards women—are remixed as masculine signs of affection. Expectation and understanding are disrupted. Absent of aloofness or rebellion, cool is made to exemplify homosexuality. Cool is transgressed. There is a rhetorical lesson here for digital writing.

The sexual transgressions a sequence like this writes, like in Smith's films, allegorize a larger understanding of signification transgression where meanings are consistently modified and mixed. The mix encourages transgression as it complicates notions of rationality and reason. This transgression is compositional, ideological, and political. Pedagogically, we might resist the compositional transgression as inappropriate or not relevant to some accepted vision of the professional sphere ("that's not how engineers write," "you will never write like that in a job"). But culturally, in light of various oppressive practices we are exposed to locally and internationally, we often encourage ideological and political transgression (like transgressing the belief in segregation or opposing an unjust war). Of all the questions to pose regarding sexuality, for instance, 1960s culture would no doubt ask (and as current discussion asks of marriage) if same sex relations, which transgress a perceived "norm," are reasonable or rational behavior. Or as Howard Becker writes in his 1963 sociological study *The Outsiders,* a likely 1960s public response would be that such relations are deviant. Becker's stance (or his rhetorical stance), similar to many within 1960s culture, signifies an accepted narrative of rational or ordered thought (homosexuality is a deviance) because of how that thought is constructed and approached. Wouldn't many of us today, however, see a need to transgress that vision of rationality? The mix offers a rhetorical transgression by complicating how belief systems (gender, writing) are portrayed as rational and by exposing the irrationality inherent in meaning systems in general. Deviancy, within commutation, is a rhetorical move meant to undermine fixed ideas; it is not a social ill as Becker claims. Within a social context, commutation asks who, in fact, best represents rationality? Becker or Smith? Within a pedagogical context, commutation asks writers to transgress and manipulate rhetorical practices. Anger and Smith demonstrate how to apply commutation (i.e., transgressive) writing for rhetorical, as well as for cultural, purposes.

Digital sampling has become the most recognizable writing space for the mix; however, its logic is seen in a variety of digital texts, not just film (or filmic soundtracks). While it's impossible to highlight all of the mixing occurring on the Web—including personal Web sites, fark contests, and song mashing.— among these kinds of mixed writings, we find Kool's Mixx and Sprite's ReMix campaign.[3] These campaigns cannot be discounted for being advertisements just as the previous examples cannot be discounted for being films (and not alphabetic-based writings). Kool's and Sprite's ads provide further examples regarding how technology shapes rhetoric, how the issue of rationality does not necessarily play into the rhetorical construction of mixes.

The image and music sampling practices both ad campaigns draw from speak to the rhetorical nature of mixing and remixing. The Kool ads comprise three separate print displays that can also be read as one large image when juxtaposed. One ad spots a DJ at a turntable; another features a series of cutout images of young people dancing around a DJ's set. The meaning of the campaign's "mixing it up" theme applies to both lifestyle choices (dances, parties) as well as taste (the cigarette's supposed "mixxed" construction of tobacco flavors). In the Sprite splash page for the ReMix Web site, the slogan reads: remix, rethink, refresh. Users of the site can work within these prescriptions by visiting The ReMix CD Creator and The ReMix Music Mixer sections, two highly interactive music generated Flash applications offered against a static image backdrop of a mixing board. The rethink and refresh tropes aligned with these sections are also commercially associated with a new "remixed" flavor the company sells. The messages of remixing flavors are complimented by a remixed style itself, a series of cut-and-paste images configured in Flash. The signifier Sprite is remixed (as is the very term *mix*) through commutated product identification (the pervious flavor "tropical" now becomes "berryclear") but also through the fluctuating meanings of youth culture, technology, and consumerism, the three items used to write the company's slogan on the Web site. That none of these items needs to be associated with the other in order to sell (or consume) cigarettes and soft drinks is irrelevant. The mere associations and connotations generated through these mixes is enough to evoke audience response (the desire to buy these products). It's a method of writing not unlike that seen in the Anger and Smith films I draw attention to as models missed by 1960s composition studies. Even without clear or permanent positions, this writing suggests, there will be various levels of meanings distributed, and there will be audience reaction. Sprite does not appear worried that mixing and remixing its product meaning will affect sales. In fact, these commutations generate the opposite effect and prove to be powerful consumer rhetorics. While consumerism stops short of allowing its own identity to be disrupted through commutation (we are encouraged, after all, to buy this drink), it does teach the potential of a digital commutative practice.

If this indeed is the logic of new media writing demonstrated through cool's usage of commutation, why are composition studies textbooks slow to respond? Because we don't want to sell cigarettes and soda, of course. Composition studies is not in the business of producing a consumer-oriented rhetoric. But composition studies does want to use visual displays as advertising does; and with that need to be visual should also be the desire to write commutative practices, much as advertising strives to accomplish. When the visually oriented textbook *Convergences* asks students to write about paintings, for instance, it, like these advertising campaigns, shows interest in art and design. But *Convergences* foregoes a commutative practice like Sprite's and chooses representational models. Among others, Normal Rockwell's early 1960s *Triple Self Portrait* is the focus of one assignment. Even though *Convergences* is marketed as a textbook designed for electronic writing, its choice of a Rockwell is perplexing, especially since the textbook's subtitle, *Message, Method, Medium* (and this subtitle's appearance at the end of every chapter), evokes McLuhan's work, which stresses the power of commutation and other related strategies. Rockwell, and his many paintings featured on the covers of *The Saturday Evening Post,* signifies representational art (and not McLuhan's cool) more so than most artists of the twentieth century. Rockwell as indicator of representational thinking is pedagogically reflected in the writing prompts that follow the painting. "What does the elaborately framed mirror resemble? How does it feature the symbol of an American Eagle?" "What do you think Rockwell is saying about the art of portraiture?" (Atwan 72). These are questions that can only be asked within a thesis-driven composition pedagogy; they demand absolute responses that directly reflect the meaning of a text. A commutated pedagogy, on the other hand, would not ask students to respond in a representational manner ("I think that the symbol represents . . .") but would instead feature a model for composing through a series of commutations or mixes.

Instead of Rockwell as inspiration, a better "art" example for electronic writing (and in particular commutation) comes from Andy Warhol. Preceding the Kool and Sprite campaign styles I draw attention to, Warhol's 1963 *Ethel Scull* performs the remix through a series of thirty-six multipanel images of the socialite in a variety of facial expressions. Each image commutates into another suggesting the exchangeability of imagery in electronic and popular culture. In his 1962 *Four Marilyns,* Warhol similarly applies commutation to the famous actress's visage in order to depict the extravagance of celebrity culture. One of Warhol's most identifiable paintings from 1963 is *Double Elvis,* a mirrored image of an Elvis Presley film still. No better figure could be used for commutation than Elvis, whose image is easily commutated from film to film (Elvis as scuba diver/Elvis as car driver), as writers like Michael Jarrett and Greil Marcus have shown. Warhol's writing with Elvis in 1963 is an important pedagogical moment for the rhetoric of cool because this writing situates the supposed cool figure (Elvis Presley) as a cool form of writing (commutation).

Appropriating Warhol's *Double Elvis* as pedagogy, I note that a better textbook for teaching commutation as digital writing than those books currently dominating the textbook market like *Convergences* is Greil Marcus's *Dead Elvis.* Marcus elaborates the commutative rhetorical move as he constructs a collage of images and references to Elvis. Lacking narrative or conventional structure, the book presents Elvis as a rhetoric of exchangeability. "There is another Elvis Presley," Marcus writes of the King, "a figure of echoes, not facts" (iv-v). In what is also appropriative and juxtapositiory, Marcus demonstrates these echoes by ignoring biography and history (the focus of referentiality) as well as argumentative claim ("my thesis is that Elvis represented X") in favor of an assemblage of Elvis references. The effect of Marcus's collection of images, textual citations, quotations, comic strips, and others is a disorganized and unclear commutated text whose effect is, nevertheless, demonstrative of the power of consumer culture. Elvis as icon, Elvis as White House press conference allusion, Elvis as morning talk show subject matter, Elvis as Elvisburger, Elvis as tabloid headline, Elvis as Joni Mabe collage, Elvis as *Life in Hell* comic strip panel; the list goes on and on.

> The controlling reason why it is so hard to think about Elvis aesthetically rather than sociologically is that his achievement—his cultural conquest—was seemingly so out of proportion to his means. Continents of meaning—of behavior, manners, identity, wish, and betrayal, continents of cultural politics—shifted according to certain gestures made on a television show, according to a few vocal hesitations on a handful of 45s. No one knows how to think of such a thing. (*Dead Elvis* 193)

Returning to the Barthes quotation I began this chapter with, how does the change in Elvis as signifier modify "the plane of content" so that we can begin to know, to produce knowledge, to alter knowledge? And how is this change indicative of digital writing? These are questions approachable if we generalize from Marcus's example of Elvis to other figures, icons, or moments. "No one knows how to think of such a thing" is, therefore, a directive for digital writing. Commutate in order to understand the complexity of meaning and the manipulations of meaning we encounter. Commutate in order to demonstrate the inventive act of not knowing previously how to think of such a thing.

To perform such a task, I have used *Dead Elvis* as a model for teaching commutation as a cool practice. Like the earlier assignments I have sketched in previous chapters, the *Dead Elvis* assignment lends itself readily to a computer medium, and in particular the Web site. Through image appropriation (the "save as" feature on the Web browser), textual appropriation (cut and paste, copying), and organization (where and how to assemble these appropriated items over a series of interlinked pages, some of which might utilize the dynamic nature of javascripting or DHTML), students compose Web sites that feature a celebrity of their choice. The Web sites are not biographical nor historical but commutative. The only criteria is that the celebrity be able to generate a significant amount of references the way Elvis does; Michael Jackson and Madonna are popular choices, but projects featuring Sid Vicious, Princess Diana, and Santa Claus have been just as compelling.

Without explanatory narrative, students write the figure they have chosen through commutative choices. Images, text, and hyperlinks are situated throughout the writing in order to evoke a desired effect or idea regarding the chosen figure. Quotations, references, collected imagery, found commodities, and personal insight are exchanged throughout each writer's Web site as indicative of the chosen figure. These digital texts do not reflect the referentiality demanded by thesis-driven assignments or the rational structure of traditional argumentation; instead they demonstrate and produce rhetorical effect through commutated signifiers. In many projects, refresh tags (HTML tags that force Web pages to change on their own) or frames (now considered outdated, but very effective for this kind of project) are employed because each allows writers to exchange chosen signifiers against other signifiers. Because they are commutative, the texts are not making a claim about an issue but instead are demonstrating an ability to rewrite figures into the digital environment. Central to this project is the ability to manipulate. The power of manipulation, which I drew attention to in chapter 3 regarding appropriation and which I note is fundamental to Anger's and Smith's texts, is highlighted in this kind of work as writers reimagine or remix the chosen figure. Manipulating Madonna or Michael Jackson alters the representation each figure demonstrates to its public audience; the manipulation as well alters the writer's engagement with an object of study (the chosen celebrity). If there exists a rhetorical stance in this writing, it becomes evident not in an achieved balance or fair approach but in how writers negotiate the ways they manipulate subject matter, in how they change meaning for specific situations and digital contexts, in how they disturb expectation.

Finally, the texts often generated through this assignment are not linear in structure, are remixed, and often reflect the larger project of the World Wide Web, itself a massive text of similarly commutated images and words. For, like readers of the Web, readers (and the writers) of these texts may follow any number of paths throughout the digital text (moving from one commutated signifier to the next) in order to grasp the text's overall commutative effect. Commutation makes no claim on linearity; its logic stems from multiple significations presented at once. With this point regarding multiple paths, I turn to nonlinearity in the next chapter in order to more fully explain its role in the rhetoric of cool.

# 6

## Nonlinearity

Welcome to CoolTown—HP Labs' vision of the future, where people, places and things are all connected to the Web.

      —Hewlett Packard, Cooltown Web site

"'Cool' is the surest sign of effectiveness; in it, each man regains the ideality of a world surrendered to a purely gestural vocabulary, a world which will no longer slow down under the fetters of language.

      —Roland Barthes, "Power and 'Cool'"

In *Research in Written Composition,* Braddock and colleagues write, "Largely ignored by people doing research in composition, variations in mode of discourse may have more effect than variations in topic on the quality of writing" (8). Almost echoing McLuhan's mantra that the structure of media is more important than the content of media, Braddock and colleagues place deserved attention on form and, in particular, on the role different forms play in composing. Yet the authors reduce their interest in modes (i.e., form) to what we have come to understand as the basis (with some variation) of current-traditional rhetoric: narration, description, exposition, argument, or criticism. As James Berlin notes, the modes enforce rationality and coherence as the primary elements of good writing, two areas I have already contrasted with the aims of the rhetoric of cool. Berlin writes:

> The writing class is to focus on discourse that deals with the rational faculties: description and narration to be concerned with sense impression and imagination (the image-making faculty), exposition with "setting forth" the generalized ideas derived from sense impression and understanding, and argument with understanding leading to conviction. (*Rhetoric and Reality* 8)

While the so-called modes don't begin with *Research in Written Composition,* the attention the authors place on the modes, no doubt, has helped propagate the myth that these structures of writing accurately reflect common writing practices when performed independently of one another. Along with *Research in Written Composition*'s scientific and rational emphasis, the modes project writing as itself always a rational act clarified in formulaic arrangements (compare and contrast/definition/classification). Braddock and colleagues felt that in order to alleviate composition's dependence on "alchemy," it should turn to science's rational methodology of observation, test, and conclusion, a formulaic, linear process of organizing material and presenting results. If are we are to reform (or give a rebirth) to composition, the argument goes, we should be rational in doing so. Our methods should be reproducible, and they should progress in linear and recognizable fashion. Hence, We can understand the modes' attractiveness as independent, rational forces within composition.

Even as they call for variations in the modes, the modes, however, limit Braddock and colleagues' recognition of an emerging technological culture of writing. Following my observations in earlier chapters, the fact that these structures reflect print culture should no longer merit mention. This same point, however, does reveal how one kind of nonprint "variation in mode of discourse" goes unnoticed by Braddock and colleagues because of its tendency to fall outside the parameters of clarity and rationality: the media-directed mode of nonlinearity. "Until now," McLuhan writes in the nonlinear *The Gutenberg Galaxy*, "a culture has been a mechanical fate for societies, the automatic interiorization of their own technologies" (95). *Research in Written Composition* maintains that interior linearity based on a scientific reasoning, even in its endorsement of "other" modes of discourse. *Research in Written Composition* reads and presents the writing process as a linear mode of composition studied, in turn, in linear ways. Derrida notes that "[w]riting in the narrow sense—and phonetic writing above all—is rooted in a past of nonlinear writing" (*Of Grammatology* 85). As *Research in Written Composition* gained momentum in 1963 (just a few years prior to Derrida's comments), composition disciplinary work, in terms of rhetoric and pedagogy, needed to become rooted in the kind of past Derrida describes.

Those aspects of juxtaposition I drew attention to in chapter 4 regarding McLuhan, Burroughs, Engelbart, and Nelson, as well as the nonlinear commutative narratives generated by Smith's and Anger's films that I detailed in chapter 5, lead me to challenge the *Research in Written Composition* preference for linearity. Because these rhetorical moves are nonlinear, I include nonlinearity as part of the rhetoric of cool and composition studies' neglected past. In terms of new media and writing, hypertext has largely garnered interest for its nonlinear structure. Since the invention of the World Wide Web, nonlinearity has been triumphed in hypertext studies as the realization of the poststructuralist theories traced to Jacques Derrida's statement in *Of Grammatology* that "the end of linear writing is indeed the end of the book" (86). Outside of the traditional (and usually romanticized) alignment with this statement, Ted Nelson's large scale, hypertext system Xanadu intended to make nonlinearity the framework out of which new media writing is created. As I note in chapter 4, in 1963, Nelson coins the term *hypertext* to describe his initial thoughts regarding an interlinking, nonlinear system of thought that creates learning in ways print is incapable of doing. In *Computer Lib/Dream Machines,* Nelson runs nonlinear threads on computing, the logic of computing, attitudes toward computing, and other related notions. The threads are textual as well as visual, appropriative (cut and pasted from other sources) as well as his own. "Everything is deeply intertwingled" one often quoted fragment reads (*Computer Lib* 166). "The *structure of ideas* are not sequential. They tie together every which way. And when we write, we are always trying to tie things together in non-sequential ways" (*Dream Machine* 29, emphasis Nelson's).

Nelson's concepts were eventually picked up by literary studies, computers and writing, and hypertext proponents who also found comfort in Derrida's declaration: George Landow, Stuart Moulthrop, and (before he announced hypertext as "dead") Robert Coover, among others. The most heralded characteristic of early hypertext fiction like Michael Joyce's *afternoon, a story* or Shelly Jackson's *Patchwork Girl* works with Nelson's sense of "intermingling" by demonstrating how nonlinearity opens up narrative possibilities for both readers and writers.[1] As Katherine Hayles notes in her recent discussion of *Patchwork Girl,* this particular hypertext's nonlinearity explores a number of cultural and fictional narratives at once; eighteenth-century copyright legislation, Mary Shelly's *Frankenstein,* and Shelly Jackson's own narrative. A narrative about monsters, *Patchwork Girl*'s nonlinearity, Hayles argues, complicates cultural and literary "monster" narratives in general. "Part of the monstrosity, then, is this mingling of the subjectivity we attribute to characters, authors, and ourselves as users with the nonanthropomorphic actions of the computer program" (Hayles 163). To refashion linear models of expression—such as a subjectivity that sees itself progressing through singular paths of experience—Hayles uses *Patchwork Girl* in order to argue for an "intermediated" subjectivity where multiple reading and writing paths can be experienced. Through narrative, nonlinear subjectivity is realized as a number of discursive, political, and cultural forces converge. Narrative paths are chosen through one's reading experiences (reading of texts and other cultural phenomenon). Similarly, Jay David Bolter underscores multiple narrative paths as the focus of electronic writing in his canonical *Writing Space.*

> In general, the connections of a hypertext are organized into paths that make operational sense to author and reader. Each topic may participate in several paths, and its significance will depend upon which paths the reader has traveled in order to arrive at that topic. In print, only a few paths can be suggested or followed. (24)

Bolter identifies "paths" as narrative devices that, in hypertext, readers choose *from* rather than *with*. "Every path defines an equally convincing and appropriate reading, and in that simple fact the reader's relationship to the text changes radically" (Bolter 25). That Bolter and others stress narrative and its paths as hypertext's most redeeming quality is not surprising; as Ong notes, narrative reflects a print logic of story telling, but also a print-oriented concept of linear progression (even if that progression can follow more than one path) that has ideologically directed contemporary notions of writing. Narrative also allowed print the ability to "close" the text within linear progression. "Print," Ong writes, "locked words into space and thereby established a firmer sense of closure than writing could" (*Orality and Literacy* 148). The "paths" concept Bolter and others foreground expands the sense of closure narrative generates, but it does not completely open up that closure. I make that point in order to note that narrative choices are not all that hypertext embodies through nonlinearity. Nonlinearity reflects openness, but an openness that extends beyond which path to follow in a piece of writing. I note this regarding textual writing (like a specific hypertext) or cultural phenomenon as writing (as in Hayle's analysis). To return to the example of film in the previous chapter, it would not have been sufficient for Smith or Anger to offer another narrative or path regarding gender acceptance. Instead, the writers had to compose multiple narratives at once, each to be read with the other, each opening up various gender references at once (gender itself representing more than one path). Commutation is partly a response for the need to write textual openness. Nonlinearity reflects another part of that gesture.

Nonlinearity, as Nelson demonstrates, maneuvers around textual closure. The open text nonlinearity poses in terms of alternative reading/writing practices is central to the rhetoric of cool for how it encourages interactivity (the contributing and deleting of text and ideas). "To call computer media 'interactive,'" Lev Manovich argues, "is meaningless—it simply means stating the most basic fact about computers" (55). Manovich's point is that computing—because of internal functions located in the machine itself—always involves interactions among components. His response is to explore interactivity beyond its "literal interpretation" of clicking on pages, pressing buttons, and (regarding hypertext fiction) following "pre-programmed, objectively existing associations" (Manovich 57, 61). A significant part of

Manovich's critique is that without expanding definitions regarding how interactivity affects nonlinear writings (film or otherwise), dependence on a fixed, and not very helpful, understanding of new media and narrative will continue. No matter how many paths (or descriptions) of new media we compose, those paths must remain open, not fixed. "In the world of new media, the word *narrative* is often used as an all-inclusive term, to cover up the fact that we have not yet developed a language to describe these new strange objects. It is usually paired with another overused word—*interactive*" (Manovich 228). Terms like *interactive* or *nonlinear* are overused when they fail to account for compositional possibilities beyond which narrative a reader or writer follows.

In 1963, Nelson offers an initial vision of hypertext that begins the process of developing a new language to describe this strange process of nonlinear writing. Exemplified in Nelson's later Xanadu project and its Parallel Textface writing system, an interactive writing space is proposed where all kinds of texts can be connected or disconnected by the writer; the text is left "open" for further work and interaction.

> The user may have a number of standby layouts, with different numbers of panels, and jump among them by stabs of the lightpen. Importantly, the panels of each can be full, each having whatever the contents were when you last used it. . . . In this approach we annotate and label discrepancies, and verbally comment on differences in separate files or documents. (*Dream Machine* 44)

This system embodies Nelson's concept of "thinkertoys," those tools (conceptual or material) that help writers "envision complex alternatives" (*Dream Machines* 50). The thinkertoy method bases itself upon a largely open-text system, one unlike the narrative bound structures hypertext theory has tended to stress. In the Xanadu model, "link types are open-ended. Searches of the link data are a specific class of user interaction. Any link to material shared between documents is available to all instances of that material" (*Dream Machine* 146). Narrative, as traditional hypertext theory utilizes it, has dominated hypertexts studies' interest in nonlinearity by limiting the scope of possible alternatives, and by placing most of its emphasis on storytelling and closed textual constructions. Nonlinear narrative involves choosing *among* various discursive strands that exist within one or more spaces. Nonlinearity, in general, is able to expand this narrative emphasis by requiring writers to work among the strands in order to complicate rhetorical options and expression. Nonlinearity asks, as Manovich might argue, that writers identify complex sets of data and form multiple texts out of the data.

Narrative is often situated within current-traditional rhetoric's modes. In itself, narrative is not a faulty mode of expression. It is, however, a print-dominated mode inherited from print's creation of self-reflection through repeated reading and the consequent need to express that reflection in essay or story form. Narrative is dependent on individual strands of thought that may, or may not, connect. I initially questioned the narratives spun around composition's beginnings because they fixate too strongly on single representations. Even if we allow for an alternative narrative to emerge, like the one I am constructing regarding cool, it is still a narrative with limited rhetorical function other than to tell *a single* story. Thus, it is not narrative that is important to the concept of nonlinearity (i.e., the choice to follow more than one narrative strand). Rather, what matters is the various overlapping, nonsequential strands that one does not choose among but composes with simultaneously. In other words, even though I tell a narrative about composition studies and cool, I do so from multiple strands (technology, cultural studies, and writing), rather than one strand of causality or narrative progression, or, as traditional hypertext studies emphasizes, individual, alternative routes. I see these multiple strands not as something that hypertext or any other new media form brings to writing but rather as the very relations among ideas that comprise new media itself–that is, the multiplicity is the rhetoric. As Foucault writes regarding the issue of multiple thoughts or ideas:

> Moreover, these relations cannot be the very web of the text—they are not by nature foreign to discourse. They can certainly be qualified as "prediscursive," but only if one admits that this prediscursive is still discursive, that is, that they do not specify a thought, or a consciousness, or a group of representations which, *a posteriori,* and in a way that is never quite necessary, are transcribed into a discourse, but that they characterize certain levels of discourse, that they define rules that are embodied as a particular practice by discourse. (76)

The multiple is the basis of Lyotard's argument in *The Postmodern Condition.* In the age of computing and technology in general, Lyotard writes, there is a "distance separating the customary state of knowledge from its state in the scientific age: the preeminence of the narrative form in the formulation of traditional knowledge" (19). Identifying the scientific age in a way far different than Braddock and colleagues do in their empirical study of variables, Lyotard challenges the contention that "narration is the quintessential form of customary knowledge" by opposing the narrative to the data-oriented information system of contemporary culture (19). "Data banks are the Encyclopedia of tomorrow," Lyotard writes. (51). They contain vast amounts of information that connect to one another depending on how the information is assembled. Manovich, as I have noted, presents all new media nonlinearity as attributable to database logic and structure. "Regardless of whether new media objects present themselves as linear narratives, interactive narratives, databases, or something else, underneath, on the level of material organization, they are all databases" (Manovich 228). In contemporary computers and writing scholarship, Johndan Johnson-Eilola considers the nonlinear aspects of databases in terms of new media writing systems like Google. "If we value this search engine," Johnson-Eilola writes,

> which is in effect the front end to a database—if we value this as a form of writing, then we can begin to argue that the sorts of choices one makes in writing the database—for example, what categories to include, what to exclude; which category to put first; etc.—we can start to argue that these choices involve responsibilities to the reader and to society, just as we now do in other, more traditional forms of writing. ("The Database and the Essay" 220)

Among choices and alternatives, among differing threads of data, then, hypertext opens up the possibility of writing. The search engine embodies one possibility, but there is the potential for other possible writing formations as well. Memorization of the hypertextual data bank, however, is not the goal of rhetorical production. Writers can never "know" all that exists in these extensive data banks of information: "It is a commonplace that what is of utmost importance is the capacity to actualize the relevant data for solving a problem 'here and now,' and to organize that data into an efficient strategy" (Lyotard 51). I understand Lyotard's remark regarding an "efficient strategy" as a move toward nonlinearity. "The transmission of knowledge should not be limited to the transmission of information," Lyotard notes (implying narrative's role in such processes), "but should include training in all of the procedures that can increase one's ability to connect the fields [of information] jealously guarded from one another by the traditional organization of knowledge" (Lyotard 52). Nonlinear systems work against disciplinary limitations (either the discipline itself or the composing it generates) because they encourage connection (via overlap and juxtaposition) where neither had been previously identified. Google might serve as one example of this database logic, as Johnson-Eilola notes, but nonlinear writing in general can perform this work as well.

Lyotard's position speaks to the central tenet of Nelson's Xanadu and the nonlinear writings McLuhan and Burroughs compose in 1963. Writing emerges and works within open databases of nonlinear information; "traditional," as Lyotard writes, organizational schemes become challenged. *Ticket That Exploded*'s "Writing Machine" section, for instance, foreshadows

Lyotard's concerns with information production; within its cut-up structure a variety of threads follow one another, contradict one another, and compliment one another. "You can say could give no information," Burroughs writes. "Dominion dwindling—we intersect on empty kingdom read to by a boy—Five times i made this dream" (65). Burroughs's media environment is a database too large to call itself anything other than an "intersection," at content and sentence structure levels. A writer following Burroughs's logic presents strands of thought and ideas compiled to a given audience, noting where they intersect instead of where they tell a story. This kind of writer performs such work more than once ("five times") as she makes her way through the informational database. This writing foregoes the option of a singular, linear mode presented in one genre or demonstration. This writing upsets McCrimmon's insistence that narrative modes follow singular sequencing or else suffer as "bad writing":

> A paragraph so written may reveal one of two flaws: (1) an obvious interruption in the sequence of ideas, caused by the introduction of irrelevant thoughts; (2) a gradual drift away from the stated purpose of the paragraph as the author lets each succeeding sentence push him farther in the wrong direction. (McCrimmon 74)

The supposed wrong direction McCrimmon emphasizes assumes the lack of a database to navigate through; it assumes a singular path to follow in order to reach a given rhetorical aim or desire. "Drifting from one side to the other frustrates the reader and proceeds a 'broken-backed' paragraph" (McCrimmon 75). Hypertext in 1963 speaks in favor of that drifting, but it does so through movements not entirely dependent on narrative, and that are anything but broken.

When we theorize nonlinearity solely through the lens of narrative, we not only concentrate on modes of knowledge production unable to accommodate the database Burroughs and Lyotard draw attention to, but we also fall victim to what McLuhan called the tendency to make the "old" do the work of the "new." We employ narrative to deal with new media and hence neglect to utilize new media for so-called "new" purposes. We rely on concepts like "sequencing" or "order" *as if* those concepts apply to new media in ways previous media allowed.

> Our official culture is striving to force the new media to do the work of the old. These are difficult times because we are witnessing a clash of cataclysmic proportions between two great technologies. We approach the new with the psychological conditioning and sensory responses of

the old. This clash naturally occurs in transitional periods. (*Medium Is the Massage* 94–95)

Thus, in *Understanding Media*, McLuhan does not write a series of alternative narratives (the old) regarding media and rhetoric whose "movement should follow some clear order" (McCrimmon 75). Instead McLuhan composes a series of nonlinear threads on the written word, the printed word, roads and paper routes, money, numbers, and other media (the new) that drift in and out of each section. It is up to the reader to engage with these strands, reading them together or separately, to see them in conversation with one another or not, and to forge a variety of connections the author intended or didn't intend to occur. I am using "new" and "old" here loosely, of course, as a generic way of understanding how a familiar mode used in a traditional context may not accommodate emerging applications.

Taking McLuhan's usage of nonlinearity, then, I want to concentrate on how it rhetorically functions in cool, and not how it suggests alternative narrative forms. I may often point to hypertext as exemplary of nonlinear practices, but I'm not restricting any of my discussion to hypertext nor to any one version of what hypertext entails. In general, nonlinearity challenges our understanding of how we order information in the digital. It also poses complex methods of information construction and distribution beyond what current writing instruction allows. I begin by recognizing that the generic insistence on singular sequencing inherited from McCrimmon's teaching has led contemporary compositionists, like Joseph Janangelo, to begin their pedagogical interest in nonlinearity by initially questioning the total-inclusive nature of hypertexts students may compose. That questioning, Janangelo eventually discovers, is ideological and institutional. "Yet a rhetoric of endless growth conflicts with the idea, endemic to academic prose, that persuasion is usually predicated on focus, selection, and strategic presentation" (Janangelo 29). Janangelo's response to the everything-can-be-included nature of nonlinear hypertexts is to ask what kinds of models composition studies might learn from in order to teach this open-ended writing. "Equipotentiality underscores the image of hypertext as an unfocused species of discourse—a kind of casual collage where texts are linked, but where the logic of the linkages can appear ambiguous and arbitrary" (Janangelo 31). To teach the collagist nature of hypertext, Janangelo studies the avant-garde work of Joseph Cornell. In the spirit of Janangelo's work, my first model for nonlinear rhetoric comes not from Cornell but from Burroughs colleague Jack Kerouac (a different type of avant-garde writer) and how his work, too, can inform the ways we teach and compose nonlinear, Web writing.

## The Kerouac Model

Jack Kerouac represents a specific 1963 literary moment when writing adopts nonlinearity for rhetorical purposes. Preempting the Web, but temporally aligned with Nelson's work, Kerouac offers an example of cool writing for how his work fashions nonlinearity out of databases of ideas. In Kerouac's 1962 *Big Sur,* associative-linked memories generate a nonlinear style that shifts suddenly from one thought to the next, each thought activated by word choices, or what we might call conceptual links.

> It reminds me of the time I once saw a whole tiptoeing gang of couples sneaking into our back kitchen door on West Street in Lowell the leader telling me to shush as I stand there 9 years old amazed, then all bursting in on my father innocently listening to the Primo Carnera-Ernie Schaaft fight on the old 1930s radio—For a big roaring toot—but Cody's oldfashioned family tiptoe sneak carries that strange apocalyptic burst of gold he somehow always manages to produce, like I said elsewhere the time in Mexico he drove an old car over a rutted road very slowly as we were all high on tea and I saw golden Heaven. (*Big Sur* 124–25)

In this passage, "tiptoe" functions as a link, an associative word connecting one memory to the next. The logic is choral, but it is also nonlinear through its presentation of a number of threads at once: living in Lowell, Massachusetts, Cody's family, and Kerouac's Duluoz character driving through Mexico with Cody. The purpose is narrative oriented; *Big Sur* is a novel after all. But the rhetoric of this text also provides a lesson for electronic writing. Kerouac's choice to compose in a nonlinear manner by following associations in place of reasoning or traditional narrative exposition grants the reader a highly cool reading experience (and it grants Kerouac a cool writing experience as well). Which thread do I follow and when? How do the threads interact and connect? Why display more than one thread at once? These are questions for electronic rhetorical production. "Today," McLuhan notes, "it is the instant speed of electric information that, for the first time, permits easy recognition of the patterns and the formal contours of change and development" (*Understanding Media* 305). Writing in the same technological environment as McLuhan and Engelbart, Kerouac poses the nonlinear process as a method for composing in an information economy dominated by too much information to reasonably navigate through individual strands. How does one achieve unified thought, *Big Sur* seems to argue, when cultural and conceptual interactions are never unified? Kerouac offers a striking contrast to the unified theory of idea representation Edward P. J. Corbett proposes when he writes in 1963, "I find that my students are most likely to produce a unified, coherent piece of writing when they are forced, before they begin to write, to state their thesis in a single declarative sentence" ("Usefulness of Classical Rhetoric" 162). Corbett's focus on the thesis, like other 1963 comments on writing, does not recognize how McLuhan's "instant speed of electric information" problematizes the dependence on one statement. With so much information to work with, how can we reduce writing to one sentence? Where, indeed, is the single declarative sentence in Kerouac's following meta-critique of the technology-driven information economy emerging in the 1960s?

> The history of everything we've seen together and separately has become a library in itself—The shelves pile higher—They're full of misty documents or documents of the Mist—The mind has convoluted in every tuckaway everwhichaway tuckered hole till there's no more the expressing of our latest thoughts let alone old—Mighty genius of the mind Cody whom I announce as the greatest writer the world will ever know if he ever gets down to writing again like he did earlier—It's so enormous we both sit here sighing in fact. (*Big Sur* 140)

This writing isn't unified, as Corbett would require, nor is it, at first, coherent. But, by following these different paths of thought presented at once, we can tease out concerns regarding information distribution. Kerouac's insight into how information is distributed and stored precedes Lyotard's uneasiness regarding how to produce information within such a system. In this nonunified passage, we discover that "[t]he mind has convoluted in every tuckaway," and one way to negotiate this convolution is nonlinearity. Kerouac quickly appends to this point a note about Cody that may or may not have anything to do with the preceding idea, though the suggestion is that an associational relationship exists. The reader will construct the meaning if needed.

The challenge for composition studies is how to write in such a manner without resorting to narrative storytelling. Like Burroughs's sense of the "how-to," *Big Sur* can be read as a rhetorical how-to approach toward generating nonlinear text.

> And it's almost tearful to realize and remember the old green T-shirt I'd found, mind you, eight years ago, mind you, on the DUMP in Watsonville, California mind you, and got fantastic use and comfort from it—Like working to fix that new stream in the creek to flow through the convenient deep new waterhole near the wood platform on the bank, and losing myself in this like a kid playing, it's the little things that count (clichés are truisms and all truisms are true)—On my deathbed I could be remembering that creek day and forgetting the day MGM bought my book, I could be

remembering the old lost green dump T-shirt and forgetting the sapphired robes. (*Big Sur* 34)

How can a writer explain the objects of desire (a T-shirt, a stream), memories (playing as a kid, getting a book published), anecdotes, history, speculation (all truisms are true), and theory all at once? Only by nonlinear patterns, Kerouac demonstrates. The formation of associative, nonlinear thoughts is itself a composing process reflective of digital media. To bring together these experiences at once, *Big Sur* instructs, write them as nonlinear points. In the cool media environments begun in the 1950s with television and updated today via Web sites, digital sampling, and TV media outlets like CNN Headline News, the ability to navigate and generate multiple lines of thinking at once is a rhetorical necessity because single, declarative sentences don't cover enough material. Single, declarative sentences leave too much information out; they restrict thought in unnecessary ways. The Kerouac nonlinear associations reflect what Matthew Fuller more recently calls "a virtual syntax" for how they motivate writers to question material under consideration for compositional inclusion. "How *can* they be connected?" Fuller asks of such material. "The heterogeneity, the massive capacity for disconnectedness of the parts, coupled with the plain evidence of their being linked by some syntax, of writing or performative action, allows for the invention of newly transversal, imaginal, technico-aesthetic or communicative dynamics to flower" (Fuller 15).

The relevancy of Kerouac's work, therefore, is in how I can appropriate its rhetorical "communicative dynamics" for writing to the Web. The Web is itself a chain of networked, and often associative pages, whose multithreaded discussions and ideas take place on Web boards, in e-mail, on Weblogs, and within Web sites. By using literature to apply a nondigital rhetorical method to digital writing, I follow Winston Weathers's work (as noted in chapter 1) as well as Kitzhaber's general interest in appropriating rhetorical approaches from literary genres: "The study of composition and the study of literature can profitably be related by showing how the principles of composition (i.e., of logic, rhetoric, and English structure) are exemplified in particular literary works" (*Themes, Theories, and Therapy* 36).

Kerouac's rhetoric of nonlinearity can be extended to the work of Tim Berners-Lee, inventor of the World Wide Web. Berners-Lee identifies information production on the Web as "cool" for how it directs writers to compose in highly interactive, nonlinear ways. Berners-Lee's concept of URIs (Universal Resource Identifiers, transitive addresses that tell browsers where to find information) as opposed to the currently used URLs (Uniform Resource Locators, the version in place today on the Web that is more static than URIs) relies on a semantic system of writing (like Ulmer's chorography or Kerouac's associative linking) at the level of cool. Berners-Lee writes:

> What makes a cool URI?
> A cool URI is one which does not change.
> What sorts of URI change?
> URIs don't change: people change them.

In the Berners-Lee excerpt, I understand "cool URI" not to mean "a worthwhile URI" but rather a URI indicative of the McLuhanist definition of cool, a highly interactive writing space. Berners-Lee's cool URI comprises a part of his semantic Web, a medium where writings relate by semantic meanings. Writers change the URIs as they compose because writers commutate and manipulate language to create a variety of rhetorical experiences that can be read at once, as overlapping, or as separate. The semantic nature of this theorized Web moves in a number of directions at once through writerly experience and rhetorical choice. Its nonlinearity is not tied to narrative (the limitations of the Kerouac model) but to expression in general. In an interview with *Technology Review,* Berners-Lee describes the nonlinear capabilities the semantic Web poses:

> When there's a web of interesting global semantic data, then you'll be able to combine the data you know about with other data that you don't know about. Our lives will be enriched by this data, which we didn't have access to before, and we'll be able to write programs that will actually help because they'll be able to *understand* the data out there rather than just *presenting* it to us on the screen. (Frauenfelder)

This matrix of data can be composed and written in any number of ways. At the technological level, the "relationship" tag, rel=",", is introduced so that the tag that links pages and ideas, <a href="">, becomes <a rel ="">.[2] At the content level, the connections writers generate come from how the data is associated to other data and how writers actualize those associations in their rhetorical choices. Writers think in terms of relationships, not separate threads of thought.[3] Such relationships have become actualized in online social network systems like the photo sharing application Flickr, the social bookmarking system Del.icio.us, and the online Web site listing service Metafilter. In these systems, markup tags (meta information attributes attached to a word or image) function as semantic exchange. They generate nonlinear, associative links among a variety of sites and images. The emphasis, in choral fashion, is not causal effect but meaning relationships, however arbitrary such meanings may, at first, appear.

Del.icio.us, in particular, changes the very hierarchical structuring book-marking initially relied upon (as early browsers followed the logic of print culture) by allowing writers to "name" their own identifiers for the places they visit on the Web. These names become hyperlinks to other Del.icio.us accounts. Writers can follow the names (and the account names) in nonlinear paths that are motivated more by association (chora) than by causality or logical progression (narrative). Writers who compose via Del.icio.us construct nonlinear organizational systems for other writers to read or (knowingly or not) contribute to. That Del.icio.us is, as of now, a bookmarking system and not a more recognizable writing practice (like an essay or story) is not important. The logic behind Del.icio.us stresses the nonlinear connections writers form at once for taxonomic purposes (and not as separate paths of thought). This logic speaks to the new media rhetoric cool creates.

Unfortunately, consumer culture appears to be the institution most interested in applying this kind of cool writing (outside of a few developers who have strong coding backgrounds and a small number of writing instructors). Best fictionalized in Cory Doctorow's science fiction novel *Eastern Standard Tribe,* this type of commercial writing is presented in a future in which consumer culture is the driving force of nonlinear rhetorics. Doctorow's concept of "The Tribe" involves a culture of information sharing, most of it based on Del.icio.us-like, semantic associations among its members (the tagging of interests, places, ideas, and words in mobile information systems). Tribes connect via a futuristic version of the Web in which all information is interlinked. "Tribes are *agendas*," Art, the novel's protagonist states. "Aesthetics. Ethos. Traditions. Ways of getting things done" (112). These agendas, or plans, include conceptualizing new ways to write or share ideas. Two particular agendas Art concocts involve a massive P2P music sharing system called MassPike and a hospital information sharing system to be used for drawing out unexpected and unexplored connections among patients' histories and medical progress. Neither of these nonlinear methods of information creation and distribution reflects the alternative "paths" Bolter's hypertext generates; but they are nonlinear, and they are writing. The rhetoric underlying this nonlinearity is association.

One reason composition studies shows little interest in semantic, association-based, nonlinear composition is that the field still clings to what Kitzhaber calls "the blunt truth" that "few faculty members outside the humanities really believe that good writing (correct, accurate, clear writing) is important" (*Themes, Theories, Therapy* 129). To contextualize "good writing" as clear and correct is to miss the possibilities the semantic Web (invented outside of the humanities) or fictionalized accounts like Doctorow's pose. If writers can change meaning, pose multiple positions at once, combine meanings, establish complex and ambiguous relationships among words or ideas, and perform other rhetorical moves associated with nonlinearity, there will always be the possibility of being unclear and not accurate. The semantic Web as a cool rhetorical space complicates Kitzhaber's (and the rest of composition's) concerns because it—like other elements of cool—displaces a tradition of accuracy and clarity. A semantic meaning may not be accurate, but it may be rhetorically powerful.

Currently, we find the most widely applied semantic moves in Web sites that track user usage or purchasing habits.[4] Amazon.com and Aol.com are two of the most dominant enterprises employing semantic information structures toward information creation and distribution; these sites generate connections among user purchases based on word choice, titles of products, or associative gestures (this book you are buying sounds like this CD, so you might want it too). The writing may or may not be correct (I don't want the CD), but such a point is immaterial. Within nonlinear threads, meaning is established. One item connects to another item in surprising or expected ways; regardless of which, there is meaning in these connections. That meaning's specificity, of course, depends on all kinds of contexts and situations. Yet in these types of examples, we find that there exists a new media logic that allows for associative nonlinear reasoning and writing. Rather than ask how we can avoid the traps such writing poses for our consumer habits, we should ask how can we use such media for a composition-oriented cool writing.

## Cooltown

Education is the space where these types of questions must be asked, and where the corporate sector—as Doctorow's novel suggests—has shown the most interest in providing some answers. In this mix of education and corporate investment, semantic writing is further related to cool in Hewlett Packard's conflation of a futuristic society that combines pedagogy and technology into an environment called Cooltown.[5] Hewlett Packard outlines the project on its Web site accordingly: "CoolTown is a place where the physical world and the virtual world meet, where technology works for you, not the other way around. It's a vision of pervasive computing, but instead of requiring new protocols and a new infrastructure, this relies on what's already there—the Web" ("Future Called CoolTown"). Cooltown positions itself as the ultimate global communicative system merging personal activity with corporate interest, one that forges semantic connections among a variety of daily activities and future plans. Drawing from cool much in the way advertising and consumerism typically do through appropriation, Hewlett Packard identifies cool as both product and discourse. Cool denotes what we buy (the company's products and services) as well as how we communicate, that is, through a series of "protocols" and an "infrastructure" Hewlett Packard has invented. Cooltown attempts to fulfill much of what McLuhan predicted the electronic age promised: The juxtaposition of consumerism and information leads to nonlinear rhetorics as opposed to the linear process of automation spurred by print.

> Grasp of this fact is indispensable to the understanding of the electronic age, and of automation in particular. Energy and production now tend to fuse with information and learning. Marketing and consumption tend to become one with learning, enlightenment, and the intake of information. (*Understanding Media* 304)

The combination of marketing and learning is what is most intriguing about Cooltown, and what I will discuss in more depth shortly. Cooltown promises to construct a society of nonlinear connections through the existing apparatus of the World Wide Web by promoting a specific commercial vision. Business meetings, catching the bus, ordering coffee, and other activities all become an interconnected experience driven by global satellite positioning systems and Web sites. "Everything has a web presence," Hewlett Packard's developers claim. "People, places, and things in the physical world will have increasingly complex online representations, allowing them to participate in Web services. They will become first-class citizens of the Web. This will enable services to become more personalized, more spontaneous, and more responsive to the wide variety of contexts in which people live their lives" ("Cooltown Beliefs"). Participation, then, is a multi-rhetorical experience driven by a variety of movements occurring concurrently in a number of directions in a number of places.

To write and participate in Cooltown, users must rethink how communication operates. Cooltown transforms the physical environment and the rhetorical strategies we associate with permanence and physicality into nonlinear spatial positionings. In Cooltown, writers compose on the fly, to a variety of places at once, from a variety of positions at once. "Cooltown is infused with the energy of the online world, and Web-based appliances and e-services give you what you need when and where you need it for work, play, life" ("What Is Cooltown"). Promotional videos for the concept demonstrate users interacting with a variety of media and information systems at once, all in nonlinear fashion (ordering products, checking the weather, looking up terms, translating words from one language to another, etc.). Each action, in turn, interlinks with another action. Cooltown promotes Berners-Lee's vision of the semantic Web, even if in unintended ways. Like Berners-Lee's cool URI, Cooltown depends on the locality of the Web space in order to commutate its physicality into something else, something not bound by any single direction of visitation or representation.

> In cooltown, URL bookmarks can be gathered from online interactions, messaging services, synchronization applications, etc. Once bookmarked, URLs can be sent to remote web locations, or beamed directly to a variety of web appliances using a beaming technology we call "e-squirt." Using this technology, your mobile phone or handheld wireless device can "squirt" the URL, enabling you to instantly put presentations on a screen, documents on a printer, or music on a connected stereo. ("Cooltown: The Ecosystem Explained")

While the computer manufacturer may not imagine a nonlinear application in its own description, it isn't hard to imagine a writer utilizing this space to present multi-threaded points and ideas; to be simultaneously in contact with multiple audiences via cell phone, laptop, or some other device; to visualize and actualize a significant portion of Nelson's initial hypertext vision of multi/dual connectivities. To transfer writing from the static, printed page to the mobile URI is to reimagine referentiality and linearity's role in the composing process. "Squirting" URIs in a assortment of directions at once from a multitude of locations could force levels of McLuhan's interactivity we haven't yet digitally experienced and could encourage writers to seek out connections in their writings that neither narrative nor traditional argumentation can account for. It could generate a new media pedagogical vision, as Hewlett Packard claims it will do.

> In Cooltown, every person, place, or thing can be connected to the web. Even a wristwatch has the capability of becoming an intelligent web appliance, for example, as a valuable extension of the schoolroom. In Cooltown a student using an e-service downloads a Spanish dictionary from her computer to her watch. Once the program is downloaded, the young Spanish student is able to access the knowledge stored in everyday objects via beacons—instantly translating that information into Spanish. ("Cooltown: The Ecosystem Explained")

Though statements like this sound like a concrete pedagogical vision, and while its hyperbolic gestures are attractive, Hewlett Packard does not move away from traditional pedagogical approaches in order to integrate this type of writing into education, specifically in the trial program established to run Cooltown.

While its promotional material for Cooltown is appealing and promising, Hewlett Packard's appropriation of Cooltown for its educational, experimental program cooltown@school does not generate a "beaming" of data in all kinds of directions but rather reinforces a traditional, linear method of thinking and expression. To return to McLuhan's point regarding education and marketing, with cooltown@school, Hewlett Packard seems content with building a system that only reestablishes the logic of print (thus excluding how marketing can shape technology) and does not structure a nonlinear writing world. The more I read the company's promotional material and the more I am exposed to this romanticized educational future, the more I hear *narratives* of nonlinearity and learning, and not database driven formations.

Based in Vancouver, cooltown@school takes the initial concept of Cooltown and, capitalizing on student enthusiasm for a word like cool, shapes an entire technology-based educational program.

> From the concept of portal-based learning and anytime, anywhere access to a student's curriculum and educational progress, to the development of community resource centers and the seamless connection of schools and other community services, Vancouver officials, with the help of HP, are about to transform the way schools educate their students and unite a community. ("School Gets Cool")

According to literature published in its own journal *mpulse,* Hewlett Packard imagines Cooltown as an advanced, technology-driven, educational mission representative of what computing offers learning.

> The Vancouver project has attracted the attention of technology-enabled education experts and advocates. They see it as a way not only to modernize the educational process, but also to test the educational system's ability to be up to the task of providing instruction that capitalizes on the underlying technology. (Coleman)

Initially, two pilot programs were planned, one at the elementary level:

> Three 5th grade classrooms at the inner-urban Eleanor Roosevelt Elementary will be equipped with laptops that will be used as the primary instruction tools. The learning portal will serve as a sort of digital enhancement of the chalkboard, and the teachers will be able to design personalized lessons based on the characteristics of each student. ("School Gets Cool")

And one at the high school level:

> A group of 30 high school students enrolled in the district's communications magnet program will spend the second half of every school day at the education, family, and community center where, using the learning portal, they will build on their interest of applying multimedia to academically challenging, relevant projects. ("School Gets Cool")

Despite such hype and despite the worthwhile goal of joining various levels of secondary education together, neither program is a database nor connects to the other as a database. Cooltown@school embodies the worst of course management. It leaves the data it stores, collects, and transmits in nonconnected forms. It works outside of database models (most prominent in social software) that are based on the basic concept of connecting data. Cooltown@school is based not on a database model nor on a nonlinear system of communication and writing, as it seems to claim, but on already familiar pedagogical methods that are superimposed onto the idea of a massive, all inclusive "Web portal."

Such an approach to database digitality is even more prominent when cooltown@school is compared to other attempts to integrate technology into education that fail to recognize how technology and databases pose new demands for learning and writing. Cooltown@school resembles many of the course management systems already in circulation in a variety of colleges and universities. Indeed, the rhetoric of the above passages closely follows popular course management system WebCT's mission statement.

> With WebCT, students get high-quality, easier-to-access education—education that not only meets their immediate needs, but that also continually adds to a foundation for lifetime learning. Each student has a single point of entry to every institutional offering that's most important to him or her, a point of entry that reflects what the system learns about the student over time and serves as a lifetime learning resource. ("WebCT Whitepaper")

Both positions embrace "anytime/anywhere" learning in which students are always connected in, what appears to be suggested, multi-threaded experiences of information gathering and production. "Cooltown is all about connectivity," Hewlett Packard's promotional video claims. "Education is more personalized, more interactive, and more stimulating" (Cooltown Videos). The promised "point of entry" WebCT describes and Hewlett Packard promotes should allow students the ability to forge nonlinear connections among a variety of resources and learning experiences and also allow for nonlinear rhetorical production, which would reflect the experiences as well. Yet nowhere in either WebCT or cooltown@school's makeup or curricula do we find the lived-out promise of nonlinear connectivity. Nowhere do we find writers performing Kerouac-like associative writing or Engelbart-oriented multiple writings. Technology keywords are present: "active learning," "full potential," "opportunities," "connectivity," "needs," "growth," "personalized learning," and "relevance" (Cooltown Videos). But little of the products' technological capabilities reflect this language. The writing students do looks like writing produced without new media exposure or influence. The writing students do looks—more or less—like any of the writing students would have done in 1963 classrooms or courses studied by Braddock and colleagues or Kitzhaber. Returning to my earlier discussion on hypertext, if a "path" is being followed here, it is the recognizable path of educational policy we have walked down many times before.

Cooltown@school.com and WebCT signify the construction of a pedagogical apparatus that does not reflect the practices it proposes teaching. While Cooltown may seem like an aberration, the WebCT/Blackboard models popular throughout higher education mimic the same type of approach to linear learning. WebCT's (like Cooltown's) point of entry is by no means a multileveled entrance; its gates and password protected barriers direct users in one, linear projection often centered around the purchasing school's own infrastructure. The work produced and maintained within the WebCT system is not multi-linear either. WebCT houses uploaded textbooks (the same versions can be found in print), bulletin boards (they can be multi-threaded but are limited in their ability only to house one section of writing at a time, not a variety of boards linked together), e-mail (not specific to WebCT), and a Web site for each course (which tends to be limited to the course itself). No evidence can be found among either WebCT's or cooltown@school.com's literature that students working in these environments write anything other than standard essays. As "connected" as these sites may claim to be, the computer languages that structure such connections—either hyperlinks or more complex markup systems like XML and XHTML—are never taught. This is hardly the vision of a nonlinear world. Once a student no longer writes within the closed-off environment of either cooltown@school.com or WebCT, where and how will the promised "lifelong learning" occur? In other words, how "lifelong" is this experience that is restricted to one kind of licensed platform? The oddest fact about any of these systems is that cooltown@school.com cannot be found on the Web through a simple Google search, and the so-called connectivity of WebCT/Blackboard keeps these systems as well outside of the Web, the medium that supposedly allows these systems to function.[6] Yet the managed courseware vision imagined in either the popular WebCT or the cool-aligned cooltown@school.com has become systematic of how nonmedia logics instill technological educational systems; the norm favors restriction in place of openness. Instead of basing their systems on the rhetoric of cool, these operations continue the nonmedia compositional tradition I have situated in 1963.

## Nonlinear Writing

Rather than resort to the simulated nonlinear proposals Cooltown or WebCT promote, I conclude with a pedagogical nod to the approach I am describing that values nonlinearity, but does so in a non-platform specific manner. To teach nonlinearity in terms of nonnarrative writing and in terms of open writing, we engage with the basic principles outlined in Kerouac's work by attempting to construct something akin to the promises put forth—but not fulfilled—by corporate technology initiatives in education. In what is a general variation of the hip-hop pedagogy assignment I described in chapter 4, one kind of nonlinear writing assignment asks students to compose for the Web via a series of threads. Based also on the Web site Everything2. com, this assignment borrows the site's language of "cooling" as a method for organizing information in nonlinear manners. As I note in chapter 4 as well, on the Everything2.com site, registered users "cool" topics by interlinking them in multiple ways. "Learning to ski," "Fermented bean curd," "Irish Girls," and "U.S. Highway 91" can all stand for individual subjects of interest interlinked in nonlinear threads.[7] The connections occur via different writers' engagement with each area of interest. In place of the linear model encouraged by the fixed places of argument (the topos), cooled topics branch out according to how users discover new connections among words, ideas, quotes, allusions, or some other issue. These places of discussion are in flux, not permanence. Within the 1963 critique the rhetoric of cool works from, Burroughs's focus on this time period as a series of multiple threads intersected seems relevant and worth mentioning—it provides its own link to the Everything2.com model.

> July 9, 1962—Disease of the image track—The onset is sudden voices screaming a steady scream—I had forgotten unseen force of memory pictures—Muttering slobbering outhouse skin seeps from his rectum— island of dying people surrounded by shallow lagoons—the boatman smiles—Wired red lips entered the '20s in drag from the Ward island natives. (*Ticket that Exploded* 98)

Like the cooled ideas on Everything2.com or the semantic nature of Berners-Lee's vision of a new Web structure, Burroughs's random topics can be expanded upon in a number of ways based on associative reasoning. Each phrase Burroughs presents can be interlinked and extended in connection with one or more of the others. Picture the student engaging with these lines of thoughts not as prompts to be developed into single standing essays but as the structure of the essay itself, interwoven threads of discursive relationships. Within these moments of observation (the boatman smiles/wired red lips), threads are generated and interlinked. The passage I reference stands not by itself but is the entryway toward multi-threaded writing; that is, it allows for a more applicable version of the WebCT "point of entry," which leads only one way. In other words, the objective is not to replicate Burroughs's passage but to use it as model for expansion. In the nonlinear model, writers explore a number of thoughts at once based on how they produce such linkages. How and why do these ideas connect?, the model queries. Everything2.com provides an electronic version of Burroughs's passage; each thread expands and shrinks based on the amount of writers engaged with the site and the compositional decisions they make.

The writing assignment that uses Everything2.com as a model can be performed in a variety of ways, but one way is to ask students to begin with a list of ideas or thoughts centered around a given topic or series of topics. Instead of transforming this list into an essay (as an outline might dictate, or a standard essay focused on a "topic" as the topos might require), students develop multiple threads around each point or idea through association, research, discussion, or another method of idea development. Working with images, quotations, new writing, allusions, and other means, students spread their threads out for concurrent and overlapping reading. These threads are then "cooled" either in a hypertext project where hyperlinks generate multiple threads interconnected or in a wiki where the texts remain forever open and expanded upon. Indeed, a wiki can serve this pedagogy better than a series of interlinked hypertexts because of how it leaves each hypertextual project always open for further changes and edits. In other words, as new associations develop, or as readers form associations with a given wiki writing done by another writer, the composition's nonlinearity grows. Each project in the course—either as stand-alone hypertexts or as wiki sections—can then be connected to the next, thus spawning an even larger nonlinear text comprised of all the writings performed in the class.

The image this kind of writing evokes is that of the multiple points of entry managed software promises but fails to deliver. That we live in a nonlinear culture of information is also an image writing instruction tends to shy away from as it supports the restricted thesis idea propagated by the McCrimmon legacy. Nonlinearity and restricted theses do not work in conjunction with one another; the choice for the thesis is a choice against nonlinearity. The compositional image of writing has thus been restricted. Because imagery is such a dominant theme in how composition studies imagines the technology-centered writer (and writings) popularized in present-day narratives regarding education, I want to turn to imagery itself in the final chapter so that I can note both its absence in the 1963 grand narrative and presence in other rhetorical moments.

# 7

## Imagery

"Image Comics Presents: 1963! A Bedazzling Brace of Barnstorming Bargains from the Bower of Brilliance!"
—Image Comics, Mystery Incorporated, Book One, 1963

An accepted trope regarding electronic writing is that writers must learn to work with images. We hear this trope in a number of places, notably in an emerging chorus of contemporary compositionists interested in visuality. "Complicating this scenario," Dean Rader remarks in a 2005 *College English* review essay, "is the realization that our beginning writing students seem to do more sophisticated interpretation with visual texts than written ones" (638). "Rhetoric has always been important in the composition classroom," Carolyn Handa writes in the introduction to Bedford St. Martin's sourcebook on visual rhetoric, "but we are *only now* beginning to understand how it might work as a device to help our students understand and create visually and verbally interwoven texts" (Handa 2, emphasis mine). "A few years ago," Marguerite Helmers and Charles Hill write in the Preface to their collection *Defining Visual Rhetorics,* "we noticed a major shift in the field of rhetoric, one in which an increasing amount of the discipline's attention was becoming focused on visual objects and the visual nature of the rhetorical process. The phrase visual rhetoric was being used more frequently in journal articles, in textbooks, and especially in conference presentations" (ix). The moment he read an airline in-flight emergency brochure comprised only of images, Bruce McComiskey notes in a 2004 *JAC* essay, he "became interested in the rhetorical functions of images; I became interested in 'visual rhetoric'" (187).

The "only now" emphasis largely implicit in Rader, Handa, Helmers, Hill, and McComiskey's observations reflects composition studies' only more recent interest regarding visuality's relationship to writing. Despite a long tradition of rhetorical *and* visual production, composition studies has only recently taken seriously the role visuality plays in meaning making and, in particular, electronic culture. "As we have more and more need to communicate across geographical, linguistic, and cultural boundaries," the editors of the 2004 textbook *Picturing Texts* reflect upon electronic writing, "the use of images will grown in importance" (8). Such use has, in fact, grown. Its growth, however, has been around longer than these writings I quote imply. "There remains much confusion," Diane George notes, "over what is meant by *visual communication, visual rhetoric,* or, more simply, *the visual* and where or whether it belongs in a composition course" (13). George traces the presence of visuality in pedagogy throughout the past sixty years and notes that this presence is often ignored in the recent enthusiasm for the visual. Agreeing with George, I also realize that this confusion is directly connected to the missed 1963 juxtapositions I have utilized to invent the rhetoric of cool. Within the structure of my project, I ask in response to these writings, why is composition studies "only now" interested in the visual?

I ask this question because many of the 1963 texts and writers I've focused on in the previous chapters conflate the border between the visual and writing in film (Anger and Smith), culture (Baraka), the computer screen (Nelson, Engelbart, and McLuhan), and even the written page (Burroughs). In these moments, visuality is either explicitly situated within electronic-based rhetorics, or it is implicitly shaped by electronic-based rhetorics. In addition to these figures and texts not being treated in the 1963 composition narrative, they are absent in the current narratives being constructed around visuality as well. There are no nods in these "only nows" to those who engaged with writing and visuality in the early 1960s.

And there were no nods to such writers in the early 1960s either. At the end of *Research in Written Composition*'s chapter "The State of Knowledge about Composition," for instance, the authors outline twenty-four areas of "unexplored territory" relevant to future disciplinary research. None deal with the visual. The absence of visuality in composition studies' rebirth narrative and its consequent delay in reaching our disciplinary vocabulary can be associated with a long-standing tradition in rhetoric and writing of favoring the word over the image, what Jacques Derrida terms *logocentrism.* As Derrida notes, our preference for the word "always assigned the origin of truth in general to the logos" *(Of Grammatology* 3). The connection between the logos and the word demands that "true" meaning derives from the printed text over the visual text. This connection has historical and pedagogical ramifications; it restricts interest in visuality as well as what the discipline is capable of visualizing. As Craig Stroupe writes, the time is long overdue for addressing the forgotten visual history intertwined with expression.

> The discipline needs to decide not only whether to embrace the teaching
> of visual and information design in addition to verbal production, which

some of the more marginalized elements of English Studies have already done, but more fundamentally, whether to confront its customary cultural attitudes toward visual discourses and their insinuation into verbal texts. (Stroupe 608)

More specifically, in the composition studies tradition, the absence of visuality can be understood as the inability to recognize the role of cool in composition in general, both its verbal and visual components. Most importantly, this absence signifies an ideological hesitation to allow imagery a place within composition studies, for most of the "only now" work done in "visual rhetoric" limits not only our understandings of visuality's relevance to composition studies history and new media but also, pedagogically, students' ability to produce their own visual-based writings in new media environments. In much of today's pedagogy, the preference is for writing about images, not with images. The preference is still for the word. Thus, we hear Rader using the word *interpretation* in his review essay of visually oriented textbooks and not the word *production*. Thus, we hear Handa—despite sporadic references to production in her introduction to the sourcebook—stress the idea of "critical thinking" repeatedly, a concept whose origins are in reading, not in producing texts. True writing can only come from reading images, these positions state, not from making images.

The "Seeing" and "Writing" components of Bedford St. Martin's two popular textbooks by that name, for instance, ask students to "see" images as texts and write about them, but never to write with images. As the editors introduce their book to prospective students, they write, "Given the fact that we're asking you to look closely at verbal and visual texts within and beyond this book, we also invite you to turn your attention to the content and design of the pages of the book. What choices have the editors and designers made in presenting the material in this way (McQuade and McQuade lv–lvi). Once that question is answered, however, it is unclear what students are to do with such information. Should they then design their own visual texts? How? Based on the choices they have discovered? Based on other rhetorical ideas? Which? For what reasons would they compose visually even if given the chance? Why isn't any instruction in this example of visual rhetorical pedagogy devoted to actual visual rhetorical production? Why is the visual something one admires but does not perform? These are questions I pose as a conclusion to my breakdown of the rhetoric of cool, for visuality is central to new media writing. Composers of new media texts, Anne Wysocki writes, "design texts that make as overtly visible as possible the values they embody" (15). No better place can this be seen than in cool that makes its meanings possible in a number of media outlets, imagery among them.

The visual, as I note early in this book, is included in my initial juxtaposition of 1963 that showcases Robert Farris Thompson observing visual writing practices in West African Yoruban culture as indicative of the idea of cool: "I recall an incident at Edunabon in the south of Oyo country in the winter of 1963–64, when a man regarded an ancient, polished blood-red carnelian bead and pronounced it 'cool' (tutu)" (*Flash of the Spirit* 43). The bead incident allows Farris Thompson to generalize to other Yoruban visual practices—sculpting, wood carving, and weaving—and conclude that in absence of alphabetic writing (print culture), Yorubans fashioned a visual language after the belief systems invested in the idea of cool (conciliation, appeasement, restoration, calmness). "The sense of certainty," he writes, "which character and àshe confer, is enriched by mystic coolness *(itutu)*, whose emblematic color is often blue or indigo or green" (*Flash of the Spirit* 12). Farris Thompson quotes a Yoruban who states that "coolness or gentleness of character is so important in our lives. Coolness is the correct way you represent yourself to a human being" (qtd. in *Flash of the Spirit* 13). Cool, in this visual discourse, is connected to representation, the ways individuals represent themselves and their thoughts to the outside world. Cool is not so much an emotional appeal (although it embodies that trait) but a visual one as well: "Coolness, then, is a part of character, and character objectifies proper custom. To the degree that we live generously and discreetly, exhibiting grace under pressure, our appearance and our acts gradually assume virtual royal power" (*Flash of the Spirit* 16). Farris Thompson's observation holds significance for a composition pedagogy increasingly interested in the visual. It speaks to the broad desire to express ideas outside of the restrictions of print. The cool, visual traditions of Yoruban culture generate concepts in ways print often cannot accommodate by itself ("appearance and acts" in one compositional gesture, for instance). Farris Thompson's work also teaches that print does not need to be the indigenous practice displaced by some other means. In other words, working with cool media (visual or not) should not be understood as the displacement of our fixation on print culture—a typical response whenever the visual is introduced into writing pedagogy ("does this mean students no longer need to be concerned with grammar?"). Cool has its origins in discourse already; it doesn't replace other concerns. The Yoruban example describes cool as a native practice outside of print, not as a displacement.

## Sketchpad

My intent is to generalize from Farris Thompson's work to other areas of visual rhetoric within 1963 and thus bring the rhetoric of cool to an expected conclusion's emphasis on visual rhetorical production. Farris Thompson's research signifies only one moment regarding visual writing that went unmentioned by composition scholars in 1963. The distance between the 1963 Los Angeles meeting of CCCC or temporal publications and West Africa cannot be minimized, but it also shouldn't be used to quantify this missed moment as a matter of cultural mis-recognition or unfair critique. In the choral tradition I have established as central to the rhetoric of cool, I am obligated to move chorally from Farris Thompson's studies to other visual moments situated in 1963 but not found in composition's paradigm shift (image motivating my choral moves). These moments connect those practices we typically associate as pertaining to literacy acquisition—as well as the ways literate individuals generate ideas—with imagery.

One notable moment I find is the invention of the personal, graphic manipulation program. Ivan Sutherland's 1963 invention of Sketchpad (and related doctoral dissertation *Sketchpad: A Man-Machine Graphical Communication System*) equated writing with visual expression. With Sketchpad, Sutherland outlined and demonstrated a computer program capable of manipulating user entered symbols (through a light pen) and then generating visual displays on TV-like monitors. Sketchpad's basic premise is identifiable today as the more contemporary commercial product Adobe Photoshop as well as its numerous clones (for images or for multimedia), tools that have become quotidian in the entertainment and advertising industries. Sketchpad is indicative of a 1963 growing interest in composing with images. "Sketchpad allowed a computer operator to use the computer to create sophisticated visual models on a display screen that resembled a television set. The visual patterns could be stored in the computer memory like any other data, and could be manipulated by the computer's processor" (Rheingold 90). Sutherland's purpose was to allow writers the ability to forge rhetorical gestures via the visual display in front of them. Sutherland recognized the importance of visuality in a world fascinated by film, television, and advertising, and he sought to locate related practices in the computer. By doing so, Sutherland tapped into the rhetorical power of visuality McLuhan described accordingly: "In visual representation of a person or an object, a single phase or moment or aspect is separated from the multitude of known and felt phases, moments and aspects of the person or object" (*Understanding Media* 291).

For McLuhan, visuality, and in particular, electronic visuality, opens up new types of senses and awareness that cannot be accounted for in alphabetic literacy. Because of its cool status (its ability to generate involvement at greater rates than print), electronic visuality has the potential to transform "fragmented and specialist extensions into a seamless Web of experience" (*Understanding Media* 292). In this sense, the question is not just of static image representation (like taking a picture or uploading an image to a Web site) but of imaging in general, of finding visual connections to work among and forge ideas out of. That process is material based (making images) and conceptual (imaging connections). It is a process that reflects Douglas Engelbart's image of connected, computerized writing, what Engelbart called "the symbol manipulator."

> This [symbol manipulator] could be a computer, with which individuals could communicate rapidly and easily, coupled to a three-dimensional color display within which extremely sophisticated images could be constructed, the computer being able to execute a wide variety of processes on parts or all of these images in automatic response to human direction. (14)

Sketchpad's usage of the visual was meant to push writers into a similar rhetorical experience. Sketchpad refigured the writing space from paper to the visual screen. Sutherland introduced his dissertation accordingly:

> The Sketchpad system makes it possible for a man and a computer to converse rapidly through the medium of line drawings. Heretofore, most interaction between men and computers has been slowed down by the need to reduce all communication to written statements that can be typed; in the past, we have been writing letters to rather than conferring with our computers. For many types of communication, such as describing the shape of a mechanical part of the connections of an electrical circuit, typed statements can prove cumbersome. The Sketchpad system, by eliminating typed statements (except for legends) in favor of line drawings, opens up a new area of man-machine communication. (Sutherland 1)

This extension of the senses Sketchpad generates is more profound today in its contemporary successors like Adobe Photoshop. Photoshop's ability to manipulate, copy, distort, fabricate, and erase visual displays at will ties into McLuhan's understanding of the visual as cool. Through these visual moves, writers extend a variety of ideas and feelings in ways print does not allow for; writers create new kinds of discursive worlds that go beyond the flatness of the page. Whereas Burroughs's cut-up was designed for text, Photoshop (via Sketchpad) puts the logic of cut and paste into visual production, a task that can make connections among images seem, in McLuhan's definition, "seamless." The point is repeated by Lev Manovich, who writes of Photoshop-like techniques in film and visuality, "[T]he problem is no longer how to generate convincing individual images but how to blend them together" (155). In other words, the problem for digital writing is how to write visually in a complex but seamless fashion.

By that, I don't mean to construct a binary between print and the visual (one creates seamless connections, one doesn't) but rather to note how Sketchpad began the process of demonstrating the rhetorical potential of the visual *to all writers* (and not just painters or artists). A writer is asked *to use* Sketchpad, not to analyze its merits or compositional potential. And Sketchpad is meant as a tool for all, not a select, talented few. An early Apple Macintosh promotional film for the Apple II called "Pencil Test" is indicative of this legacy. In the film, the pencil icon for drawing leaves its place in the drawing program, considers itself as a writing instrument by taking the place of a "real" pencil laying on the table, and eventually returns to the computer, the very computer we are to believe created this short film we are watching. In the spirit of Sketchpad, everyday writing with text transforms into everyday writing with images. The interaction between developing an idea and writing that idea now must include the visual, the film claims. "Sketchpad exemplified a new paradigm for interacting with computers," Lev Manovich writes. "By changing something on the screen, the operator changed something in the computer's memory. The real-time screen became interactive" (102). That interactivity, I claim, alters rhetorical expression dramatically, for Manovich's sense of "interaction" is not just pushing buttons or pulling down drop menus on an interface, as I remarked in the previous chapter. It is a reflection of a new dimension of cultural and rhetorical interactivity: connecting a variety of experiences and ideas at once visually, treating "Pencil Test" as a metaphor for an emerging digital practice.

No doubt such thinking regarding visuality and writing would be difficult to understand for those 1963 compositionists translating students into written variables or debating the effectiveness of sentence construction. "If the new grammar is to be brought to bear on composition," Francis Christensen begins his well-known essay in the 1963 October *College Composition and Communication,* "it must be brought to bear on the rhetoric of the sentence" (155). Christensen's concerns with a rhetoric of the sentence reflect the logocentrism Derrida critiques, but Christensen also draws attention to the literate emphasis on learning and meaning making as a print phenomenon despite technological influence already in existence. McLuhan notes, "Our Western values, built on the written word, have already been considerably affected by the electric media of telephone, radio, and TV. Perhaps that is the reason why many highly literate people in our time find it difficult to examine this question without getting into a moral panic" (*Understanding Media* 85). Whether or not Christensen would have entered a "moral panic" over a writing application like Sketchpad is not obvious. But one can assume that the definition of writing as purely text based and alphabetic would lead compositionists like Christensen to reject Sketchpad's premise that writing may be visual as well. How does one teach a rhetoric of the sentence for a compositional text that lacks a sentence or has images in addition to sentences? After all, we see such reactions even today.

Without displacing alphabetic writing entirely, Sketchpad serves the teaching of electronic writing by drawing attention to the additional importance imagery plays in digital communication. This last point is no doubt evident to those compositionists in the twenty-first century who have begun to make visual rhetoric a trope within their pedagogy. That trope, though, still seems to be neglecting the rhetorical issues Sketchpad poses for writing, that sense of "seamless" Web experience McLuhan describes. Mostly, imagery's role in electronic writing is currently reduced to rhetorical analysis and not production. When that is the case, as popular textbooks like *Seeing and Writing* or *Convergences* demonstrate, writing is still a print-directed concept. Students write *about* images, but not with images. Students "see" images but don't use them for generating new experiences. Students observe images but are not asked to find correlations between an image-based experience and their own.

Thus, we are still caught in a bind of print-based literacy assumptions regarding writing. "What will be the new configurations of mechanisms and of literacy," McLuhan concludes *The Gutenberg Galaxy*, "as these older forms of perception and judgment are interpenetrated by the new electric age?" (330). McLuhan's question is a direct challenge not only to the definition of writing as print based but to an entire vision of literacy acquisition. The difference in these two positions (print and electronic) is the continuing motif regarding how each relates to rhetorical production found outside of the classroom. To imagine or engage with a visual rhetoric, one must write as visual writers do outside of the classroom. For 1963 compositionists, that kind of imagination is hard to acquire. Braddock and colleagues, like my other principle composition figures, symbolize a classroom-only attitude, for they work exclusively with the categorization of factors that influence *student* writing and not just writing. A glimpse at their brief mentioning of technology is revealing in this regard for how it shapes a non-imagery-based teaching.

Students in the 1960s write in classrooms with pens and paper, and maybe with the time period's most prominent form of writing technology, typewriters. The typewriter, one would think, would be the most easily adopted technology for writing pedagogy because of its direct relationship to producing alphabetic literacy. However, even this emerging image of writing—writing produced by new technology—was difficult to deal with for the image it evoked of writing. McLuhan recognized this difficulty when he cast doubt on how readily teachers would accept the move toward teaching with typewriters. "In 1882, ads proclaimed that the typewriter could be used as an aid in learning to read, write, spell, and punctuate. Now, eighty years later, the typewriter is used only in experimental classrooms" (*Understanding Media* 227). In terms of composition, McLuhan's critique sounds accurate. This supposedly novel way of writing (via the machine) was still framed by many educators as experimental, and thus, it was not seriously considered as an already conventional practice. The typewriter's "experimental" nature garners a brief mention in *Research in Written Composition,* but not for its ability to change how individuals write or how the very image of writing might be altered by this new device. Instead, in *Research in Written Composition,* the typewriter is still classified as a device devoted to print, and even more so, to typed student essays—an understandable point given that *Research in Written Composition*'s focus is student writing. But even with this point anticipated, Braddock and colleagues convey a limited understanding of technology and writing. The typewriter's influence on student writing, the authors argue, needs to be studied more before the typewriter is used pedagogically on a larger scale (58). The typewriter, in other words, is still too experimental. That the typewriter may already be in use outside of the classroom, that its image as a writing tool may already be in the public imaginary, that almost seventy years earlier—to accept McLuhan's point—advocates called for its inclusion in pedagogy, none of these points are mentioned or considered.

Studying the typewriter more seems an irrelevant point for the kinds of writing 1960s business culture generates using typewriters, but it also shows a lack of recognition of the ways media shapes thought in anticipated and unanticipated ways. One place such recognition surfaced was in 1960s avant-garde practices. Alan Kaprow, for example, found the typewriter to be indicative of visuality and visual-based expression. In his 1963 Happening *Words,* an interactive installation featuring typewritten and handwritten banners to be read or written on, Kaprow turned this print-oriented device into a tool for generating a visual rhetoric.

> Overhead are crudely-lettered signs urging the visitors to roll the rolls, to tear off more word strips from stacks nailed to a center-post, and to staple them over the ones already there; in addition, they are exhorted to play the Victorolas and listen to the records I had made, of talk, lectures, shouts, advertisements, ramblings of nonsense, etc.—either singly or all together. ("Words: An Environment" 446)

One selection in Kaprow's performance read: "Try a record, try a poem. Listen to the word on the Victorolas. Words. Words. Words!" Words, indeed. Words as text and words as image, both occupying the same compositional space. Why call for further study, then, when the typewriter's application was already in circulation in nonclassroom rhetorical moments that posed its usage in complex ways? As Fredric Kittler has more recently demonstrated in *Gramophone, Film, Typewriter,* the tradition of the typewriter cannot easily be disconnected from the overall history of modern writing (and consequently, new media) even if it is not taken seriously by writing pedagogy. "Writing as keystrokes, spacing, and the automatics of discrete block letters bypassed a whole system of education," Kittler notes (193). Kaprow's work marks one effort to teach an emerging model of education (at least in the realm of the plastic arts), a technology-based composition practice. Braddock and colleagues' demand for "further study" of typewriting before approving its usage belongs within the tradition of "bypassing" that Kittler highlights; it is a failure to recognize that outside of the classroom, typewriters were being used extensively.[1]

Moreover, the nonalphabetic usage of typewriters in installations like Kaprow's (or McLuhan's example of poet Charles Olson and his influence on the Visual Poets) shows writing taking place visually as well as typographically. "The typewriter," McLuhan writes, "fuses composition and publication, causing an entirely new attitude to the written and printed word" (*Understanding Media* 228). With this comment, McLuhan makes the broad intellectual jump Braddock and colleagues do not; he connects the typewriter to an even newer invention, the computer. The ability to produce new knowledge via the mechanics of the typewriter—be it typographic or visual—leads to the kinds of visual knowledge computing can allow for via its manipulation of programmed language into alternative kinds of representations. Without this kind of understanding, Sketchpad cannot be invented, and current interest in visual rhetoric cannot develop.

> Especially with the computer, the work effort is applied at the "programming" level, and such effort is one of information and knowledge. In the decision-making and "make happen" aspect of the work operation, the telephone and other such speed-ups of information have ended the divisions of delegated authority in favor of the "authority of knowledge." (*Understanding Media* 232)

While Braddock and colleagues are waiting for "further study" that will justify a pedagogy of typing, McLuhan is already looking ahead to the typewriter's successor. As much as typing can allow writers to visualize their work through inventive typographic display or alternative poetic style (McLuhan quotes e. e. cummings extensively), the computer display (though not yet a classroom tool in the early 1960s) will lead to a new kind of visualization of composition. The computer display, McLuhan contends, allows writers to become involved in a visual composing process in ways movable type (which is performed elsewhere, and not by the writer) did not allow. Visuality, McLuhan notes, extends writers' ability to generate knowledge because of how it extends perception. This perception may be reduced to the page or screen (what something physically looks like), but it is also an expansion of an overall ability to understand and connect. My argument throughout this book has been concerned with that latter point. The connections, commutations, and juxtapositions the rhetoric of cool teaches are meant to produce a type of new media writing while also altering a perception of what composition entails.

Braddock and colleagues' quick rejection of new media tools (in this case, the typewriter) is illuminating, for outright rejection of the new without regard to popular usage demonstrates a lack of perception, or as McLuhan would say, a lack of in-depth involvement. Composition cannot perceive new media's role in writing if the field is not involved in new media innovations. Hence, this rejection has also become a dominant theme in contemporary composition pedagogy. Early rejection of word processing, later dismissal of hypertext, and, even now, the shrugging off of widely popular media like Weblogs or social software is indicative of the attitudes Braddock and colleagues proliferate in their study regarding typewriters (and as I noted earlier, film). The *Research in Written Composition* claim is that the tool is either not applicable or it must be studied in depth empirically before it can be evaluated for pedagogical usage. Its usage must be controlled for its value to be determined. Meanwhile, generations grow up using these tools daily, generations learn their application without controlled study, and, in turn, generations grow up internalizing new kinds of thought processes (the visual functioning by a different logic than the typographic) that affect communicative practices outside of a given classroom situation.[2] The mass proliferation of Weblogs and related applications reflects this point. While Weblogs (as of 2006) are still fairly new and novel, the application's quick and widespread acceptance for composing purposes (food blogs, academic blogs, political blogs, music blogs, personal blogs) has resulted from how the Web alters recognizable writing spaces, how it mixes print literacy with visual literacy. The millions of new writers discovering how to interlink (hyperlinks), visualize (posting of images found or created), and reimagine the writing space (on Blogger, WordPress, or MySpace) are perceiving writing spaces as total in-depth involvement. Each site, as Webloggers often show through quotes, comments, daily posts, and links, is involved with every other writing experience other blogs generate. Popular sites like BoingBoing, Metafilter, and Waxy[3] represent the Web's contents as an always interlinked network of ideas. These sites list (following literacy's tradition of listing) selections from and links to other eclectic, personal, and serious Web sites and, in turn, revisualize the writing space. As if trying out the Web (a picture here, a phrase there), the generic Weblog experience, at times, revisualizes Kaprow's *Words:* "Try a record, try a poem. Listen to the word on the Victorolas. Words. Words. Words!" What television was for McLuhan—"With TV, the viewer is the screen"—the Weblog or social software variant is partly for current electronic discourse (*Understanding Media* 272). And this has all occurred without "further study."

## Television

As McLuhan reminds any investigation into 1963 and composing, television dominated the post-World War II communicative revolution. Regarding technology, and aside from their dismissal of typewriters, the closest Braddock and colleagues come to the visual and the recognition that rhetoric takes place outside of the classroom is their brief mention of television. Without any acknowledgment of theoretical or practical work done regarding television (such as McLuhan's work or the ETV nationwide television systems in place in many universities and colleges),[4] they offer a negative assessment of its value to writing pedagogy: "Despite the fact that much money has been granted by foundations for experiments in the use of television as an instructional aid, little of the research, as published, seems convincing, at least where instruction in written composition is concerned" (47). Despite the skepticism of Braddock, Lloyd-Jones, and Schoer, education had turned to technology's visual component somewhat, and that includes television. In 1962, Walter Ong notes in a republished essay from *College English* that

> [t]elevision is a more feasible means of education than radio. This is not because it can use visual aid devices (figures written on a blackboard on television cannot be seen by any viewer unless the camera is turned on them—they lack the permanent availability of figures on a classroom blackboard). It is because television better implements personal rapport between instructor and student. ("Wired for Sound" 226)

Ong's support for television is actualized in the popularity of ETV (closed-circuit education television) and in 1963 journals like *American School and University,* which are full of advertisements for television and other related media equipment. One would assume that such equipment would be used in various classrooms, including those where composition was taught. These ads include Kodak Pageant Film projectors, Kodak sound recording tapes, the Ampex E-65 tape recorder, 3M tapes, Astatic's Astatiphone headphones, Sony video recorders, and Magnavox TVs. In fact, one advertisement in the *American School and University*'s March 1964 issue asks: "Will the Sony Videocorder Replace Teachers?" "Of course not," the ad comforts.

> Nothing will every replace the teacher. But the new Sony Videocorder will go a long way toward alleviating the shortage of good teachers, of multiplying the efficiency of the school teaching staff and making the tax dollar go a lot further in this era of increasing costs.

Nothing might replace the teacher, but evidence demonstrates some degree of interest in applying visual-oriented technology to pedagogical usage, and, in particular, to *using* visual-based tools. What exactly teachers were doing with Sony video recorders or Magnavox TVs is not clear. Yet someone was using them; teachers were being solicited to purchase these devices. Increasing attention to the visual in the early 1960s signifies an attempt to split with the typographic centrism central to much of composition's pedagogical practice. There are more significant consequences of typographic centrism than not teaching students how to use cameras or work with television. Like other aspects of cool, those consequences are ideological as well as practical. The decision to study student writers and not *writers* because of such centrism led Braddock and colleagues (and consequently a significant body within composition studies) to not include visuality as part of future work until visual culture became too dominating a force to ignore—as evidenced by the Handa collection. The preponderance of imagery on the Web, on television, in film, in games, on video, and elsewhere is not as much a recent phenomenon as the phrase "visual culture" might lead us to believe. Even though Sketchpad would not have been a common item or known item to composition teachers still concerned with handwritten essays, its emergence in 1963 is a reflection (not a cause) of increasing interest in visuality and expression. Visual writing already had been in circulation in areas composition studies should have noticed and expressed interest in thinking about in terms of writing and writing instruction. In the age of new media, pedagogy cannot remain insular. It must be aware of all media in order to better understand the dynamics of rhetoric within digital culture. Often, such media are objects we encounter daily, like typewriters in the 1960s or Web sites and Weblogs in the twenty-first century. To make my point more explicit, I turn from more obvious, general examples like television to a specific visual example in popular circulation, the record album cover. The record cover identifies the gap between 1963 writing instruction and 1963 writing with images.

## Blue Note Records

One place I can develop my initial ideas regarding visual rhetoric (and how writers compose with images) in 1963 is Blue Note Records' influential covers from that year. Even if these examples are not digital texts, they are, as records, intertwined in the emerging electronic apparatus of the 1960s that fused technological innovations with sound recording. "The brief and compressed history of the phonograph," McLuhan comments, "includes all phases of the written, the printed and the mechanized word" (*Understanding Media* 243). By looking at the rhetoric of record covers, I'm trying to expand further the notion of what constitutes writing in the popular sphere. As I have shown, many of the models digital culture draws upon come from nondigital sources and media (film, literature, urban affairs, cultural critique, etc.), especially those familiar to popular spheres of influence. Music, of all forms of composition, is a popularly distributed form of writing. Record covers as well are popular forms of writing, and they circulate in popular vocabularies in complex ways. My interest in studying record covers is similar to what textbook author Robert Atwan instructs writing students to think about when examining visual texts: "In visual texts, composition is often a matter of spatial relations: How has the artist, designer, film director, or photographer first framed a space and then arranged the various elements inside it? How are images grouped? How is your eye drawn to particular features? What do you tend to notice first?" (liii). Blue Note, one of the most prolific producers of jazz in the postwar period, gives me a place to interlink Atwan's questions into a specific way writers can utilize imagery in the rhetoric of cool. Unlike Atwan's textbook *Convergences,* however, which is too fixated on observing images only, I turn to Blue Note to learn how *to teach* its visual methods for electronic writing and not only *to understand* how the images rhetorically function.

Blue Note produced a number of record covers in 1963 distinct in their style: Freddie Roach's *Mo' Greens Please,* Donald Byrd's *A New Perspective,* Jackie McLean's *One Step Beyond,* Hank Mobley's *No Room For Squares,* Blue Mitchell's *Step Lightly,* and Horace Silver's *Silver's Serenade.* Marked by geometric shapes and patterns, tilted angles and sharp recolorations and shadings, these record covers, all designed by Reid Miles, revealed a new aesthetic for jazz and marketing, what Felix Cromey calls "an abstract design hinting at innovations, cool strides for cool notes, the symbolic implications of typeface and tones" (Marsh, Cromey, and Callingham 7). In the tradition of cool rhetorical production (as seen in Beat writings and underground film, for instance), Miles's methods juxtaposed low financial budgets with innovations on previous forms. Speaking about Blue Note's reaction to his work, Miles noted, "Fifty bucks an album . . . they loved it, thought it was modern, they thought it went with the music . . . one or two colours to work with at that time and some outrageous graphics!" (qtd. in Marsh, Cromey, Callingham 72). Blue Note's cover designs commutated the symbols of both urban and pop culture into a cool aesthetic. In addition to the covers' usage of abstract shapes and angles (a marker of pop art influence[5]), Reid's designs often troped the themes of 1950s and 1960s cool: sexy women, cars, and aloof posing. Lou Donaldson's *Good Gracious* comically features Donaldson ogling a passing woman. Herbie Hancock's *Inventions and Dimensions* isolates the pianist's image in the middle of a fairly empty commercial district; his cool look is the recognizable loner in the Baraka sense of political, racial, and economic detachment. Hank Mobley's *No Room for Squares* spotlights Mobley demonstrating the cool look. Wearing dark sunglasses and positioned in an indifferent stance, Mobley inhales nonchalantly on a cigarette, its long ash about to fall. His posture repeats the album's title: There is no room for squares in this cool scene. The circle outline of a trumpet frames Mobley's stance so that the identity of the figure represented and the musical instrument merge. The medium, in this case, distinctly is the message. Another example of Reid's work, Donald Byrd's *A New Perspective,* foregrounds the image of an automobile headlight directing immediate attention; the rest of the vehicle drifts back into the distance, where Byrd stands cross-armed, cool, removed from everything but his car.[6] Similar to the Mobley design, Byrd's identity is formed by the automobile, the urban-ideal media form[7] where utility gives way to aesthetic appeal. The design suggests that driving a car poses less importance than becoming a car; technology and personality, user and design, all juxtapose into one.

These covers construct a variation of what we now often refer to as visual arguments, and they represent what we have come to call visual rhetoric. The visual displays produced by consumer products, of course, are highly contested for how such designs encourage spending rather than disseminate a given idea. Even Thomas Frank's poignant description of 1960s co-optations of youth values is meant to reveal how consumerist ideology eventually maintains a dominant force on visual communication. It's a point well taken like any other aspect of cool, but one that must be aligned with the overall potential visual writing has for teaching writings *other* than advertising. Blue Note, like other early 1960s producers of consumer goods, uses specific Afrocentric or cool-aesthetic imagery to appeal to record buyers, much in the way, Mina Hamilton and Malcolm Brookes discuss in a 1963 essay, that record packaging is meant to do. "The package must carry some point-of-sale message to inform the prospective purchaser, or to attract him so that he becomes a prospective purchaser" (78). When that place of attraction taps into specific attitudes, as Frank indicates regarding cool and consumer culture, writing (as record packaging) shapes the individual's perception of selfhood (much in the way film or an essay creates similar experiences). Those ads that succeeded in the 1960s, Frank writes, were those that shaped a sense of selfhood. "The basic task of advertising, it seemed in the 1960s, was not to encourage conformity but a never-ending rebellion against whatever it is that everyone else is doing, a forced and exaggerated individualism" (Frank 90). Record covers, of course, are ads as much as they are displays of what a purchaser will discover within the product, and possibly within herself. But it is that question of selfhood that is most important to writing with images. Blue Note shapes selfhood; in particular, its images expand temporal interest in equality, African-American identity, and economics—all complex areas of study that overlap in intriguing ways in the 1960s as well as today. Blue Note Records, then, marks a notable place for me to consider how the label teaches a rhetoric of imagery as well as how such a rhetoric shapes our understandings of writers and writing.

An important writing lesson I find in Blue Note involves the discovery of another method for displaying iconic imagery for rhetorical purposes. Blue Note's visual displays tend to deal with the very explicit, temporal issue of civil rights and black power. Many of the artists recording with Blue Note in the 1960s, like Horace Silver, Herbie Hancock, and Art Blakey's Jazz Messengers, carried these visual arguments into their music, which eventually became known as soul jazz. Soul jazz (or hard bop as it is also called) emphasized the self-proclaimed return to black cultural production. Paralleling the growing influence of the early 1960s civil rights movement, soul jazz highlighted black culture's promise and positive social constructions, even if the iconic markers it chose often bordered on the stereotypical. For example, Freddie Roach's *Mo' Greens Please* record cover features Green ordering soul food, a prominent iconic display of African-American eating habits. Covers like Roach's used iconic display to emphasize black pride and power, stressing the African-American right to choose what to eat as opposed to what white-dominated advertising often tells its audiences to eat through targeted commercials or print ads.

The visual, then, was being used commercially to discuss and respond to difficult subject matter (race relations). Teaching students in 1963 to write about civil rights would seem an obvious pedagogical move for a discipline concerned with treating writing as a "serious intellectual activity that, like all human behavior, has social and ethical consequences," as Kitzhaber writes in his 1963 *College Composition and Communication* essay "4C, Freshman English, and the Future" (134). No better example of social and ethical issues could be found in 1963 than Martin Luther King's 1963 "Letter From Birmingham Jail." As I note in chapter 4, King's work has since become a canonical essay in many contemporary first-year rhetoric readers. Both King's essay and Blue Note's covers treat race as a topic of discussion; King does so through the essay, and Blue Note does so visually. The overlap of the two might allow a reborn discipline to think further about the possibilities of both, where each might fit in a newly created composition curriculum, where one might juxtapose with the other. Yet nowhere in a textbook like James McCrimmon's *Writing with a Purpose* do we find writing instruction either promoting visuality to deal with these issues or, at the very least, touching upon the issues that record covers like *Mo' Greens Please* do, or that King's essay fittingly describes.

I make this distinction because the pedagogical decision to not teach students how to work with imagery reflects not only an anti-visual ideological position but also a desire to use print in order to de-emphasize the existence of nonconventional or disruptive subject matter *along with* perceived nonconventional forms of writing (like images). Much in the way that McLuhan's collagist/juxtaposition approach employs a cool rhetoric in order to disrupt the scholarly essay through the fairly nonconventional tactic of collage, Blue Note confronts 1960s conventional attitude toward race through a cool application of images. We see this approach as well on the cover of Dexter Gordon's 1963 *One Flight Up*. Gordon, nicely dressed in a dapper suit, stands in front of a dilapidated, tenement housing project. As an African-American celebrity in the limited-reaching, jazz world, Gordon, the image seems to argue, is only "one step up" from the low-income status most African-Americans living in the inner city experience in the early 1960s. Expressing this point as image and not as text, Blue Note disrupts an accepted manner of discourse in order to, at the very least, begin to form an argument regarding race, economic success, and social status. Who can ascend any kind of flight, this cover seems to argue, when social issues prevent racial success?

For me, or anyone else, to come to that reading (or another), of course, I must interact with the imagery in a way McLuhan defines as cool; I must juxtapose the iconic markers the image displays, and I must create a reading based on association. I cannot read the argument from a series of observations or linear supports in order to understand the cover. And neither, it seems, could 1963 students learning writing from McCrimmon. Instead of confronting and working with complex issues like civil rights (which speak to the very nature of argumentation) through iconography and association, in *Writing with a Purpose*, students learn argumentation from the non-cool method of syllogistic reasoning (a method still dominant in contemporary textbooks). McCrimmon presents the syllogism as a simple and safe exercise in analysis whose linear reasoning keeps subjects under control in terms of comprehension and clearness. Consider the iconic display on *Mo' Greens Please*'s cover, which juxtaposes eating habits with race. Then consider McCrimmon's teaching of argumentative reasoning as a print-based logic.

> She cannot love me and tell lies about me.
> She does tell lies about me.
> She cannot love me.
>
> (McCrimmon 333)

Useful for teaching major and minor premises, McCrimmon's example of the syllogism nevertheless represents a method of writing instruction insistent on leaving difficult issues outside of student writing. In place of civil rights, we find school love. Instead of complexity, we find logical, ordered reasoning ("if she lies, she obviously doesn't love me!"). When McCrimmon does delve into "controversial" topics, such as his example of an argumentative debate entitled "Should Communism Be Studied in Our Schools," his conclusion is that both sides of the debate have done a fair job presenting their case, but both could use more work. In other words, no side wins; no one feels threatened; no beliefs are challenged. "Logic," interpreted as coherence, reins in this kind of pedagogy. Students, the pedagogy calls out to the writers studying this method, always make yourselves logical. "To be reliable, a syllogism must be both true and valid—that is, the information provided in the premises must accord with the facts, and the conclusion must necessarily follow from the premises" (McCrimmon 329). It's a reasonable reflection on how syllogisms work. Yet when questions of "fact" are disputable—such as a government clinging to the validity of segregation—and when conclusions don't always flow from given premises ("all men are created equal" but what to make of segregation? If all "men" are equal, why is Dexter Gordon still in the projects?), how do writers compensate? To read or to write the Blue Note record cover is not to encounter a fact or a reliable conclusion or a logical response to tense social conditions. The Blue Note rhetoric is not a replication of traditional syllogistic argumentation. Its mix of iconic display and juxtaposition propose a more complex construction of ideas. Is *Mo' Greens Please* actually a plea for African-American empowerment as I initially suggested? Or does it comment on how stereotypical African-American habits (like eating soul food) are picked up uncritically by African-American culture itself? Or can both arguments be read off of the cover? Or is the argument something else entirely?

It is the nature of ambiguity that challenges the conventional notion of argumentation demonstrated in a book like McCrimmon's. Students asked to engage with social and cultural issues should encounter such topics not from the point of certainty but from the position of ambiguity, ambiguity regarding what the issues concern as well as how to engage with such issues if at all. Social conflict is a site of ambiguous meaning; issues must be recognized for their complex histories, makeups, and effects, not for how one premise may be followed by a next in reliable order. By writing with photographs and other images, the Blue Note example pushes writing instruction to locate practices that utilize imagery for such tasks. McLuhan writes, "The logic of the photograph is neither verbal or syntactical, a condition which renders literary culture quite helpless to cope with the photograph" (*Understanding Media* 177). We can say the same about record covers and why the "literate" method of instruction (syllogistic reasoning) does not acknowledge their visual displays.

## A Pedagogy of the Image

What I find in Blue Note record covers is a pedagogy of the image foreign to even those fleeting moments in composition's rebirth that did devote some attention to the visual. In the December 1963 *College Composition and Communication* Staffroom Interchange section, Charlotte Winzeler writes in her brief essay "The Visual Written Image" about her usage of the visual to teach writing. Winzeler describes using an overhead projector in order to "correct" grammar mistakes students typically make. The presentation is meant to teach students what not to do in their own work. Winzeler's short essay stands for a larger trend within composition pedagogy that situates new media only in terms of print culture or the reproduction of existing practices. Like McCrimmon's pedagogy of the syllogism, Winzeler understands the usefulness of visuality in the classroom through the concepts of correctness and simple language structure. What she cannot imagine is the conflicted world visualized in McLuhan's collagist galaxy or Blue Note's imagery, for neither of these options accommodate the print directive for clear and coherent prose. Notice Winzeler describing how she teaches with the overhead: "A grammatical problem, as whether to separate clauses by semicolons or commas, becomes much simpler when I place a red overlay on the independent clauses and a green overlay on the dependent clauses" (Winzeler 265). Even in 1963, the overhead is not the most elaborate form of technology one could employ for writing instruction; yet any application of technology introduced into the classroom should make significant strides toward achieving what may be done differently than if the technology was never used at all. An overhead projector is not needed to demonstrate faulty usage. One could teach the same principles without it. Winzeler's overhead projection of grammar errors is symptomatic of McLuhan's frustration over trying to explain the visual electronic world to those still devoted to a print only world. "A few decades hence it will be easy to describe the revolution in human perception and motivation that resulted from beholding the new mosaic mesh of the TV image. Today it is futile to discuss it at all" (*Gutenberg* 323). Today, forty years after Winzeler, it can feel just as futile to push the visual in a field that still obsesses not over printed words as much as it does over print logic. In a typical contemporary classroom, Power Point's slide show of bullet points and static clipart replaces Winzeler's overhead projector because it is the technology that most closely duplicates print logic.[8] Those other logics of visual construction—advertising examples, comic strips, film stills, and Web page displays, which many contemporary textbooks reprint for students, also become places to maintain an already prescribed way of thinking. Textbooks don't ask students to write comic strips, for instance, only to point out the faulty logic or correct reasoning one may embody; in place of identifying incorrect clauses, students are now asked to identify incorrect representations. Even if we are not using overhead transparencies to reveal student error, we are still teaching in manners similar to Winzeler's approach.

The current manifestation of Winzeler's work is the pedagogical directive in many image-oriented textbooks that ask students to decode an image's meaning or analyze its overall rhetorical effect. This kind of exercise offers little more than Winzeler's overhead projector demonstration does; students identify errors in visual logic, note how images and typeface work, respond to faulty visual representations of race, gender, or class, and then offer detailed explanations of these processes in essay form. "What is more effective," Donald and Christine McQuade ask students regarding a Sequoia Citrus Association advertisement, "the image or the language—in ads like these? Choose one such advertisement or commercial—whether the product is an orange, an automobile, or a sneaker—and write an essay in which you explain why you think the ad or commercial does or does not 'work'" (17). "Write an essay" is the prescriptive. Find the errors in the image you are examining (why the ad does or does not work). Construct your response within the logic of print (the essay). One might wonder the purpose of reading an advertisement at all. Why don't these authors ask students to write their own set of images? Could McQuade and McQuade imagine media-oriented prompts like, for example, compose with a series of iconic gestures the way the citrus ad does; critique the ad through your own ad; complicate the ad's pro-citrus message by juxtaposing new images which challenge the ad's stance; further the ad's stance with a new series of ads that promote the same message; or use the ad's logic of juxtaposition to create your own series of ads? None of these assignments are offered, of course, because the logic of McQuade and McQuade's *Seeing and Writing,* despite all its glossy imagery and heavy promotion by its publisher, is still print directed; it is still McCrimmon oriented in its focus.

To compose the Blue Note way, writers assemble iconic imagery into a space like a Web site (though a Photoshop composite, Flash site, or even animated gif would suffice) in order to construct an argument, present a position, express an idea, or perform any other rhetorical act. The iconic, the juxtaposed moment, the cultural signifier are items writers use (among others) to visualize their position. In place of the *Seeing and Writing* assignment, one kind of visual assignment might be to ask students to compose an autobiographical statement only with visual icons. Much in the spirit of *Mo' Greens Please* or any of the other Blue Note covers, the assignment asks writers to contextualize personal positions with cultural issues. Updated for the Web, it would be demonstrated over a series of interlinked Web pages with minimal text (or text that is not narrative but additive to the imagery). Chosen imagery can come from one's area of study, interests, cultural identification, fears, desires, and so forth. Another assignment I suggest is to turn the focus to advertising (a popular trope in texts like *Seeing and Writing*) and ask students to study a particular advertising campaign, like the Absolut Vodka ads whose rhetoric involves the juxtaposition of iconic moments into the repetitive (and appropriated) image of a bottle. These juxtapositions work with familiar icons from popular culture, literature, history, and elsewhere. Instead of analyzing these ads, students use them as models in order to construct a series of iconic self-portraits, advertisements for themselves. What Absolute does with the bottle (how it both appropriates and commutates popular imagery and references), the assignment asks, do with another shape or figure.[9] The challenge of these kinds of visual assignments I contrast with textbook offerings is to invent ways to compose with images, whether to follow the Sketchpad legacy and use a graphic manipulation program or to simply allow for likely and unlikely juxtapositions to motivate the project.

## The Cool Writer

The bias I draw attention to throughout this chapter extends beyond working with images; it also shapes composition studies' *image* of the writer. When I began this book, I commented on how the courses I have taught entitled Writing about Cool often generate questions from colleagues regarding whether I or the students I work with consider ourselves "cool." These are questions of image, of how we imagine ourselves in writing instruction and how we imagine the individuals we work with as a part of or not a part of digital culture. Even in Alan Liu's lengthy breakdown of electronic culture, the networked society, and what he terms *knowledge work,* the narrative eventually settles on some variation of the troped question of cool, and thus the troped image of cool, which only reflects personality: "I work here, but I'm cool" (*Laws of Cool* 299). Liu writes, "This is why 'cool!' exclaimed about any new toy, dress, high-tech gadget, or Web page always hovers ambiguously between the subjective and objective ('I'm cool/it's cool'). 'Cool!' is the song of a subject robbed of any voice except that of the technological subject" (299–300). Liu's mistake, like composition studies' general error in reducing technology to only the tools of technology, is in ignoring a rich rhetorical tradition associated with cool and digital culture that does not depend on personality. Liu's own vision of technology robs it of the rhetorical possibilities I have drawn attention to in this book and reduces technology and rhetoric to mere catch phrases and latest gadgets. No wonder Liu is overtly fascinated with the declaration "it's cool." His own ability to *imagine* cool is restricted to the popular trope. If the rhetoric of cool succeeds in only producing this kind of image of the new media-oriented writer, the so-called "cool figure," then the project of cool as writing has terribly failed. It has failed because it has maintained a specific image's status quo in our disciplinary vocabulary. It has failed for continuing the dead-end circulation of a trope with limited to little meaning outside of popularity.

When the popular meaning of the word is stressed over the various meanings I have brought together in this book, we foreground the non-digital. When we do that, we find it increasingly difficult to visualize a type of writing or writing situation different from what we currently know and accept as the status quo. The status quo is itself an imagined state. How could the 1963 compositionist imagine the writer any differently than she did, a critique of my own critique in this book might ask? What about the specific apparatus 1963 compositionists worked within? How was that apparatus ideologically constructed? How could she have seen what you, in the twenty-first century and in a different type of apparatus, now see? Indeed, how could she? The images of writing and writers circulating in that time period prevented any kind of image not imagined in the status quo from being entered into the disciplinary discussions taking place. The fault is not with the individual instructor or theorist I draw attention to periodically. The fault is in the ways the discipline itself—as a whole—imagines writing and writers. If the classroom writer, like the cliché cool figure, is the only kind of writer we imagine, then our perception of writing will remain narrow in scope. in 1963 we miss out on cool. Today we miss out on something else. The fault is large scale and ideological, not personal.

While I hope that the complexities cool poses as a rhetoric of electronic writing have made an impact by this point of the book, I also know that by retaining an image of writers who somehow work and live separate from digital culture, composition studies resists the idea of a cool writer being someone outside of personality or status, and it eventually preserves the image of the student as writer as only student writer. In the age of new media, this kind of classification no longer maintains relevance. In his textbook *Internet Invention*, Gregory Ulmer contextualizes the cool writer as a participant in electracy. "'Cool' is a practice of impersonation that accords with the becoming-image that is the emerging subject of electrate people" (309). To be electrate, that is, to compose electronically through the various rhetorical strategies I have described in the preceding chapters, is to be cool. But this version of cool differs drastically from the throwaway term we have culturally grown comfortable using, a comfort expressed in even the most accepted efforts to move into unfamiliar ground, like Gerald Graff's limited vision of "hidden intellectualism." "What is most great criticism, after all," Graff asks, "but an elaborated way of saying in effect, 'It sucks' or 'It's cool?'" (Graff 35). At some point, we must begin the process of imagining intellectualism (of which pedagogy is a part of) to be more than it sucks or it's cool. Cool writing signifies more than sucking or being good; it stands for an electronic rhetoric.

This is a form of coolness that differs from that associated with figures like James Dean or Marlon Brando. In rhetoric, cool does not merely reflect the brooding, male figure; the marginal, African-American; the hipster; the rebel; or any other cliché. The cool writer encompasses what Burroughs calls a "media being," an individual who mixes and is mixed, who composes with media by commutating, appropriating, visualizing, and chorally structuring knowledge. "The basic law of association and juxtaposition," Burroughs writes, "the basic law of association and conditioning is known to college students even in America: Any object, feeling, odor, word, image in juxtaposition with any other object feeling, odor, word, or image will be associated with it" (*Nova Express* 85). The cool writer understands how media shapes her view of the world and her ability to communicate within that world. The composition program, in general, does not yet understand that fact. Even as it hypes media as something to be studied (as its current crop of popular textbooks do), composition studies still does not envision the media shaped writer. It has refused to give up its grasp on the print shaped writer, an image cherished in our profession for so long. Where is the writing student whose juxtapositions, appropriations, commutations, nonlinear thoughts, choral moves, and visual displays mark a significant body of writing production taught and encouraged? Where is the curriculum whose outcomes speak to these rhetorical gestures? Where is the discussion—beyond the fixation on assessing (and, one assumes, controlling)—of this type of digital rhetoric? These are not questions of accusation but genuine inquiries for a field that still struggles to see relevance in such thinking. These are genuine questions for a field still fixated on the topos of writing as controlled experience, on the topos of composition as a single identity, a single locale, for writing. These are questions that remind us of Diane Davis's sharp critique of writing instruction.

> It follows that there is a precious little bit of writing going in comp classes today, where students are commanded to "know" their audience and their (lone) purpose, where they are rewarded for grounding their inscriptions in "common places" (the same), for pretending to have mastered something, and for perpetuating the myths of community and identity via the strategies of clarity and linear presentations. (238–39)

These are genuine inquiries I pose throughout this book because the story I am telling challenges such myths but still asks if our research and pedagogies will respond to such challenges and consequently change in this age of new media.

One reason many compositionists are not convinced that such questions are relevant is because composition studies does not fully recognize the image of the media being, or even the influence of media on composition practices. In *Themes, Theories, and Therapy*, Kitzhaber asks, "Suppose that after a course in English composition the student does *not* write better than he did at the beginning. What then?" Kitzhaber proceeds to offer a number of reasons why a student hasn't improved, among them many we might find familiar today:

> It may be that his English teacher's efforts to instill habits of correctness and coherence and precision of statement have been nullified by counterinfluences in other courses where teachers tolerate sloppy writing and say that "it's only the ideas that count." The student's friends may exert the same kind of counterinfluence; so may newspapers, radio, television, magazines. (5–6)

This brief excerpt goes a long way toward explaining why composition studies cannot imagine the cool writer as a media being or composition itself as a media being (a media-based body of ideas and practices). Whether it is his preference of form over content (his rejection of the claim that "it's only the ideas that count") or his dismissal of the media's role in shaping writing (newspapers, radio, television, magazines), Kitzhaber encapsulates a disciplinary rejection of those areas I have aligned with the rhetoric of cool. Viewing media as a "counterinfluence" works against imagining the student writer as anything but a *student*. Students don't engage with media, this argument claims. They use only those forms and genres native to the university-accepted curriculum of exams, essays, and other print-related assessment procedures. Thus, when Kitzhaber adds to his diatribe above and claims, "The effects of the English course cannot be isolated from the effects of a myriad of other influences which lie entirely outside the English teacher's control," he is not suggesting that English, or composition, consider these effects for their rhetorical value (6). He is placing these effects within the counterinfluence sphere, as influences to avoid or struggle against.

And here lies composition studies' greatest dilemma regarding media. Are media a counterinfluence, or are they, in fact, *influences*? If we choose the latter, we begin the work necessary to integrate electronic writing into our curricula. If we recognize influence as broader than classroom study, as the 1963 story I am telling dictates we should do, then we can also understand how media is writing. But to make the claim for broad influence, we have to expand the types of writing students do so that they better reflect the kinds of writing media generate. To write to a Weblog is not the same as to write a personal essay; to engage with a wiki is not the same as to write a thesis; to construct a hypertextual project is not the same as to create a print-based research essay. To even conduct research is no longer the same. Media dictate otherwise. Media change us, and media change the nature of our work.

Image is everything, the popular Sprite commercial declares. Image is everything, including how composition studies imagines writing in general. Is writing still the dominance of alphabetic notation, or does writing include imagery as well? Is writing the teaching of thesis-driven representation, is it a rhetoric devoted largely to the concepts of audience and purpose, or is it only logical reasoning? Does a writer really need purpose or a sense of audience each time she sits down to write? Should she be inventing the university or media culture? Or—and possibly in addition to these items—does writing also include those items I note as central to the rhetoric of cool?

These are questions for the future work of composition studies. These are questions 1963 composition studies was unable to address because of the range of its vision regarding writing and writing instruction. These are questions I'm still not confident composition studies today takes seriously. Despite some emerging calls to reconsider the role of media in writing instruction, notably Kathleen Blake Yancey's well received CCCC chair address in 2004, we are not too removed from the very nonmedia outlook embraced in 1963. "Sometimes, you know, you have a moment," Yancey begins her address. "For compositionists, of time and of this place, this moment—this moment right now—is like none other" (297). Sometimes disciplines, writers, and texts have moments, and sometimes these items and moments, indeed, are like no others. As I have tried to show, one particular moment, 1963, was in fact like no other moment, but what made it unique has gone unnoticed until now. Our task today is to reimagine our status quos, to reconceptualize writing so that it includes, among other things, the notion of cool. Our task is to live up to the "moment," as Yancey requests. The positive composition studies response to Yancey's address might also remember her call for

> developing a new curriculum for the 21st century, a curriculum that carries forward the best of what we have created to date, that brings together the writing outside of school and that inside. This composition is located in a new vocabulary, a new set of practices, and a new set of outcomes;…it will focus our research in new and provocative ways; it has as its goal the creation of thoughtful, informed, technologically adept writing publics. (308)

To do all that Yancey requests, and to do all of this in terms of supposedly "provocative" approaches like the one I have outlined in this book, we can more fully realize electronic writing in our work, our teaching, our research, and elsewhere. To do all of this, we can become cool in ways we haven't yet begun to imagine. To do any of this, we must reimagine ourselves and our work entirely.

# Notes

# Works Cited and Consulted

# Index

# Notes

## Introduction

1. http://www.educationworld.com/cool_school/2003/index.shtml.

2. See http://www.educationworld.com/cool_school/2005/cool_school1005-17.shtml.

3. See http://coolschool.k12.or.us/.

4. Just because I won't write this book in slang, I don't deny slang's important rhetorical role in cool, particularly how it carries over from hip-hop. When celebrities like Snoop Dogg introduce sayings like "Fo Shizzle" into popular vocabulary, we are witnessing various elements of cool (puns, appropriation, etc.) that I will describe in this book.

## 1. The Story of Composition Studies and Cool

1. See Lester Faigley, *Fragments of Rationality*; Geoffrey Sirc, "English Composition as a Happening II, Part One"; and Robert Connors, Andrea Lunsford, and Lisa Ede, eds., *Essays on Classical Rhetoric and Modern Discourse*.

2. Vitanza is discussing "Philosophical Rhetoric," but the point of sub/versive histories I generalize to rhetoric and composition.

3. For a brief survey of some of these tools' relationship to new media practices, see Johndan Johnson-Eilola's *Datacloud*, particularly the chapters "Articulating (in) the Datacloud" and "Some Rearticulations." Johnson-Eilola gives short overviews of specific tools' usage.

4. As I write this, McCrimmon's textbook is in its thirteenth edition and has been retitled (or remixed) as *The New Writing with a Purpose*. The new edition, written by Joseph Trimmer and published by Houghton Mifflin, boasts Web assignments with its chapters, but as I will show in later chapters, the ideology of the initial textbook still continues despite such superficial changes.

## 2. Chora

1. See http://www.keds.com.

2. There exist too many advertising examples that appropriate cool. Two recent examples include Sears' 2005 "Cooler Every Day" campaign and Gatorade Rain's 2006 series of commercials that begin with the statement "Introducing the rebirth of cool." Gatorade appropriates and remixes the title of Miles Davis's

1950 album *The Birth of Cool*. One Gatorade commercial features basketball star Kevin Garnet, drawing attention to the role of celebrity in this process (a point I make here regarding James Dean and will continue with in later chapters).

3. See my articles "The Handbook of Cool" in *Kairos* and "Writing about Cool: Teaching Hypertext as Juxtaposition" in *Computers and Composition*.

4. See http://en.wikipedia.org/wiki/Wik.

5. MediaWiki is the type of wiki (there are many kinds) Wikipedia runs on. Examples of other usages of MediaWiki can be found at the Wayne State University Composition wikis I run, http://englishweb.clas.wayne.edu/~1020/1020/ and http://englishweb.clas.wayne.edu/~3010/3010, and at Bradley Dilger's Glossolalia, http://wrecking.org/glossolalia/index.php?title=Main_Page, used for computers and writing and composition courses he teaches at Western Illinois University.

## 3. Appropriation

1. See http://home.netscape.com/netcenter/cool/editorial.html.

2. See http://iat.ubalt.edu/kaplan/lit/.

3. For further work on how retailers like the Gap play off of the images of the Beats, see the collection of essays from the *Baffler, Commodify Your Dissent*. Thomas Frank's "Why Johnny Can't Dissent"states,

> The GAP may have since claimed Ginsberg and *USA Today* may run feature stories about the brilliance of the beloved Kerouac, but the rebel race continues today regardless, with ever-heightening shit-references calculated to scare Jesse Helms, talk about sex and smack that is supposed to bring the electricity of real life, and more determined defiance of the repressive rules and mores of the American 1950s—rules and mores that by now we know only from the movies. (33)

> In "Back in Black: Here Come the Beatniks!" Maura Mahoney writes,

> The Gap's 1993 celebrities-who-wore-khakis ad campaign included Jack Kerouac, looking hardened and compelling in pants you too can buy. . . . His aesthetic, the transcendence of sensation and onrushing action, and his pursuit of slick style over substantive content, lend themselves nicely both to advertising and that ineluctable late-twentieth century 'art form'—the video image. (59–60)

4. The images were displayed in a *New York Times* op-ed piece by Adbuster Tibor Kalman ("Losing Their Cool," 15 Jan. 1997), which read, "I'm a designer. I've worked all my life to make different products (including cigarettes) cool. Now I'm thinking about how to make smoking uncool."

5. As I write this, I also note the irony that I cannot quote lyrics from the songs (i.e., I cannot appropriate) that compliment various parts of my argument

without paying exorbitant fees to publishers for the right to do so. The problems copyright poses for intellectual work have been raised by noted media scholars and intellectual property advocates like Lawrence Lessig and Siva Vaidhyanathan, and it is an issue always present within the rhetoric of cool even if I don't explicitly address it. If anything, composing to a print space foregrounds these restrictions more than it would if I were composing to my own Weblog or Web site, where I would pay little attention to the restrictions because of how I understand my own publishing sites' relationship to new media. See Steven Westbrook's "Visual Rhetoric in a Culture of Fear: Impediments to Multimedia Production," *College English* (May 2006): 457–80, for the ideological issues at stake regarding the stranglehold copyright places on intellectual and pedagogical work within composition studies.

6. The alter ego is also a trope circulated in other media shaped by technology, like late-nineteenth-century and early-twentieth-century literature. The Portuguese poet Fernando Pessoa, for instance, appropriated a number of identities to write under. His work could be read as the by product of late-nineteenth-century technological innovations in communication. One could extend, therefore, the alter ego argument by beginning with a figure like Pessoa, examining Hollywood stars asked to change their names, and considering a more recent film like *Fight Club*, which is about the struggle with an alter ego.

7. Eminem's alter ego, Slim Shady, heads the alter ego "band" (each member taking on a different name as well), which asks fans sarcastically if they know the name of "my band." Eminem, itself, is an alter ego for Marshall Mathers. In my online writing, I've adopted the alter egos of out-of-control academic Dr. Fabulous and forgotten rap star Pelzure.

## 4. Juxtaposition

1. See Adam Greenfield's *Everyware: The Dawning Age of Ubiquitous Computing* for a more complete discussion of juxtaposition in new media applications. In Thesis 47, Greenfield draws a parallel between the logic of music mashups (combining two distinct songs as one) and business and professional concerns where different goals and applications are juxtaposed for new purposes (like HousingMaps' juxtaposition of Craigslist with Google Maps). See also Kevin Kelly's *New York Times Magazine* essay "Scan This Book!" 14 May 2006:43. Kelly, too, draws larger conclusions from mashups, noting that in a culture of mashups, "[e]very object, event or location on earth would 'know' everything that has ever been written about it in any book, in any language, at any time. From this deep structuring of knowledge comes a new culture of interaction and participation."

2. Nor are these kinds of juxtapositions the focus of contemporary textbooks that make the claim for juxtaposition, like, for example, Marlene Clark's *Juxtapositions: Ideas for College Writers* (Boston: Pearson, 2006). The textbook's promo-

tional material makes my point clear; its emphasis is on the textbook's teaching of "The Five-Part Essay," one of the most non-juxtapositional writing strategies composition studies has embraced in its over one-hundred-year history.

3. By this I do not mean that composition practices are all drill and answer. However, a good deal of formulaic writing (write on a topic of your own choosing) and assessment, either within the institution or preenrollment (like, for example, placement exams or the S.A.T.), do revolve around this type of thinking to some extent. In addition, a continued emphasis on "error" (despite much scholarship that argues to the contrary) is a reflection of this drill and answer legacy.

4. While North dismisses the academic anecdote, the juxtaposition of the two writing machines I introduce here prompts my own anecdote. Early in my teaching career, I taught basic writing and ESL at Santa Fe Community College in Gainesville, Florida. The Writing Center—which all basic writers attended—was outfitted with new PCs. In the tradition of Kitzhaber's writing machine, students used the computers to complete fill in the blank grammar drills that duplicated the same exercises in their workbooks. At that time, I had discovered the Web and how to make Web pages. After sharing this insight with the ESL students I worked with, I received numerous requests to help them get on the Web as well. Many of the students were from Central America and wanted to share photos and thoughts with relatives in their home countries. Already aware of how to copy HTML (view source) and of the availability of free Web space via the local Freenet and sites like Geocities, I went to the Writing Center to ask for permission to teach ESL students how to put their work online. The Writing Center administrator was not convinced that the PCs should be used for non-drill purposes. The anecdote teaches me a moment of misrecognition: Whereas the students understood how Web space could be used to juxtapose experiences across countries, the professors who ran the Writing Center and whose ideology was dictated by the textbook used did not share the same experience.

5. See Nelson's Web site: http://www.sfc.keio.ac.jp/~ted/TN/WhoIAm.html.

6. See http://www.everything2.com for examples of this kind of writing.

7. See also Cynthia Haynes's work on "offshore writing" as another investigation into nonargumentative writing and pedagogy. As Haynes notes, not all writing needs to be reduced to argument.

8. See "The 1963 Hip Hop Machine: Hip Hop Pedagogy as Composition," *CCC* (Feb. 2003): 453–71.

## 5. Commutation

1. Barthes is working with semiotics, or semiology, of course. But as he moves away from structuralism in later books, we can see an implied digital influence on his thinking. Referentiality yields to nonrepresentational systems of thinking: the punctum, the third meaning, and *jouissance*.

2. While McLuhan argues that film is not a cool medium because of how the film is structured by complete images (frames), I am arguing that Smith's rhetoric of commutation is cool for how it forces high levels of participation in order to come to any kind of meaning.

3. See Rob Walker, "Consumed: Sprite Remix," The Way We Live Now, *New York Times* 28 Mar. 2004: 24.

## 6. Nonlinearity

1. See John Slatin's "Reading Hypertext: Order and Coherence in a New Medium," *College English* 52.8 (Dec.1990): 870-83; Jane Yellowlees Douglas's "Gaps, Maps, and Perception: What Hypertext Readers (Don't Do)," *Perforations* 2.3 (1992), http://www.pd.org/topos/perforations/perf3/douglas_p3.html; and Nancy Kaplan's "E-literacies: Politexts, Hypertexts and Other Cultural Formations in the Late Age of Print."

2. Following this logic, the XHTML Friends Network (http://gmpg.org/xfn/) is one site that uses this semantic logic to build friendship networks. My examples here, of course, only reflect one aspect of the semantic web, that based on relationships, and not the issue of standards it often proposes.

3. At the 2004 Convergences symposium held at North Carolina State University, Collin Brooke referred to a rhetoric of network relationships as Rhetworks. His work on networks and rhetoric will help the field better understand this new media-oriented method of expression, which I believe, cool also draws upon.

4. Another notable exception, in addition to the already mentioned Del.icio.us and Flickr, is the FOAF-a-matic Web site Berners-Lee mentions in his interview with *Technology Review*. Located at http://www.ldodds.com/foaf/foaf-a-matic.html, the site generates a user profile that, when uploaded to the Web, is meant to semantically connect to other profiles that contain some kind of associative semblance. It's a simple application whose long range goals could include more complex nonlinear linkings of information.

5. See http://www.hpl.hp.com/archive/cooltown/. For a fascinating look at the theoretical work driving this project, see the Hewlett Packard paper "People, Places, Things: Web Presence for the Real World" at http://www.hpl.hp.com/techreports/2001/HPL-2001-279.html?jumpid=reg_R1002_USEN.

6. Indeed, since originally writing this, I have noticed that all the promotional videos created for these projects—both Cooltown and the Cooltown@school.com educational plan—have been taken off of Hewlett Packard's Web site. The implication is that the projects failed. One can guess as to why (no reason is given anywhere on the HP site), but I would suggest that these failures stem from much of the argument I have been drawing out in this book; HP, like education in general, has been unable to integrate the new logics of new media into its given strategies. We can understand the metaphoric value of HP's failure

and seriously consider our own failures in education regarding technology and writing. One such failure can be found in the pedagogies endorsed by platforms still active on the market, WebCT and Blackboard. They are not financial failures but pedagogical ones.

7. These topics were listed on the site's Page of Cool on September 26, 2004. See http://www.everything2.com/index.pl?node=Cool%20Archive for more current listings of diverse subjects interlinked.

## 7. Imagery

1. A more contemporary example—and one that continues this thought I introduce—can be found in Kid Koala and Money Mark's song "Carpal Tunnel Syndrome," which can be found on the *Funkungfusion* album (Ninja Tune, 1998). The song begins with the sampled sound of a typewriter clicking away. As further samples and music are juxtaposed into the composition, the typing merges with the music. The importance of this example is how it demonstrates that in non-classroom-based writing, tools are often used in a variety of ways to compose. That activity occurs in 1963 as well as 1998. How a writer *imagines* a tool's usage is what is important.

2. Steven Johnson's *Everything Bad Is Good for You* does an excellent job fleshing out the role media play in generating complex thinking, an act that occurs because of how media structures are internalized.

3. See http://www.boingboing.net, http://www.metafilter.com, and http://www.wayxy.org/links.

4. See also Wilbur Schramm, Kack Lyle, and Ithiel de Sola Pool's 1963 *The People Look at Educational Television: A Report of Nine Representative ETV Stations* (Stanford: Stanford UP) a study of television's affects on education. Prior to 1963, NCTE issued its 1961 report *Television and the Teaching of English* (New York: Appleton) an argument for television's pedagogical usage.

5. See the cover of Cecil Taylor's 1966 *Unit Structures* (Blue Note). An almost exact replication of Warhol's 1963 Marilyn paintings, it depicts rows of the same image in different silk screen colors.

6. Blue Note Records 2004 release *Blue Note Revisited* remixes the Byrd cover with new images of an attractive African-American woman leaning on an automobile foregrounded in the frame. The songs on the album are remixes of Blue Note recordings as well, making the album a fine example of cool writing visually and compositionally.

7. Following McLuhan's inclusion of the automobile as a media form in *Understanding Media*, I comment likewise.

8. For a specific contemporary example, see Gerald Graff's interview with the online publication Academic Commons, http://www.academiccommons.org/commons/interview/graff. Asked how he uses technology in his courses,

Graff responds: "I love using e-mail for writing instruction. I can get right inside my students' sentences and paragraphs, stop them and ask them 'can you see a problem with this phrase?' or 'can you think of an alternative to this formulation?' or 'please improve on this sentence,' with an immediacy and turnaround speed that handing papers back with comments cannot begin to match." Graff repeats Winzeler's usage of the overhead, replacing it with e-mail.

9. This assignment can be viewed in more detail in the online version of *Writing about Cool: Hypertext and Cultural Studies in the Computer Classroom*, located at Ablongman.com.

# Works Cited and Consulted

Aderman, Ralph, and Elizabeth Kerr, eds. *Aspects of American English*. New York: Harcourt, 1963.

Alexander, Donnell. "Are Black People Cooler Than White People?" *Might* Jul.-Aug. 1997. 44–53.

Aristotle. *The Rhetoric of Aristotle*. Englewood Cliffs, NJ: Prentice-Hall, 1960.

Atwan, Robert. *Convergences: Message, Method, Medium*. Boston: Bedford–St. Martin's, 2004.

Axelrod, Rise B., and Charles R. Cooper. *The St. Martin's Guide to Writing*. 5th ed. New York: St. Martin's, 1997.

Baker, Sheridan. *The Practical Stylist*. New York: Crowell, 1962.

Baraka, Amiri. *Black Music*. New York: Morrow, 1967.

———. *Blues People: Negro Music in White America*. New York: Morrow, 1963.

Bardini, Thierry. *Bootstrapping: Douglas Engelbart, Coevolution, and the Origins of Personal Computing*. Stanford, CA: Stanford UP, 2000.

Barnett, Sylvan, and Marcia Stubbs, eds. *The Little, Brown Reader*. New York: Harper, 1996.

Barthes, Roland. *Camera Lucida*. New York: Hill, 1981.

———. *Elements of Semiology*. Trans. Annette Lavers and Colin Smith. New York: Noonday, 1988 (1964).

———. *Image/Music/Text*. New York: Hill, 1997.

———. "On Film." *The Grain of the Voice. Interviews: 1962–1980*. Trans. Linda Coverdale. New York: Hill, 1985.

Bartholomae, David. "Inventing the University." *Composition in Four Keys: Inquiring into the Field*. Ed. Mark Wiley, Barbara Gleason, and Louise Wetherbee Phelps. Mountain View, CA: Mayfield, 1996.

Baty, Paige S. *American Monroe: The Making of a Body Politic*. Berkeley: U of California P, 1985.

Baudrillard, Jean. *Simulacra and Simulation*. Trans. Sheila Faria Glaser. Ann Arbor: U of Michigan P, 1994.

———. *Symbolic Exchange and Death*. Trans. Iain Hamilton Grant. London: Sage, 1993.

Becker, Howard S. *The Outsiders: Studies in the Sociology of Deviance*. New York: Free Press, 1963.

Bell, Dawson. "Hip Michigan: Let's Talk about Cool Cities, Hot Coffee." *Detroit Free Press* 31 May 2003 <http://www.freep.com/news/politics/gran31_20030531.htm>.

Ben Folds Five. "That's Robert Sledge." No publication information.

Benjamin, Walter. *Charles Baudelaire: A Lyric Poet in the Era of High Capitalism*. Trans. Harry Zohn. London: NLB, 1973.

———."The Work of Art in the Age of Mechanical Reproduction." *Illuminations*. Trans. Harry Zohn. New York: Harcourt, 1968.

Berlin, James. "Composition and Cultural Studies." *Composition and Resistance*. Ed. C. Mark Hurlbert and Michael Blitz. Portsmouth, NJ: Boyton, 1991.

———. "Rhetoric and Ideology in the Writing Class." *College English* 50.5 (Sept. 1988): 477–94.

———. *Rhetoric and Reality: Writing Instruction in American Colleges, 1900–1985*. Carbondale: Southern Illinois UP, 1987.

Berners-Lee, Tim. "Hypertext Style: Cool URIs Don't Change." WW3 25 Jan. 2002 <http://www.w3.org/Provider/Style/URI.html>.

Billsion, Janet Mancini, and Richard Majors. *Cool Pose: The Dilemmas of Black Manhood in America*. New York: Lexington, 1992.

Bolter, Jay David. *Writing Space: The Computer, Hypertext, and the History of Writing*. Hillsdale, NJ: Erlbaum, 1991.

Booth, Wayne. "The Rhetorical Stance." *College Composition and Communication* 14.3 (Oct. 1963): 139–45.

———. "The Scholar in Society." *Introduction to Scholarship in Modern Languages and Literatures*. Ed. Joseph Gibaldi. New York: MLA, 1981.

Boyer, Troy B. "Flash Is Fast, Flash Is Cool." *Schtick* 47.1 (1997): 3–12.

Braddock, Richard, Richard Lloyd-Jones, and Lowell Schoer. *Research in Written Composition*. Champaign, IL: NCTE, 1963.

Brookes, Malcolm, and Mina Hamilton. "Off the Record." *Industrial Design* (Mar.1963): 78–81.

Brooks, Gwendolyn. "Negro Hero." *Selected Poems*. New York: Harper, 1963.

———. "We Real Cool." *Selected Poems*. New York: Harper, 1963.

Brow, Francis. *Collage*. New York: Pitman, 1963.

Brown, James. *Live at the Apollo Vol. 1*. King Records, 1963.

Burroughs, William S. *Naked Lunch*. New York: Grove, 1982 (1959).

———. *Nova Express*. New York: Grove, 1992 (1964).

———. *The Ticket That Exploded*. New York: Grove (1987 (1964).

———. *Yage Letters*. 1963. San Francisco: City Lights, 1978 (1963).

Burroughs, William S., and Byron Gysin. *The Third Mind*. New York: Viking, 1978.

Calloway, Cab. *Cab Calloway's Cat-ologue: A Hepster's Dictionary. Just the Swing* 10 Feb. 2004 <http://just-the-swing.com/liv/jive>.

Caponi, Dagel Gina, ed. *Signifyin[g], Sanctifyin' and Slam Dunking.* Amherst, MA: U of Massachusetts P, 1999.

Carney, Ray. *Beat Culture and the New America: 1960–1965.* Paris: Flammarion, 1995.

Casey, Edward S. *The Fate of Place: A Philosophical History.* Berkeley: U of California P, 1998.

Christensen, Francis. "A Generative Rhetoric of the Sentence." *College Composition and Communication* 14.3 (Oct. 1963): 155–61.

———. "Notes toward a New Rhetoric." *College English* 14.3 (Oct. 1963): 17–11.

Coleman, Anthony. "School Gets Cool." *mpulse: A Cooltown Magazine* 28 Dec. 2002 <http://www.cooltown.hp.com/mpulse/0901atschool.asp>.

*College Composition and Communication* 14.3 (Oct. 1963).

Connor, Marlene Kim. *What Is Cool? Understanding Black Manhood in America.* New York: Crown, 1995.

Connors, Robert J. "Current-Traditional Rhetoric: Thirty Years of *Writing with a Purpose.*" *Rhetoric Society Quarterly* 11.4 (Fall 1981): 208–21.

Connors, Robert J., Andrea Lunsford, and Lisa Ede, eds. *Essays on Classical Rhetoric and Modern Discourse.* Carbondale: Southern Illinois UP, 1984.

Cool Cities. "Background." 2 Feb. 2003 <http://www.coolcities.com>.

"Cool Issue, The." *Rolling Stone* 11 Apr. 2002.

Corbett, Edward P. J. "Teaching Composition: Where We've Been and Where We're Going." *College Composition and Communication* 38.4 (Dec.1987): 444–52.

———. "The Usefulness of Classical Rhetoric." *College Composition and Communication* 14.3 (Oct. 1963): 162–64.

Danesi, Marcel. *Cool: The Signs and Meanings of Adolescence.* Toronto, Canada: U of Toronto P, 1994.

Davis, Diane D. *Breaking Up (at) Totality: A Rhetoric of Laughter.* Carbondale: Southern Illinois UP, 2000.

Davis, Erik. "The Future Mix." 18 Mar. 2001 <http://www.techgnosis.com/futuremix.html>.

Derrida, Jacques. *Limited Inc.* Evanston, IL: Northwestern UP, 1988.

———. *Of Grammatology.* Baltimore: Johns Hopkins UP, 1974.

———. "Plato's Pharmacy." *Dissemination.* Trans. Barbara Johnson. Chicago: U of Chicago P, 1981.

Dery, Mark. "Culture Jamming: Hacking, Slashing and Sniping in the Empire of Signs." 15 Jan. 2000 <http://gopher.well.sf.ca.us:70/0/cyberpunk/cultjam.txt>.

———. *Escape Velocity: Cyberculture at the End of the Century.* New York: Grove, 1996.

Digable Planets. "Cool Like Dat." *Reachin' (A New Refutation of Time and Space)*. EMD-Pendulum, 1993.

Dinnerstein, Joel. "Lester Young and the Birth of the Cool." *Signifyin[g], Sanctifyin' and Slam Dunking*. Caponi 239–76.

DJ Spooky (Paul Miller). "Algorithms: Erasures and the Art of Memory." *Audio Culture: Readings in Modern Music*. Ed. Christoph Cox and Daniel Warner. New York: Continuum, 2004.

———. "Living through the Past as a Kind of Reflection Site for Future Permutations." *Afrofuturism* 9 June 2000 <http://www.afrofuturism.net/text/Manifestos/Miller03.html>.

———. *Rhythm Science*. Cambridge: MIT, 2004.

Doctorow, Cory. *Eastern Standard Tribe*. New York: Tor, 2004.

Eagles, The. "James Dean." *On the Border*. Elektra Asylum, 1985 (1974).

*Education U.S.A. A Special Weekly Report on Educational Affairs* 7 Nov. 1963.

*Education World*. 14 Feb. 2005 <http://www.education-world.com/best_of/1997/cool_school.shtml>.

Elbow, Peter. *Writing with Power: Techniques for Mastering the Writing Process*. Oxford: Oxford UP, 1981.

Engelbart, Douglas. "A Conceptual Framework for Augmenting Man's Intellect." *Vistas in Information Handling*. Washington, DC: Spartan, 1963.

Eshun, Kodowo. *More Brilliant Than the Sun: Adventures in Sonic Fiction*. London: Quartet, 1999.

Esther, Polly. "Filler: 4.22: Pretension: You've Come a Long Way Baby." 22 Apr. 1998. Suck.com. 12 Feb. 2000 <http://www.suck.com/daily/98/04/22/nc_index5.html>.

Faigley, Lester. *Fragments of Rationality: Postmodernity and the Subject of Composition*. Pittsburgh: U of Pittsburgh P, 1992.

Farris, Christine. "Too Cool for School? Composition as Cultural Studies and Reflective Practices." *Preparing College Teachers of Writing: Histories, Theories, Programs, and Practices*. Ed. Betty Pytlik and Sarah Liggett. New York: Oxford UP, 2001. 97–107.

Farris Thompson, Robert. "An Aesthetic of Cool." *Signifyin[g], Sanctifyin' and Slam Dunking*. Caponi 77–86.

———. *Flash of the Spirit: African and Afro-American Art and Philosophy*. New York: Vintage, 1983.

Fernando, S. H. Jr. "Back in the Day: 1975–1979." *The Vibe History of Hip Hop*. Light 13–21.

Florida, Richard. *The Rise of the Creative Class . . . And How It's Transforming Work, Leisure, Community, and Everyday Life*. New York: Basic, 2002.

Foucault, Michel. *The Archeology of Knowledge and the Discourse on Language*. Trans. A. M. Sheridan Smith. New York: Pantheon, 1972.

# Works Cited and Consulted

Frank, Thomas. *The Conquest of Cool: Business Culture, Counterculture, and the Rise of Hip Consumerism*. Chicago: U of Chicago P, 1997.

———. "Why Johnny Can't Dissent." *Commodify Your Dissent: Salvos from the Baffler*. New York: Norton, 1997. 31–45.

Frauenfelder, Mark. "Sir Tim Berners-Lee." *Technology Review* 30 Oct. 2004 <http://www.technologyreview.com/InfoTech/13784/>.

Freund, John. "McLuhan's Galaxy." *College Composition and Communication* 14.12 (May 1963): 112–16.

Fuller, Matthew. *Media Ecologies: Materialist Energies in Art and Technoculture*. Cambridge: MIT, 2005.

George, Diane. "From Analysis to Design: Visual Communication in the Teaching of Writing." *College Composition and Communication* 54.1 (Sept. 2002): 11–39.

George, Diane, Anna Palchik, Cynthia Selfe, and Lester Faigley, eds. *Picturing Texts*. New York: Norton, 2005.

Gladwell, Malcolm. "The Coolhunt." *New Yorker* 17 Mar.1997. 78–88.

Gooch, Bryan. "ETV and NET: Humanities and Mass Media." *The Humanities Association Review* 20.2 (1969): 34–41.

Goody, Jack, and Ian Watt. "The Consequences of Literacy." *Literacy in Traditional Societies*. Ed. Jack Goody. Cambridge: Cambridge UP, 1968. 27–68.

Graff, Gerald. "Hidden Intellectualism." *Pedagogy* 1.1 (Winter 2001). 21–36.

Gray, Kathleen. "Detroit's U.S. Rankings Drop." *Detroit Free Press* 30 June 2005 <http://ww.freep.com/news/locway/census30e_20050630.htm>.

Greenfield, Adam. *Everyware: The Dawning Age of Ubiquitous Computing*. Berkeley, CA: New Riders, 2006.

Greenhunt, Morris. "Great Books and English Composition." *College English* 24.2 (Nov. 1962): 136–40.

Hacker, Diane. *A Writer's Reference*. Boston: Bedford–St. Martin's, 1999.

Hall, Stuart, and Paddy Whannel. *The Popular Arts*. New York: Pantheon, 1964.

Handa, Carolyn. *Visual Rhetoric in a Digital World: A Critical Sourcebook*. Boston: Bedford–St. Martin's, 2004.

Harris, Joseph. "Revision as Critical Practice." *College English* 65.5 (July 2003): 77–92.

Havelock, Eric. *Preface to Plato*. Cambridge, MA: Belknap of Harvard UP, 1963.

———.*The Muse Learns to Write*. New Haven: Yale UP, 1986.

Hayles, Katherine N. *My Mother Was a Computer: Digital Subjects and Literary Texts*. Chicago: U of Chicago P, 2005.

Haynes, Cynthia. "Writing Offshore: The Disappearing Coastline of Composition Theory." *JAC* 23.4 (2003): 607–724.

Hewlett Packard. "Cooltown Beliefs." 15 Mar. 2001 <http://www.cooltown.hp.com/dev/beliefs.asp>.

——. "Cooltown: The Ecosystem Explained." 15 Mar. 2001 <http://www.cooltown.hp.com/mpulse/backissues/0601/0601-cooltown.asp>.

——. "Cooltown Videos." 10 Dec. 2002 <http://www.cooltown.hp.com/cooltownhome/cooltown-video.asp>.

——. "A Future Called CoolTown." 15 Mar. 2001 <http://www.hpl.hp.com/news/cooltown.html>.

——. "School Gets Cool." 15 Mar. 2001 <http://www.cooltown.hp.com/mpulse/0901-atschool.asp>.

Hill, Charles, and Marguerite Helmers. *Defining Visual Rhetorics.* Mahwah, NJ: Erlbaum, 2004.

Hult, Christine A., and Thomas N. Huckin. *The New Century Handbook.* Needham, MA: Allyn, 1999.

Irmscher, William F. "Finding a Comfortable Identity." *College Composition and Communication* 38.1 (Feb. 1987): 81–87.

Jameson, Fredric. *Postmodernism, or the Logic of Late Capitalism.* Durham, NC: Duke UP, 1991.

——."Nostalgia for the Present." *Classical Hollywood Narrative.* Ed. Jane Gaines. Durham and London: Duke UP, 1992.

Janangelo, Joseph. "Joseph Cornell and the Artistry of Composing Persuasive Hypertexts." *College Composition and Communication* 49.1 (Feb. 1998): 24–44.

Johndan, Johnson-Eilola. "The Database and the Essay." *Writing New Media: Theory and Applications for Expanding the Teaching of Composition.* Logan: Utah State UP, 2004.

——. *Datacloud: Toward a New Theory of Online Work.* Cresskill, NJ: Hampton, 2005.

Johnson, Steven. *Everything Bad Is Good for You: How Today's Popular Culture Is Actually Making Us Smarter.* New York: Riverhead, 2005.

Journet, Debra, Mary Rosner, and Beth Boehm, eds. *History, Reflection, and Narrative: The Professionalization of Composition, 1963–1983.* Greenwich, CT: Ablex, 1999.

Kaplan, Nancy. *E-literacies: Politexts, Hypertexts and Other Cultural Formations in the Late Age of Print.* 20 Dec. 2000 <http://raven.ubalt.edu/staff/kaplan/lit/index.cfm?whichOne=Hypertexts_601.cfm>.

Kaprow, Allan. "Happenings' in the New York Scene." *ArtNews* (May 1961): 36–39, 58– 62.

——. "Words: An Environment." *A Book of the Book: Some Words and Projections about the Book and Writing.* Ed. Jerome Rothenberg and Steven Clay. New York: Granary, 2000.

Kelman, Ken. "Anticipations of the Light." *The New American Cinema.* Ed. Gregory Battcock. New York: Dutton, 1967.

Kennedy, George. *The Art of Persuasion in Greece*. Princeton, NJ: Princeton UP, 1963.

Kerouac, Jack. *Big Sur*. New York: Penguin, 1992 (1962).

———. *On the Road*. New York: Signet, 1957.

———. *Visions of Cody*. New York: McGraw, 1970.

———. *Visions of Gerard*. New York: Farrar, 1963.

King, Martin Luther, Jr. "Letter from Birmingham Jail." *The Little, Brown Reader*. Ed. Marcia Stubbs and Sylvan Barnet. New York: Harper, 1996. 763–78.

Kittler, Friedrich A. *Gramophone, Film, Typewriter*. Trans. Geoffrey Winthrop-Young and Michael Wutz. Stanford: Stanford UP, 1999.

Kitzhaber, Albert. "4C, Freshmen English, and the Future." *College Composition and Communication* (Oct 1963): 129–38.

———. *Themes, Theories, and Therapy: The Teaching of Writing in College*. New York: McGraw, 1963.

Koala, Kid. *Some of My Best Friends Are DJs*. Ninja Tunes, 2003.

Landow, George. *Hypertext 2.0*. Baltimore: Johns Hopkins UP, 1997.

———. "The Paradigm Is More Important than the Purchase: Educational Innovation and Hypertext Theory." *Digital Media Revisited*. Ed. Gunnar Liestøl, Andrew Morrison, and Terje Rasmussen. Cambridge: MIT, 2003.

Lasn, Kalle. *Culture Jam: The Uncooling of America*. New York: Eagle Brook, 1999.

Lhamon, W. T., Jr. *Deliberate Speed: The Origins of a Cultural Style in the American 1950s*. Washington, DC: Smithsonian, 1990.

Light, Alan, ed. *The Vibe History of Hip Hop*. New York: Three Rivers, 1999.

Liu, Alan. *The Laws of Cool: Knowledge Work and the Culture of Information*. Chicago: U of Chicago P, 2004.

———. *Voice of the Shuttle: Laws of Cool Page* 20 Dec. 2000 <http://vos.ucsb.edu/shuttle/cool.html>.

Lyman and Scott. "Coolness in Everyday Life" *The Sociology of the Absurd*. New York: Appleton, 1970.

Lyotard, Jean-François. *The Postmodern Condition: A Report on Knowledge*. Trans. Geoff Bennington and Brian Massumi. Minneapolis: U of Minnesota P, 1997.

McAdams, Lewis. *Birth of the Cool: Beat, Bebop, and the American Avant-Garde*. New York: Free Press, 2001.

McComisky, Bruce. "Visual Rhetoric and the New Public Discourse." *JAC* 24.1 (2004): 187–206.

McCrimmon, James. *Writing with a Purpose*. Boston: Houghton, 1963.

McElfresh, Suzanne. "DJs Vs. Samplers." Light 170–72.

McLuhan, Marshall. "A Dialogue." *McLuhan Hot and Cool*. New York: Dial, 1967.

————. *The Gutenberg Galaxy.* Toronto: University of Toronto, 1962.

————. *The Medium Is the Massage.* San Francisco: Hardwired, 1996 (1967).

————. *Understanding Media.* New York: Signet, 1964.

McQuade, Donald, and Christine McQuade. *Seeing and Writing.* New York: Bedford–St. Martin's, 2000.

Macrorie, Ken. *Uptaught.* Portsmouth, NH: Boynton, 1996 (1970).

Madlib. *Shades of Blue.* Blue Note Records, 2003.

Mahoney, Maura. "Back in Black: Here Come the Beatniks." Frank, *Commodify Your Dissent* 57–61.

Mailer, Norman. "The White Negro." *Advertisements for Myself.* Great Britain: Panther, 1968.

Mancini Billson, Janet, and Richard Majors. *Cool Pose: The Dilemmas of Black Manhood in America.* New York: Lexington, 1992.

Manovich, Lev. *The Language of New Media.* Cambridge: MIT, 2000.

Marcus, Greil. *Dead Elvis.* Cambridge: Harvard UP, 1991.

————. *Lipstick Traces: A Secret History of the Twentieth Century.* Cambridge: Harvard UP, 1989.

Marsh, Graham, Felix Cromey, and Glyn Callingham. *Blue Note: The Album Cover Art.* San Francisco: Chronicle, 1991.

Miller, Warren. *The Cool World.* New York: Crest, 1959.

A Modern Program in a Traditional Setting. Advertisement. *English Record.* Feb. 1965.

Mulderig, Gerald P. "Is There Still a Place for Rhetorical History in Composition Studies?" Journet, Rosner, and Boehm 163–76.

Murray, Donald M. *Write to Learn.* New York: Holt, 1984.

"My Coolest Years." VH1.com. 25 Aug. 2005. <www.vh1.com/shows/dyn/my_coolest_years/series_about.jhtml>.

Nelson Ted. *Computer Lib/Dream Machines.* Redmond, WA.: Tempus of Microsoft, 1987.

————. "Opening Hypertext: A Memoir." *Literacy Online: The Promise (and Peril) of Reading and Writing with Computers.* Ed. Myron C. Tuman. Pittsburgh: U of Pittsburgh P, 1992.

————. *Ted Nelson Home Page.* 20 July 2000 <http://www.sfc.keio.ac.jp/~ted/TN/WhoIAm>.

North, Stephen. *The Making of Knowledge in Composition: Portrait of an Emerging Field.* Upper Montclair, NJ: Boynton, 1987.

Ong, Walter. *Orality and Literacy: The Technologizing of the Word.* New York: Routledge, 1982.

————. *Ramus, Method, and the Decay of Dialogue.* Cambridge: Harvard UP, 1983 (1958).

————. "Wired for Sound: Teaching, Communications, and Technological

Culture." *The Barbarian Within: And Other Fugitive Essays and Studies*. New York: MacMillan, 1962.

Poschardt, Ulf. *DJ Culture*. London: Quartet, 1998.

Potter, Russell A. *Spectacular Vernaculars: Hip-Hop and the Politics of Postmodernism*. New York: State U of New York P, 1995.

Pountain, Dick, and David Robbins. *Cool Rules: Anatomy of An Attitude*. London: Reaktion, 2000.

Public Enemy. "Caught, Can We Get a Witness!" *It Takes a Nation of Millions to Hold Us Back*. Def Jam Recordings, 1987.

———. "Fight the Power." *Fear of a Black Planet*. Def Jam Recordings, 1990.

Pynchon, Thomas. *V*. New York: Bantam, 1963.

Quasimoto. *The Unseen*. Stones Throw, 2000.

Rader, Dean. "Composition, Visual Cultures, and the Problems of Class." *College English* 67.6 (July 2005): 636–50.

Random House. Advertisement. *English Record* Feb.1963: 54.

Rheingold, Howard. *Virtual Reality*. New York: Touchstone, 1991.

Rice, Jeff. "The Handbook of Cool." *Technology, Popular Culture, and the Writing Classroom*. Ed. James Inman and Cheryl Reed. *Kairos Special Issue* 7.2 (Summer 2002) <http://www.english.ttu.edu/Kairos/7.2/sectiontwo/rice/>.

———. "Writing about Cool." Teaching Hypertext as Juxtaposition." *Computers and Composition* 20.3 (Sept. 2003): 221–36.

Rohman, Gordon D., and Albert O. Wlecke. *Pre-Writing: The Construction and Application of Models for Concept Formation in Writing*. East Lansing: Michigan State UP, 1964.

RZA, The. *The Wu-Tang Manual*. New York: Berkley, 2005.

Schramm, Wilbur, Kack Lyle, and Ithiel de Sola Pool. *The People Look at Educational Television: A Report of Nine Representative ETV Stations*. Stanford, CA: Stanford UP, 1963.

Schultz, Charles. *You Can't Win Them All, Charlie Brown*. Greenwich, CT: Fawcett, 1972.

Selber, Stuart A. *Multiliteracies for a Digital Age*. Carbondale: Southern Illinois UP, 2004.

Sirc, Geoffrey. *English Composition as a Happening*. Logan: Utah State UP, 2002.

———. "English Composition as a Happening II, Part One." *Pre/Text* 15.3–4 (1994): 265–93.

———. "Virtual Urbanism." *Computers and Composition* 18.1 (2001): 11–19.

Sitney, P. Adams. *Visionary Film: The American Avant-Garde*. New York: Oxford UP, 1974.

Sontag, Susan. "Jack Smith's Flaming Creatures." *Against Interpretation*. New York: Noonday, 1966 (1964).

Sony. Advertisement. *American School and University* 36 (1964).

"Special Advertising Section, A." *Wired* Nov. 2001: ix–xv.

Stroupe, Craig. "Visualizing English: Recognizing the Hybrid Literacy of Visual and Verbal Authorship on the Web." *College English* 62.5 (May 2000): 607–32.

Suck.com. "Stupe Du Jour." 6 Nov. 1995. 13 Feb. 2001 <http://www.suck.com/daily/95/11/06/daily.html>.

Sutherland, Ivan. *Sketchpad: A Man-Machine Graphical Communication System.* Diss. MIT, 1963.

Tate, Gary, Amy Rupiper, and Kurt Schick, eds. *A Guide to Composition Pedagogies.* New York: Oxford UP, 2001.

"'Team Cool' in Da House: Attention to Young Workers Vital to Region's Success." *Michigan Daily* 2 June 2003 <http://www.michigandaily.com/vnews/display.v/ART/2003/06/02/3edaf250dff5f>.

Trimbur, John. "Composition Studies: Postmodern or Popular." *Into the Field: Sites of Composition Studies.* Ed Anne Ruggles Gere. New York: MLA, 1993.

Trimbur, John, and Diane George. "The Communication Battle or Whatever Happened to 4th C?" *College Composition and Communication* 50 (1999): 682–98.

Ulmer, Gregory L. *Heuretics: The Logic of Invention.* Baltimore: Johns Hopkins UP, 1994.

———. "I Untied the Camera of Tastes (Who Am I?): The Riddle of Chool (A Reply and Alternative to A. Sahay)." *New Literary History* 28.3 (1997): 569–94.

———. *Internet Invention: From Literacy to Electracy.* New York: Longman, 2003.

———. "The Miranda Warnings." *Hyper/Text/Theory.* Ed. George Landow. Baltimore: Johns Hopkins UP, 1994.

———. "The Object of Post-Criticism." *The Anti-Aesthetic: Essays on Postmodern Culture.* Port Townsend, WA.: Bay, 1983.

———. "Textshop for Post(e)pedagogy." *Writing and Reading Differently: Deconstruction and the Teaching of Composition and Literature.* Ed. G. Douglas Atkins and Michael L. Johnson. Lawrence: UP of Kansas, 1985.

Vitanza, Victor J. "Critical Sub/Versions of the History of Philosophical Rhetoric." *Rhetoric Review* 6.1 (1987): 41–66.

"Watch That Man: The Many Phases of Paul D. Miller." *Beam Monthly Magazine* 11 July 2001 <http://www.radio-v.com/main/beam/innerviews/spooky/>.

Weathers, Winston. *An Alternative Style: Options in Composition.* Rochelle Park, NJ: Hayden, 1980.

Weaver, Richard. *Language Is Sermonic: Richard Weaver and the Nature of Rhetoric.* Ed. Richard L. Johannesen, Rennard Strickland, and Ralph T. Eubanks. Baton Rouge: Louisiana State UP, 1970.

"WebCT Whitepaper: Leveraging Technology to Transform the Educational Experience." 23 March 2003 <http://webct.com/Communities/library/itemi nformation?source=browse&objectID=4464759>.

Weir, John. "The Beautiful American Word 'Cool.'" "The Cool Issue." *Rolling Stone* 11 Apr. 2002: 67.

Whiting, Cécile. *A Taste for Pop: Pop Art, Gender, and Consumer Culture.* Cambridge: Cambridge UP, 1997.

Williams, Cecil B., and Allan H. Stevenson. *A Research Manual: For College Studies and Papers.* New York: Harper, 1963.

Williams, Raymond. *Keywords: A Vocabulary of Culture and Society.* New York: Oxford UP, 1985.

Winzeler, Charlotte. "The Visual Written Image." *College Composition and Communication* 14.4 (Dec. 1963): 264–65.

Wysocki, Anne Francis. "Opening New Media to Writing: Openings and Justifications." *Writing New Media: Theory and Applications for Expanding the Teaching of Composition.* Ed. Anne Frances Wysocki, Johndan Johnson-Eilola, Cynthia Selfe, and Geoffrey Sirc. Logan: Utah State UP, 2004.

Yancey, Kathleen Blake. "Made Not Only in Words: Composition in a New Key." *College Composition and Communication* 56.2 (Dec. 2004): 297–328.

Young, Richard. "Paradigms and Problems: Needed Research in Rhetorical Invention." *Research on Composing: Points of Departure.* Ed. Charles Cooper and Lee Odell. Urbana IL: NCTE, 1978.

# Index

Index

**Jeff Rice** is an assistant professor of English at Wayne State University, where he teaches courses in rhetoric, composition, new media, and pedagogy. He is the author of the textbook *Writing about Cool: Hypertext and Cultural Studies in the Computer Classroom* and the coeditor of *New Media/New Methods: The Turn from Literacy to Electracy*. He is currently working on a project that poses Detroit as metaphoric of digital culture and networks. He blogs at Yellow Dog: http://www.ydog.net.